No. 21.

LIBRARY OF CHOICE NOVELS.

CONTARINI FLEMING.

AN AUTOBIOGRAPHY.

BY THE

RIGHT HON. BENJAMIN DISRAELI,

AUTHOR OF

"LOTHAIR," "VENETIA," "HENRIETTA TEMPLE," "VIVIAN GREY," "ALROY," "CONINGSBY," ETC., ETC.

NEW YORK:

D. APPLETON & COMPANY,

90, 92 & 94 GRAND STREET.

1870.

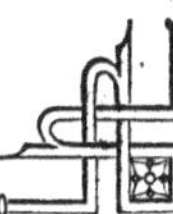

CONTARINI FLEMING.

AN AUTOBIOGRAPHY.

BY THE

RIGHT HON. BENJAMIN DISRAELI,

AUTHOR OF

"LOTHAIR," "VENETIA," "HENRIETTA TEMPLE," "VIVIAN GREY," "ALROY," "CONINGSBY," ETC., ETC.

NEW YORK:
D. APPLETON AND COMPANY,
90, 92 & 94 GRAND STREET.
1870.

CONTARINI FLEMING.

I.

Wandering in those deserts of Africa that border the Erythræan sea, I came to the river Nile, to that ancient, and mighty, and famous stream, whose waters yielded us our earliest civilization, and which, after having witnessed the formation of so many states, and the invention of so many creeds, still flow on with the same serene beneficence, like all that we can conceive of Deity; in form sublime, in action systematic, in nature bountiful, in source unknown.

My solitary step sounded in the halls of the Pharaohs. I moved through those imperial chambers, supported by a thousand columns, and guarded by colossal forms seated on mysterious thrones; I passed under glittering gates meet to receive the triumphal chariot of a Titan; I gazed on sublime obelisks pointing to the skies, whose secrets their mystic characters affected to conceal. Wherever I threw my sight, I beheld vast avenues of solemn sphinxes reposing in supernatural beauty, and melancholy groups of lion-visaged kings; huge walls vividly pictured with the sacred rites and the domestic offices of remote antiquity, or sculptured with the breathing forms of heroic warfare.

And all this might, all this magnificence, all this mystery, all this beauty, all this labour, all this high invention—where were their originators? I fell into deep musing. And the kingdoms of the earth passed before me, from the thrones of the Pharaohs to those enormous dominations that sprang out of the feudal chaos, the unlawful children of Ignorance and Expediency. And I surveyed the generations of man from Rameses the Great, and Memnon the Beautiful, to the solitary pilgrim, whose presence now violated the sanctity of their gorgeous sepulchres. And I found that the history of my race was but one tale of rapid destruction or gradual decay.

And in the anguish of my heart, I lifted up my hands to the blue ether, and I said, "Is there no hope? What is knowledge, and what is truth? How shall I gain wisdom?"

The wind arose, the bosom of the desert heaved, pillars of sand sprang from the earth and whirled across the plain, sounds more awful than thunder came rushing from the south; the fane and the palace, the portal and the obelisk, the altar and the throne, the picture and the frieze, disappeared from my sight, and darkness brooded over the land. I knelt down and hid my face in the movable and burning soil, and as the wind of the desert passed over me, methought it whispered, "Child of nature, learn to unlearn!"

We are the slaves of false knowledge. Our memories are filled with ideas that have no origin in truth. We learn nothing from ourselves. The sum of our experience is but a dim dream of the conduct of past generations, generations that lived in a total ignorance of their nature. Our instructers are the unknowing and the dead. We study human nature in a charnel-house, and, like the nations of the East, we pay divine honours to the maniac and the fool. A series of systems have mystified existence. We believe what our fathers credited, because they were convinced without a cause. The faculty of thought has been destroyed. Yet our emasculated minds, without the power of fruition, still pant for the charms of wisdom. It is this that makes us fly with rapture to false knowledge—to tradition, to prejudice, to custom. Delusive tradition, destructive prejudice, degenerating custom! It is this that makes us prostrate ourselves with reverence before the wisdom of by-gone ages, in no one of which has man been the master of his own reason.

I am desirous of writing a book which shall be all truth, a work of which the passion, the thought, the action, and even the style, should spring from my own experience of feeling, from the meditations of my own intellect, from my own observation of incident, from my own study of the genius of expression.

When I turn over the pages of the metaphysician, I perceive a science that deals in words instead of facts. Arbitrary axioms lead to results that violate reason; imaginary principles establish systems that contradict the common sense of mankind. All is dogma, no part demonstration. Wearied, perplexed, doubtful, I throw down the volume in disgust.

When I search into my own breast, and trace the developement of my own intellect, and the formation of my own character, all is light and order. The luminous succeeds to the obscure, the certain to the doubtful, the intelligent to the illogical, the practical to the impossible, and I experience all that refined and ennobling satisfaction that we derive from the discovery of truth and the contemplation of nature.

I have resolved, therefore, to write the history of my own life, because it is the subject of which I have the truest knowledge.

At an age when some have scarcely entered upon their career, I can look back upon past years spent in versatile adventure and long meditation. My thought has been the consequence of my organization; my action the result of a necessity not less imperious. My fortune and my intelligence have blended together, and formed my character.

I am desirous of executing this purpose while my brain is still fed by the ardent though tempered flame of youth; while I can recall the past with accuracy, and record it with vividness; while my memory is still faithful, and while the dewy freshness of youthful fancy still lingers on the flowers of my mind.

I would bring to this work the illumination of an intellect emancipated from the fatal prejudices of an irrational education. This may be denied me. Yet some exemption from the sectarian prejudices that imbitter life may surely be expected from one who, by a curious combination of circumstances, finds himself without country, without kindred, and without friends; nor will he be suspected of indulging in the delusion of worldly vanity, who, having acted in the world, has retired to meditate in an inviolate solitude, and seeks relief from the overwhelming vitality of thought in the flowing spirit of creation.

II.

When I can first recall existence, I remember myself a melancholy child. My father, Baron Fleming, was a Saxon nobleman of ancient family, who, being opposed to the French interest, quitted, at the commencement of this century, his country, and after leading for some years a wandering life, entered into the service of a northern court. At Venice, yet a youth, he married a daughter of the noble house of Contarini, and of that marriage I was the only offspring. My entrance into this world was marked with evil, for my mother yielded up her life while investing me with mine. I was christened with the name of her illustrious race. Thus much, during the first years of my childhood, I casually learned, but I know not how; I feel I was early conscious that my birth was a subject on which it was proper that I should not speak, and one, the mention of which, it was early instilled into me, would only occasion my remaining parent bitter sorrow. Therefore upon this topic I was ever silent, and with me, from my earliest recollection, Venice was a name to be shunned.

My father again married. His new bride was a daughter of the country which had adopted him. She was of high blood, and very wealthy, and beautiful in the fashion of her land. This union produced two children, both males. As a child, I viewed them with passive antipathy. They were called my brothers, but nature gave the lie to the reiterated assertion. There was no similitude between us. Their blue eyes, their flaxen hair, and their white visages claimed no kindred with my Venetian countenance. Wherever I moved, I looked around me, and beheld a race different from myself. There was no sympathy between my frame and the rigid clime whither I had been brought to live. I knew not why, but I was unhappy. Had I found in one of my father's new children a sister, all might have been changed. In that sweet and singular tie, I might have discovered solace, and the variance of constitution would perhaps, between different sexes, have fostered, rather than discouraged affection. But this blessing, which I have ever considered the choicest boon of nature, was denied me. I was alone.

I loved my father dearly and deeply, but I seldom saw him. He was buried in the depth of affairs. A hurried kiss and a passing smile were the fleeting gifts of his affection. Scrupulous care however was taken that I should never be, and should never feel, neglected. I was overloaded with attentions, even as an infant. My stepmother, swayed by my father, and perhaps by a well-regulated mind, was vigilant in not violating the etiquette of maternal duty. No favour was shown to my white brethren which was not extended also to me. To me also, as the eldest, the preference, if necessary, was ever yielded. But for the rest, she was cold, and I was repulsive, and she stole from the saloon, which I rendered interesting by no infantile graces, to the nursery, where she could lavish her love upon her troublesome, but sympathizing offspring, and listen to the wondrous chronicle which their attendants daily supplied of their marvellous deeds and almost oracular prattle.

Because I was unhappy, I was sedentary and silent, for the lively sounds and the wild gambols of children are but the unconscious outpourings of joy. They make their gay noises, and burst into their gay freaks, as young birds in spring chant in the free air, and flutter in the fresh boughs. But I could not revel in the rushing flow of my new blood, nor yield up my frame to its dashing and voluptuous course. I could not yet analyze my feelings; I could not indeed yet think; but I had an instinct that I was different from my fellow-creatures, and the feeling was not triumph, but horror.

My quiet inaction gained me the reputation of stupidity. In vain they endeavoured to conceal from me their impression. I read it in their looks; in their glances of pity full of learned discernment, in their telegraphic exchanges of mutual conviction. At last, in a moment of irritation, the secret broke from one of my white brothers. I felt that the urchin spoke truth, but I cut him to the ground. He ran howling and yelping to his dam. I was surrounded by the indignant mother and the domestic police. I listened to their agitated accusations, and palpitating threats of punishment, with sullen indifference. I offered no defence. I courted their vengeance. It came in the shape of imprisonment. I was conducted to my room, and my door was locked on the outside. I answered the malignant sound by bolting it in the interior. I remained there two days deaf to all their entreaties, without sustenance, feeding only upon my vengeance. Each fresh visit was an additional triumph. I never answered; I never moved. Demands of apology were exchanged for promises of pardon: promises of pardon were in turn succeeded by offers of reward. I gave no sign. I heard them stealing on tiptoe to the portal, full of horrible alarm, and even doubtful of my life. I scarcely would breathe. At length the door was burst open, and in rushed the half-fainting baroness, and a posse of servants, with the children clinging to their nurses' gowns. Planted in the most distant corner, I received them with a grim smile. I was invited away. I refused to move. A man-servant advanced and touched me. I stamped, I gnashed my teeth, I gave a savage growl, that made him recoil with dread. The baroness lost her remaining presence of mind, withdrew her train, and was obliged to call in my father, to whom all was for the first time communicated.

I heard his well-known step upon the stair, I beheld the face that never looked upon me without a smile, if in carelessness, still, still a smile. Now it was grave, but sad, not harsh.

"Contarini," he said, in a serious, but not angried voice, "what is all this?"

I burst into a wild cry, I rushed to his arms. He pressed me to his bosom. He tried to kiss away the flooding tears, that each embrace called forth more plenteously. For the first time in my life I felt happy, because for the first time in my life I felt loved.

III.

It was a beautiful garden, full of terraces and arched walks of bowery trees. A tall fountain sprang up from a marble basin, and its glittering column broke in its fall into a thousand coloured drops, and woke the gleamy fish that would have slept in the dim water. And I wandered about, and the enchanted region seemed illimitable, and at each turn more magical and more bright. Now a white vase shining in the light, now a dim statue shadowy in a cool grot. I would have lingered a moment at the mossy hermitage, but the distant bridge seemed to invite me to new adventures.

It was only three miles from the city, and belonged to the aunt of the baroness. I was brought here to play. When the women met there was much kissing, and I also was kissed, but it gave me no pleasure, for I felt even then that it was a form, and I early imbibed a hatred of all this mechanical domestic love. And they sat together, and took out their work, and talked without ceasing, chiefly about the children. The baroness retold all the wonderful stories of the nurses, many of which I knew to be false. I did not say this, but the conviction gave me, thus early, a contempt for the chatter of women. As soon as I was unobserved, I stole away to the garden.

Even then it was ravishing to be alone. And although I could not think, and knew not the cause of the change, I felt serene, and the darkness of my humour seemed to leave me. All was so new and so beautiful. The bright sweet flowers, and the rich shrubs, and the tall trees, and the flitting birds, and the golden bees, and the gay butterflies, and that constant and soothing hum, broken only ever and anon by a strange shrill call, and that wonderful blending of brilliancy and freshness, and perfume and warmth, that strong sense of the loveliness and vitality of nature which we feel amid the growing life of a fair garden, entered into my soul, and diffused themselves over my frame, softened my heart, and charmed my senses.

But all this was not alone the cause of my happiness. For to me the garden was not a piece of earth belonging to my aunt, but a fine world. I wandered about in quest of some strange adventure, which I would fain believe, in so fair a region must quickly occur. The terrace was a vast desert over which I travelled for many days, and the mazy walks, so mysterious and unworldly, were an unexplored forest fit for a true knight. And in the hermitage, I sought the simple hospitality of a mild and aged host, who pointed to the far bridge as surely leading to a great fulfilment, and my companion was a faithful esquire, whose fidelity was never wanting, and we conversed much, but most respecting a mighty ogre, who was to fall beneath my puissant arm. Thus glided many a day in unconscious and creative revery, but sometimes, when I had explored over again each nook and corner, and the illimitable feeling had worn off, the power of imagination grew weak. I found myself alone amid the sweets and sunshine, and felt sad.

But I would not quit this delicious world without an effort, and invented a new mode of mingling in its life. I reclined beneath a shady tree, and I covered my eyes with my little hand, and I tried to shut out the garish light, that seemed to destroy the visions which were ever flitting before me. They came in their beauty, obedient to my call. And I wandered in strange countries, and achieved many noble acts, and said many noble words, and the beings with whom I acted were palpable as myself, with beautiful faces and graceful forms. And there was a brave young knight, who was my friend, and his life I ever saved, and a lovely princess, who spoke not, but smiled ever, and ever upon me. And we were lost in vast forests, and shared hard food, and as the evening drew on, we came to the gates of a castle.

"Contarini! Contarini!" a voice sounded from the house, and all the sweet visions rushed away like singing birds scared out of a tree. I was no longer a brave knight: I was a child. I rose miserable and exhausted, and in spite of a repeated cry, I returned with a slow step and a sullen face.

I saw there was an unusual bustle in the house. Servants were running to and fro doing nothing, doors were slammed, and there was much calling. I stole into the room unperceived. It was a new comer. They were all standing around a beautiful girl, expanding into prime womanhood, and all talking at the same time. There was also much kissing.

It appeared to me that there could not be a more lovely being than the visiter. She was dressed in a blue riding-coat, with a black hat, which had fallen off her forehead. Her full chestnut curls had broken loose. Her rich cheek glowed with the excitement of the meeting, and her laughing eyes sparkled with social love.

I gazed upon her unperceived. She must have been at least eight years my senior. This idea crossed me not then, I gazed upon her unperceived, and it was fortunate, for I was entranced. I could not move or speak. My whole system changed. My breath left me. I panted with great difficulty. The colour fled from my cheek, and I was sick from the blood rushing to my heart.

I was seen, I was seized, I was pulled forward. I bent down my head. They lifted it up, drawing back my curls; they lifted it up covered with blushes. She leant down, she kissed me—O! how unlike the dull kisses of the morning. But I could not return her embrace; I nearly swooned upon her bosom. She praised, in her good-nature, the pretty boy, and the tone in which she spoke made me doubly feel my wretched insignificance.

The bustle subsided; eating succeeded to talking. Our good aunt was a great priestess in the mysteries of plum-cake and sweet wine. I had no appetite. This was the fruitful theme of much discussion. I could not eat: I thought only of the fair stranger. They wearied me with their wonderment and their inquiries. I was irritated and I was irritable. The baroness schooled me in that dull tedious way which always induces obstinacy At another time, I should have been sullen, but my heart was full and softened, and I wept. My stepmother was alarmed lest, in an unguarded moment, she should have passed the cold, strict line of maternal impartiality which she had laid down for her constant regulation. She would have soothed me with commonplace consolation. I was miserable and disgusted. I fled again to the garden.

I regained with hurrying feet my favourite haunt, again I sat under my favourite tree. But not now to build castles of joy and hope, not now to commune with my beautiful creation, and revel in the warm flow of my excited fancy. All, all had fled all, all had changed. I shivered under the cold horror of reality.

I thought I heard beautiful music, but it was only the voice of a woman.

"Contarini," said the voice, "why do you weep?"

I looked up; it was the stranger, it was Christiana. "Because," I answered, sobbing, "I am miserable."

"Sweet boy," she said, as she knelt down beside me, "dry, dry your tears, for we all love you. Mamma meant not to be cross."

"Mamma! She is not *my* mamma."

"But she loves you like a mother."

"No one loves me."

"All love you, dearest—I love you," and she kissed me with a thousand kisses.

"O! Christiana," I exclaimed, in a low, tremulous voice, "love me, love me always. If *you* do not love me I shall die!"

I threw my arms around her neck, and a gleam of rapture seemed to burst through the dark storm of my grief. She pressed me to her heart a thousand times, and each time I clung with a more ardent grasp—and by degrees, the fierceness of my passion died away, and heavy sobs succeeded to my torrents of tears, and light sighs at last came flying after, like clouds in a clearing heaven. Our grief dies away like a thunder-storm.

IV.

The visit of Christiana was the first great incident of my life. No day passed without my seeing her, either at the garden-house, or at our town, and each day I grew happier. Her presence, the sound of her voice, one bright smile, and I was a different being; but her caresses, her single society, the possession of her soft hand—all this was maddening. When I was with her in the company of others, I was happy, but I indicated my happiness by no exterior sign. I sat by her side, with my hand locked in hers, and I fed in silence upon my tranquil joy. But when we were alone, then it was that her influence over me broke forth. All the feelings of my heart were hers. I concealed nothing. I told her each moment that I loved her, and that until I knew her I was unhappy. Then I would communicate to her in confidence all my secret sources of enjoyment, and explain how I had turned common places into enchanted regions, where I could always fly for refuge. She listened with fondness and delight, and was the heroine of all my sports. Now I had indeed a princess. Strolling with her, the berceau was still more like a forest, and the solace of the hermit's cell still more refreshing.

Her influence over me was all-powerful, for she seemed to change my habits and my temper. In kindness she entered into my solitary joys; in kindness she joined in my fantastic amusements; for her own temper was social, and her own delight in pastimes that were common to all. She tried to rouse me from my inaction, she counselled me to mingle with my companions. How graceful was this girl! Grace was indeed her characteristic, her charm. Sometimes she would run away swifter than an arrow, and then, as she was skimming along, suddenly stop, and turn her head with an expression so fascinating, that she appeared to me always like a young sunny fawn.

"Contarini!" she would cry, in a clear flute-like voice. How I rushed to her!

I became more amiable to my brothers. I courted more the members of my little society. I even joined in their sports. It was whispered that Contarini was much improved, and the baroness glanced at me with a kind of patronising air, that seemed to hint to the initiated not to press me too heavily with their regulations, or exercise towards one so unpractised, perhaps so incapable, all the severity of their childish legislation.

The visit of Christiana drew to a close. There was a children's ball at our house, and she condescended to be its mistress. Among my new companions, there was a boy who was two years my senior. He had more knowledge of the world than most of us, for he had been some time at school. He was gay, vivacious, talkative. He was the leader in all our diversions. We all envied him his superiority, and all called him conceited. He was ever with Christiana. I disliked him.

I hated dancing, but to-night I had determined to dance, for the honour of our fair president. When the ball opened, I walked up to claim her hand as a matter of course. She was engaged—she was engaged to this youthful hero. Engaged! Was it true? Engaged! Horrible jargon! Were the hollow forms of mature society to interfere with our play of love? She expressed her regret, and promised to dance with me afterward. She promised what I did not require. Pale and agitated, I stole to a corner, and fed upon my mortified heart.

I watched her in the dance. Never had she looked more beautiful; what was worse, never more happy. Every smile pierced me through. Each pressure of my rival's hand touched my brain. I grew sick and dizzy. It was a terrible effort not to give way to my passion. But I succeeded, and escaped from the chamber, with all its glaring lights and jarring sounds.

I stopped one moment on the staircase for breath. A servant came up and asked if I wanted any thing. I could not answer. He asked if I were unwell. I struggled with my choking voice, and said I was very well. I stole up to my bed-room. I had no light, but a dim moon just revealed my bed. I threw myself upon it and wished to die.

My forehead was burning hot, my feet were icy cold. My heart seemed in my throat. I felt quite sick. I could not speak; I could not weep; I could not think. Every thing seemed blended in one terrible sensation of desolate and desolating wretchedness.

Much time perhaps had not elapsed, although it seemed to me an age, but there was a sound in the room, light and gentle. I looked around, I thought that a shadowy form passed between me and the window. A feeling of terror crossed me. I nearly cried out; but as my lips moved, a warm mouth sealed them with sweetness.

"Contarini," said a voice I could not mistake, "are you unwell?"

I would not answer.

"Contarini, my love, speak to Christiana!"

But the demon prevailed, and I would not speak.

"Contarini, you are not asleep?"

Still I was silent.

"Contarini, you do not love me."

I would have been silent, but I sighed.

"Contarini, what has happened? Tell me, tell me, dearest. Tell your Christiana. You know you always tell her every thing."

I seized her hand—I bathed it with my fast-flowing tears.

She knelt down as she did on our first meeting in the garden, and clasped me in her arms; and each moment the madness of my mind grew greater. I was convulsed with passion.

And when I grew more calm, she again spoke, and asked me what made me so unhappy; and I said, between my wild sobs, "O! Christiana, you too have turned against me!"

"Dear, sensitive child," she said, as she pressed me to her bosom, "if you feel so keenly, you will never be happy. Turn against you! O! Contarini, who is your friend if not Christiana! Do I not love you better than all the world? Do I not do all I can to make you happy and good? And why should I turn against Contarini when he is the best and dearest of boys, and loves his Christiana with all his heart and soul?"

She raised me from the bed, and placed me in her lap. My head reposed upon her fond and faithful heart. She was silent, for I was exhausted, and I felt her sweet breath descending upon my cheek.

"Go," I said, after some little time, and in a feeble voice, "go, Christiana. They want you."

"Not without you, dearest. I came to fetch you."

"I cannot go. It is impossible; I am so tired."

"O! come dearest! I shall be so unhappy if you do not come. You would not have me unhappy the whole evening, this evening that we were to be so gay. See! I will run and fetch a light, and be with you in a moment." And she kissed me and ran away, and in a moment returned.

"Dearest Christiana! I cannot go. What will they think of me?"

"Nobody knows even that you are away; all are busy."

"What will they think of me? Really I cannot go, and my eyes are so red."

"Nonsense! They are the blackest and most beautiful eyes I ever saw."

"O! they are horridly red," I answered, looking in the glass. "I cannot go, Christiana."

"They are not the least red. I will wash them with some eau de Cologne and water."

"O! Christiana, do you really love me? Have you really made it up?"

"I love you more than ever, dear! There, let me brush your curls. Is this your brush? What a funny little brush! Dear Contarini, how pretty you look!"

V.

When I was eight years of age, a tutor was introduced into the house, and I was finally and formally emancipated from the police of the nursery, and the government of women. My tutor was well qualified for his office, according to the existing ideas respecting education, which substitute for the noblest of sciences the vile art of teaching words. He was learned in his acquirements, and literary in his taste, with a calm mind, a bland manner, and a mild voice. The baroness, who fancied herself a great judge of character, favoured him, before the commencement of his labours, with an epitome of mine. After a year's experience of his pupil, he ventured to express his opinion, that I was by no means so slow as was supposed, that although I had no great power of application, I was not averse to acquiring knowledge, and that if I were not endowed with any very remarkable or shining qualities, my friends might be consoled for the absence of these high powers by my being equally destitute of those violent passions and that ungovernable volition which were usually attendant upon genius, and too often rendered the most gifted miserable.

I was always a bad learner, and although I loved knowledge from my cradle, I liked to acquire it in my own way. I think that I was born with a detestation of grammars. Nature seemed to whisper to me the folly of learning words instead of ideas, and my mind would have grown sterile for want of manure, if I had not taken its culture into my own hands, and compensated by my own tillage for my tutor's bad husbandry. I therefore, in a quiet way, read every book that I could get hold of, and studied as little as possible in my instructer's museum of verbiage, whether his specimens appeared in the anatomy of a substantive, or the still more disgusting form of a dissected verb.

This period of my life was too memorable for a more interesting incident than the introduction of my tutor. For the first time I visited the theatre. Never shall I forget the impression. At length I perceived human beings conducting themselves as I wished. I was mad for the playhouse, and I had the means of gratifying my mania. I so seldom fixed my heart upon any thing, I showed, in general, such little relish for what is called amusement, that my father accorded me his permission with pleasure and facility, and as an attendant to this magical haunt, I now began to find my tutor of great use.

I had now a pursuit, for when I was not a spectator at the theatre, at home I was an actor. I required no audience—I was happier alone. My chivalric reveries had been long gradually leaving me; now they entirely vanished. As I learned more of life and nature, I required for my private world something which, while it was beautiful and uncommon, was nevertheless natural and could live. Books more real than fairy tales and feudal romances had already made me muse over a more real creation. The theatre at once fully introduced to me this new existence, and there arose accordingly in my mind new characters. Heroes succeeded to knights, tyrants to ogres, and boundless empire to enchanted castles. My character also changed with my companions. Before all was beautiful and bright, but still and mystical. The forms that surrounded me were splendid, the scenes through which I passed glittering, but the changes took place without my agency, or if I acted, I fulfilled only the system of another—for the foundation was the supernatural. Now, if every thing were less beautiful, every thing was more earnest. I mingled with the warlike and the wise, the crafty, the suffering, the pious—all depended upon our own exertions, and each result could only be brought about by their own simple and human energies—for the foundation was the natural.

Yet at times even this fertile source of enjoyment failed, and the dark spirit which haunted in my first years would still occasionally descend upon my mind. I knew not how it was, but the fit came upon me in an instant, and often when least counted on. A star, a sunset, a tree, a note of music, the sound of the wind, a fair face flitting by me in unknown beauty, and I was lost. All seemed vapid, dull, spiritless, and flat. Life had no object and no beauty; and I slunk to some solitary corner, where I was content to lie down and die. These were moments of bitter agony, these were moments in which if I were spoken to I had no respect for persons. Once I remember my father found me before the demon had yet flown, and, for the first time, he spoke without being honoured.

At last I had such a lengthened fit that it attracted universal attention. I would scarcely move, or speak, or eat for days. There was a general alarm. The baroness fell into a flutter, lest my father should think I had been starved to death, or ill-used, or poisoned, and overwhelmed me with inquiries, each of which severally procrastinated my convalescence. For doubtless, now that I can analyze my past feelings, these dark humours arose only from the want of being loved. Physicians were called in. There were immense consultations. They were all puzzled, and all had recourse to arrogant dogmas. I would not, nay, I could not assist them. Lying upon the sofa with my eyes shut, as if asleep, I listened to their conferences. It was settled that I was suffering from a want of nervous energy. Strange jargon, of which their fellow-creatures are the victims! Although young, I looked upon these men with suspicion, if not contempt, and my after life has both increased my experience of their character, and confirmed my juvenile impression.

Change of air and scene were naturally prescribed for an effect by men who were ignorant of the cause. It was settled that I should leave town, accompanied by my tutor, and that we should reside for a season at my father's castle.

VI.

"And I, too, will fly to Egeria!"

We were discoursing of Pompilius when the thought flashed across me. I no longer listened to his remarks, and ceased also to answer. My eyes were indeed fixed upon the page, but I perceived nothing; as it was not yet my hour of liberty, I remained in a soft state of dreamy abstraction.

When I was again free I wandered forth into the park, and I hastened, with a rushing, agitated step, to the spot on which I had fixed.

It was a small dell, and round it grew tall trees with thin and light-coloured leaves; and the earth was everywhere covered with thick fern and many wild flowers. And the dell was surrounded at a very slight distance by a deep wood, out of which white glancing hares each instant darted to play upon the green sunny turf. It was not indeed a sparry grot, cool in the sparkling splendour of a southern scene; it was not indeed a spot formed in the indefinite, but lovely, mould of the regions of my dreams, but it was green, and sweet, and wondrous still.

And I threw myself upon the soft yielding fern, and covered my eyes. And a shadowy purple tint was all that I perceived, and as my abstraction grew more intense, the purple lightened into a dusky white, and this new curtain again into a glittering veil, and the veil mystically disappeared, and I beheld a beautiful and female face.

It was not unlike Christiana, but more dazzling, and very pensive. And the eyes met mine, and they were full of serious lustre, and my heart beat, and I seemed to whisper with a very low, but almost ecstatic voice, "Egeria!" Yet indeed my lips did not move. And the vision beamed with a melancholy smile. And suddenly I found myself in a spacious cave, and I looked up into the face of a beautiful woman, and her countenance was the countenance of the vision. And we were in deep shade, but far out I could perceive a shining and azure land. And the sky was of a radiant purple, and the earth was streaming with a golden light. And there were blue mountains, and bright fields, and glittering vineyards.

And I said nothing, but I looked upon her face, and dwelt upon her beauty. And hours flew, and the sun set, and the dew descended. And as the sky became less warm, the vision gradually died away, and I arose in the long twilight, and I returned home pensive and grave, but full of a soft and palpitating joy.

And when I returned, I could not eat. My tutor made many observations, many inquiries, but he was a simple man, and I could always quiet him. I sat at the table full of happiness, and almost without motion. And in the evening I stole into a corner, and thought of the coming day with all its rich strange joys.

My life was now one long stream of full felicity. It was indeed but one idea, but that idea was as beautiful as it was engrossing. Each day I hastened to the enchanted dell, each day I returned with renewed rapture. I had no thought for any thing but my mystic mistress. My studies, always an effort, would now have been insupportable, had I not invented a system by which I rendered even their restraint a new source of enjoyment. I had now so complete a command of my system of abstraction, that while my eye apparently was employed and interested with my allotted page, I in fact perceived nothing but my visionary nymph My tutor, who observed me always engrossed, could not perceive that I was otherwise than a student, and when I could remember, I would turn over a leaf, or affect with much anxiety to look out a word in the lexicon, so that his deception was perfect. Then at the end of the day I would snatch some hasty five minutes to gain an imperfect acquaintance with my task, imperfect enough to make him at length convinced that the baroness's opinion of my intellect was not so erroneous as he had once imagined.

A short spring and a long summer had passed away thus delightfully, and I was now to leave the castle and return to the capital. The idea of being torn away from Egeria was harrowing. I became again melancholy, but my grief was tender, not savage. I did not recur to my ancient gloom, for I was prevented by the consoling conviction that I was loved. Yet to her the sad secret must be confided. I could not quit her without preparation. How often in solitary possession of the dreadful fact, have I gazed upon her incomparable face, how often have I fancied that she was conscious of the terrible truth, and glanced reproachfully even amid her looks of love.

It was told: in broken acts of passionate wo, with streaming eyes, and amid embraces of maddening rapture, it was told. I clung to her, I would have clung to her forever, but a dark and irresistible destiny doomed us to part, and I was left to my uninspired loneliness.

Returning home from my last visit to the dell, I met my tutor. He came upon me suddenly, otherwise I would have avoided him, as at this moment I would have avoided any thing else human. My swollen cheeks, my eyes dim with weeping, my wild and broken walk, attracted even his attention.

He inquired what ailed me. His appearance, so different from the radiant being from whom I had lately parted, his voice so strange after the music which yet lingered in my ear, his salutation so varying in style to the one that ever welcomed me, and ever and alone was welcome, the horrible contrast that my situation formed with the condition I had the instant quitted—all this overcame me. I expressed my horror by my extended arms and my averted head. I screamed, I foamed at the mouth, I fell into violent convulsions.

VII.

Although I have delineated with some detail the feelings of my first boyhood, I have been indebted for this record to the power of a faithful and analytic memory, and not to any early indulgence in the habits of introspection. For indeed, in these young years I never thought about myself, or if some extraordinary circumstances impelled me to idiosyncratic contemplation, the result was not cheering. For I well remember that when, on the completion of my eleventh year, being about to repair to a college where I was to pass some years preparatory to the university, I meditated on this great and coming change,—I was impressed with a keen conviction of inferiority. It had sometimes indeed crossed my mind that I was of a different order to those around me, but never that the difference was in my favour, and brooding over the mortifying contrast which my exploits exhibited in my private and my public world, and the general opinion which they entertained of me at home, I was at times strongly tempted to consider myself even half a fool.

Though change was ever agreeable, I thought of the vicissitude that was about to occur with the same apprehension that men look forward to the indefinite horror of a terrible operation. And the strong pride that supported me under the fear, and forbade me to demonstrate it, was indeed the cause of my sad forebodings. For I could not tolerate the thought that I should become a general jest, and a common agent. And when I perceived the state preparing for me, and thought of Egeria, I blushed. And that beautiful vision that had brought me such delicious solace was now only a source of depressing mortification. And for the first time in my life, in my infinite tribulation, and in the agony of my fancy, I mused why there should be such a devilish and tormenting variance between my thought and my action.

The hour came, and I was placed in the heart of a little and a busy world. For the first time in my life I was surrounded by struggling and excited beings. Joy, hope, sorrow, ambition, craft, courage, wit, dulness, cowardice, beneficence, awkwardness, grace, avarice, generosity, wealth, poverty, beauty, hideousness, tyranny, suffering, hypocrisy, truth, love, hatred, energy, inertness—they were all there, and all sounded, and moved, and acted about me. Light laughs, and bitter cries, and deep imprecations, and the deeds of the friendly, the prodigal, and the tyrant, and the exploits of the brave, the graceful, and the gay, and the flying words of native wit, and the pompous sentences of acquired knowledge—how new, how exciting, how wonderful!

Did I tremble? Did I sink into my innermost self? Did I fly? Never As I gazed upon them, a new principle rose up in my breast, and I perceived only beings whom I was determined to control. They came up to me with a curious glance of half-suppressed glee, breathless and mocking. They asked me questions of gay nonsense with a serious voice and a solemn look. I answered in their kind. On a sudden I seemed endowed with new powers, and blessed with the gift of tongues. I spoke to them with a levity which was quite new to me, a most unnatural ease. I even, in my turn, presented to them questions to which they found it difficult to respond. Some ran away to communicate their impressions to their comrades, some stayed behind, but these became more serious and more natural. When they found that I was endowed with a pregnant and decided character, their eyes silently pronounced me a good fellow, they vied with each other in kindness, and the most important led me away to initiate me in their mysteries.

Weeks flew away, and I was intoxicated with my new life and my new reputation. I was in a state of ceaseless excitement. It seemed that my tongue never paused: yet each word brought forth a new laugh, each sentence of gay nonsense fresh plaudits. All was rattle, frolic, and wild mirth. My companions caught my unusual manner, they adopted my new phrases, they repeated my extraordinary apophthegms. Every thing was viewed and done according to the new tone which I had introduced. It was decided that I was the wittiest, the most original, the most diverting of their society. A coterie of the most congenial insensibly formed around me, and my example gradually ruled the choice spirits of our world. I even mingled in their games, although I disliked the exertion, and in those in which the emulation was very strong, I even excelled. My ambition conquered my nature. It seemed that I was the soul of the school. Wherever I went, my name sounded, whatever was done, my opinion was quoted. I was caressed, adored, idolized. In a word, I was popular.

Yet sometimes I caught a flying moment to turn aside, and contrast my present situation with my past one. What was all this? Was I the same being? But my head was in a whirl, and I had not time, or calmness, to solve the perplexing inquiry.

There was a boy, and his name was Musæus. He was somewhat my elder. Of a kind, calm, docile, mellow nature, moderate in every thing, universally liked, but without the least influence,—he was the serene favourite of the school. It seemed to me that I never beheld so lovely and so pensive a countenance. His face was quite oval, his eyes deep blue: his rich brown curls clustered in hyacinthine grace upon the delicate rose of his downy cheeks, and shaded the light blue veins of his clear white forehead.

I beheld him: I loved him. My friendship was a passion. Of all our society, he alone crowded not around me. He was of a cold temperament, shy and timid. He looked upon me as a being whom he could not comprehend, and rather feared. I was unacquainted with his motives, and piqued with his conduct. I gave up my mind to the acquisition of his acquaintance, and of course I succeeded. In vain he endeavoured to escape. Wherever he moved, I seemed unintentionally to hover around him: whatever he wanted, I seemed providentially to supply. In the few words that this slight intercourse called forth, I addressed him in a tone strange to our rough life; I treated him with a courtesy which seemed to elevate our somewhat coarse condition. He answered nothing, was confused, thankful, agitated. He yielded to the unaccustomed tenderness of my manner, to the unexperienced elegance of my address. He could not but feel the strange conviction, that my conduct to him was different to my behaviour to others, for in truth his presence ever subdued my spirit, and repressed my artificial and excited manner.

Musæus was lowly born, and I was noble; he poor, and I wealthy; I had a dazzling reputation, he but good report. To find himself an object of interest, of quiet and tender regard, to one to whose notice all aspired, and who seemed to exist only in a blaze of cold-hearted raillery and reckless repartee, developed even his dormant vanity. He looked upon me with interest, and this feeling soon matured into fondness.

O! days of rare and pure felicity, when Musæus and myself, with our arms around each other's neck, wandered together amid the meads and shady woods that formed our limits. I lavished upon him all the fanciful love that I had long stored up, and the mighty passions that yet lay dormant in my obscure soul, now first began to stir in that glimmering abyss. And indeed conversing with this dear companion was it, that I first began to catch some glimpses of my yet hidden nature. For the days of futurity were our usual topic, and in parcelling out their fortunes, I unconsciously discovered my own desires. I was to be something great, and glorious, and dazzling, but what we could not determine. The camp and the senate, the sword and the scroll, that had raised, and had destroyed, so many states—these were infinitely discussed. And then a life of adventure was examined, full of daring delight. One might be a corsair or a bandit. Foreign travel was what we could surely command, and must lead to much. I spoke to him, in the fulness of our sweet confidence, of the strangeness of my birth, and we marvelled together over mysterious Venice. And this led us to conspiracies, for which I fancied that I had a predisposition. But in all these scenes, Musæus was to be never absent. He was to be my heart's friend from the beginning to the death. And I mourned that nature had given me no sister, wherewith I could bind him to me by a still stronger and sweeter tie. And then, with a shy, hesitating voice, for he delighted not in talking of his home, he revealed to me that he was more blessed: and Caroline Musæus rose up at once to me like a star, and without having seen her, I was indeed her betrothed.

Thus, during these bright days, did I pour forth all the feelings I had long treasured up, and in endeavouring to communicate my desires to another, I learned to think. I ascended from indefinite revery to palpable cogitation.

I was now seldom alone. To be the companion of Musæus, I participated in many pastimes which otherwise I should have avoided, and in return he, although addicted to sports, was content, for my sake, to forego much former occupation. With what eagerness I rushed, when the hour of study ceased—with what wild eagerness I rushed to resume our delicious converse! Nor indeed was his image ever absent from me, and when, in the hour of school, we passed each other, or our countenances chanced to meet, there was ever a sweet, faint smile, that, unmarked by others, interchanged our love

A love that I thought must last forever, and forever flow like a clear, bright stream, yet at times my irritable passions would disturb even these sweet waters. The temperament of Musæus was cold and slow. I was at first proud of having interested his affection, but, as our friendship grew apace, I was not contented with this calm sympathy and quiet regard. I required that he should respond to my affection with feelings not less ardent, and energetic than mine own. I was sensitive, I was jealous. I found a savage joy in harrowing his heart—I triumphed when I could draw a tear from his beautiful eye; when I could urge him to unaccustomed emotion; when I forced him to assure me, in a voice of agitation, that he loved me alone, and prayed me to be pacified.

From sublime torture to ridiculous teasing, too often Musæus was my victim. One day I detected an incipient dislike to myself, or a growing affection for another: then, I passed him in gloomy silence, because his indispensable engagements had obliged him to refuse my invitation to our walk. But the letters with which I overwhelmed him under some of these contingencies—these were the most violent infliction. What pages of mad eloquence! —solemn appeals, bitter sarcasms, infinite ebullitions of frantic sensibility. For the first time in my life, I composed. I grew intoxicated with my own eloquence. A new desire arose in my mind, novel aspirations which threw light upon old and often-experienced feelings. I began to ponder over the music of language; I studied the collocation of sweet words, and constructed elaborate sentences in lonely walks. Poor Musæus quite sunk under the receipt of my effusions. He could not write a line, and had he indeed been able, it would have been often difficult for him to have discovered the cause of our separations. The brevity, the simplicity of his answers were irresistible and heart-rending. Yet these distractions brought with them one charm, a charm to me so captivating, that I fear it was sometimes a cause—reconciliation was indeed a love-feast.

The sessions of our college closed. The time came that Musæus and myself must for a moment part, but for a moment, for, I intended that he should visit me in our vacation, and we were also to write to each other every week. Yet even under these palliating circumstances parting was anguish.

The eve of the fatal day, we took our last stroll in our favourite meads. The whole way I wept, and leaned upon his shoulder. With what jealous care I watched to see if he too shed a tear. One clear drop at length came quivering down his cheek, like dew upon a rose. I pardoned him for its beauty. The bell sounded. I embraced him, as if it sounded for my execution, and we parted.

VIII.

I WAS once more at home, once more silent, once more alone. I found myself changed. My obscure aspirations after some indefinite happiness, my vague dreams of beauty, or palpable personifications of some violent fantastic idea, no longer inspired, no longer soothed, no longer haunted me. I thought only of one subject, which was full of earnest novelty, and abounded in interest, curious, serious, and engrossing. I speculated upon my own nature. My new life had developed many qualities, and had filled me with self-confidence

The clouds seemed to clear off from the dark landscape of my mind, and vast ambition might be distinguished on the far horizon; rearing its head like a mighty column. My energies stirred within me, and seemed to pant for the struggle and the strife. A deed was to be done, but what? I entertained at this time a deep conviction that life must be intolerable, unless I were the greatest of men. It seemed that I felt within me the power that could influence my kind. I longed to wave my inspiring sword at the head of armies, or dash into the very heat and blaze of eloquent faction.

When I contrasted my feelings and my situation I grew mad. The constant jar between my conduct and my conceptions was intolerable. In imagination a hero, I was in reality a boy. I returned from a victorious field to be criticised by a woman: in the very heart of a deep conspiracy, which was to change the fate of nations, to destroy Rome or to free Venice, I was myself the victim of each petty domestic regulation. I cannot describe the insane irritability which all this produced. Infinite were the complaints of my rudeness, my violence, my insufferable impertinence: incessant the threats of pains and penalties. It was universally agreed that college had ruined me. A dull, slow boy I had always been, but, at least, I was tolerably kind and docile. Now, as my tutor's report correctly certified, I was not improved in intellect, and all witnessed the horrible deterioration of my manners and my morals.

The baroness was in despair. After several smart skirmishes, we at length had a regular pitched battle.

She began her delightful colloquy in the true style of domestic reprimand; dull, drony nonsense, adapted, as I should hope, to no state in which human intellect can ever be found, even if it have received the full benefit of the infernal tuition of nurses, which would be only ridiculous, if its effects were not so fatally and permanently injurious. She told me that whenever I spoke I should speak in a low voice, and that I should never think for myself. That if any thing were refused, I should be contented, and never ask the reason why, because it was not proper ever to ask questions, particularly when we were sure that every thing was done for our good. That I should do every thing that was bidden, and always be ready to conform to everybody's desires, because at my age no one should have a will of his own. That I should never, on any account, presume to give my opinion, because it was quite impossible that one so young could have one. That on no account, also, should I ever be irritable, which never could be permitted; but she never considered that every effect has a cause, and never attempted to discover what might occasion this irritability. In this silly, superficial way she went on for some time, repeating dull axioms by rote, and offering to me the same useless advice that had been equally thrown away upon the tender minds of her generation.

She said all this, all this to me, all this to one who, a moment before, was a Cæsar, an Alcibiades. Now I had long brooded over the connexion that subsisted between myself and this lady. I had long formed in my mind and caught up from books, a conception of the relations which must exist between a stepmother and her unwelcome son. I was therefore prepared. She grew pale as I described in mad heroics our exact situation. She had no idea that any people, under any circumstances, could be influenced by such violent, such wicked, such insane sentiments. She stared, in stupid astonishment, at my terrible and unexpected fluency. She entirely lost her presence of mind, and burst into tears—tears not of affection, but of absolute fright, the hysteric offspring of a cold, alarmed, puzzled mind.

She vowed she would tell my father. I inquired, with a malignant sneer, of what? She protested she certainly would tell. I dilated on the probability of a stepdame's tale. Most certainly she would tell. I burst into a dark, foaming rage. I declared that I would leave the house, that I would leave the country, that I would submit no longer to my intolerable life, that suicide (and here I kicked down a chair) should bring me immediate relief. The baroness was terrified out of her life. The fall of the chair was the perfection of fear. She was one of those women who have the highest respect for furniture. She could not conceive a human being, much less a boy, voluntarily kicking down a chair, if his feelings were not very keen indeed. It was becoming too serious. She tried to soothe me. She would not speak to my father. All should be right, all should be forgotten, if I only would not commit suicide, and not kick down the chairs.

After some weeks, Musæus paid his long meditated visit. I had never, until I invited him, answered his solitary letter. I received him with a coldness which astonished me, and must have been apparent to any one but himself. I was distressed by the want of unction in my manner, and tried to compensate by a laboured hospitality which, like ice, was dazzling, but frigid. Many causes, perhaps, conduced to occasion this change, then inscrutable to me. Since we had parted, I had indulged in lofty ideas of self, and sometimes remembered, with a feeling approaching to disgustful mortification, the influence which had been exercised over me by a fellow-child. The reminiscence savoured too much of boyish weakness, and painfully belied my proud theory of universal superiority. At home, too, when the permission for the invitation was accorded, there was much discussion as to the quality of the invited. They wished to know who he was, and when informed looked rather grave. Some caution was muttered about the choice of my companions. Even my father, who seldom spoke to me, seemed alarmed at the prospect of a bad connexion. His intense worldliness was shocked. He talked to me for an unusual time upon the subject of school friendships, and his conversation, which was rare, made an impression. All this influenced me, for at that age I was, of course, the victim of every prejudice. Must I add to all this, what is perhaps the sad and dreary truth, that in loving all this time Musæus with such devotion, I was in truth rather enamoured of the creature of my imagination than the companion of my presence. Upon the foundation which he had supplied, I had built a beautiful and enchanted palace. Unceasing intercourse was a necessary ingredient of the spell. We parted, and the fairy fabric dissolved into the clouds.

Certain it is, that his visit was a failure. Musæus was too little sensitive to feel the change of my manner, and my duty, as his host, impelled me to conceal it. But the change was great. He appeared to me to have fallen off very much in his beauty. The baroness thought him a little coarse, and praised the complexion of her own children, which was like chalk. Then he wanted constant attention, for it was evident that he had no resources of his own, and certainly he was not very refined. But he was pleased, for he was in a new world. For the first time in his life he moved in theatres and saloons, and mingled in the splendour of high civilization. I took him everywhere; in fact, I could bear every thing but to be alone with him. So he passed a very pleasant fortnight, and then quitted us. How different from our last parting! Cheerful indeed it was, and, in a degree, cordial. I extended him my hand with a patronising air, and mimicking the hollow courtesy of maturer beings, I expressed, in a flimsy voice of affected regard, a wish that he might visit us again. And six weeks before I had loved this boy better than myself, would have perilled for him my life, and shared with him my fortune!

IX.

I RETURNED to college gloomy and depressed. Not that I cared for quitting home: I hated home. I returned in the fullness of one of my dark humours, and which promised to be one of the most terrible visitations that had ever fallen upon me. Indeed, existence was intolerable, and I should have killed myself had I not been supported by my ambition, which now each day became more quickening, so that the desire of distinction and of astounding action raged in my soul, and when I recollected that at the soonest many years must elapse before I could realize my ideas, I gnashed my teeth in silent rage and cursed my existence.

I cannot picture the astonishment that pervaded our little society, when they found the former hero of their gayety avoiding all contact and conversation, and moving about always in gloomy silence. It was at first supposed, that some great misfortune had happened to me, and inquiries were soon afloat, but nothing could be discovered. At length one of my former prime companions, I should say, perhaps, patrons, expostulated with me upon the subject: I assured him with grim courtesy that nothing had happened, and wished him good morning. As for Musæus, I just contrived the first day to greet him with a faint agonizing smile, and ever after I shunned him. Nothing could annoy Musæus long, and he would soon have forgotten his pain, as he had already perhaps freed his memory of any vivid recollection of the former pleasure which our friendship had undoubtedly brought him. He welcomed enjoyment with a smile, and was almost as cheerful when he should have been much less pleased.

But although Musæus was content to be thus quiet, the world in which he lived determined that he should be less phlegmatic. As they had nothing better to do, they took his quarrel upon themselves. "He certainly has behaved infamously to Musæus. You know they were always together. I wonder what it can be! As for the rest of the school, that is in comparison nothing; but Musæus—you know they were decided cronies. I never knew fellows more together. I wonder what it can be! If I were Musæus, I certainly would come to an explanation. We must put him up to it. If Musæus asks him, he cannot refuse, and then we shall know what it is all about."

They at length succeeded in beating it into poor Musæus's head, that he had been very ill-treated, and must be very unhappy, and they urged him to insist upon an explanation. But Musæus was no hand at demanding explanations, and he deputed the task to a friend.

I was alone, sitting on a gate in a part of the grounds which was generally least frequented, when I heard a shout which, although I could not guess its cause, sounded in my ear with something of a menacing and malignant expression. The whole school, headed by the deputy, were finding me out, in order that the important question might be urged, that the honour of Musæus might be supported, and their own curiosity gratified.

Now at that age, whatever I may be now, I could not be driven. A soft word, and I was an Abel; an appearance of force, and I scowled a Cain. Had Musæus, instead of being a most commonplace character, which assuredly he was, had it been in his nature to have struck out a single spark of ardent feeling, to have indulged in a single sigh of sentiment, he might perhaps yet have been my friend. His appeal might have freed me from the domination of the black spirit, and in weeping over our reconciliation upon his sensitive bosom, I might have been emancipated from its horrid thrall. But the moment that Musæus sought to influence my private feelings by the agency of public opinion, he became to me, instead of an object of indifference, an object of disgust, and only not of hatred, because of contempt.

I did not like the shout, and when, at a considerable distance, I saw them advancing towards the gate with an eager run, I was almost tempted to retire; but I had never yet flinched in the course of my life, and the shame and sickness which I now felt at the contemplation of such an act impelled me to stay.

They arrived, they gathered round me, they did not know how to commence their great business: breathless and agitated, they looked first at their embarrassed leader, and then at me.

When I had waited a sufficient time for my dignity, I rose to quit the place.

"We want you, Fleming," said the chief.

"Well!" and I turned round and faced the speaker.

"I tell you what, Fleming," said he, in a rapid nervous style, "you may think yourself a very great man; but we do not exactly understand the way you are going on. There is Musæus; you and he were the greatest friends last half, and now you do not speak to him, nor to any one else. And we all think that you should give an explanation of your conduct. And, in short, we come here to know what you have got to say for yourself."

"Do you!" I answered, with a sneer.

"Well, what have you got to say?" he continued in a firmer voice and more peremptory tone.

"Say! say that either you or I must leave this gate. I was here first, but as you are the largest number, I suppose I must yield."

I turned my heel upon him and moved. Some one hissed. I returned, and inquired in a very calm, mild voice, "Who hissed?"

Now the person who hissed was a boy, who was indeed my match in years, and perhaps in force, but a great coward. I knew it was he, because he was just the fellow who would hiss, and looked quite pale when I asked the question. Besides, no one answered it, and he was almost the only boy who, under such circumstances, would have been silent.

"Are you afraid to own it?" I asked, in a contemptuous tone, but still very subdued.

This great mob of nearly two hundred boys were very much ashamed at the predicament in which their officious and cowardly member had placed them. So their leader, proud in a fine frame, a great and renowned courage, unrivalled achievements in combat, and two years of superiority of age over myself, advanced a little and said, "Suppose I hissed, what then?"

"What then!" I exclaimed, in a voice of thunder, and with an eye of lightning—"what then! Why, then I will thrash you."

There was an instantaneous flutter and agitation, and panting monosyllabic whisper in the crowd; they were like birds when the hawk is first detected in airy distance. Unconsciously, they withdrew like waves, and the arena being cleared, my opponent and I were left in opposition. Apparently there never was a more unequal match: but indeed he was not fighting with Contarini Fleming, but with a demon that had usurped his shape.

"Come on, then," he replied, with brisk confidence.

And I came—as the hail upon the tall corn. I flew at him like a wild beast; I felt not his best blow, I beat down his fine guard, and I sent him to the ground, stunned and giddy.

He was up again in a moment, and indeed I would not have waited for their silly rules of mock combat, but have destroyed him in his prostration. But he was up again in a moment. Again I flew upon him. He fought with subtle energy, but he was like a serpent with a tiger. I fixed upon him: my blows told with the rapid precision of machinery. His bloody visage was not to be distinguished. I believe that he was terrified with my frantic air.

I would never wait between the rounds. I cried out in a voice of madness for him to come on. There was breathless silence. They were thunderstruck. They were too generous to cheer their leader. They could not refrain from sympathizing with inferior force and unsupported courage. Each time that he came forward, I made the same dreadful spring, beat down his guard, and never ceased working upon his head, until at length my fist seemed to enter his very brain, and after ten rounds he fell down quite blind. I never felt his blows—I never lost my breath.

He could not come to time—I rushed forward—I placed my knee upon his chest. "I fight no more," he faintly cried.

"Apologize," I exclaimed; "apologize."

He did not speak.

"By heavens, apologize," I said, "or I know not what I shall do."

"Never!" he replied.

I lifted up my arm. Some advanced to interfere. "Off, dogs," I shouted; "Off, off." I seized the fallen chief, rushed through the gate, and dragged him like Achilles through the mead. At the bottom there was a dung hill: upon it I flung the half-inanimate body.

X.

I STROLLED away to one of my favourite haunts; I was calm and exhausted; my face and hands were smeared with gore. I knelt down by the side of the stream, and drank the most delicious draught that I had ever quaffed. I thought that I should never have ceased. I felt invigorated, and a plunge in the river soon completed my renovation.

I reclined under a branching oak, and moralized on the part. For the first time in my life, I had acted. Hitherto I had been a creature of dreams, but within the last month unconsciously I found myself a stirrer in existence. I perceived that I had suddenly become a responsible agent. There were many passions, many characters, many incidents, Love, hatred, faction, vengeance, Musæus, myself, my antagonist, his followers, who were indeed a world; our soft walks, the hollow visit, the open breach, the organized party, the great and triumphant struggle.

And as I mused, all these things flitted across my vision, and all that had passed was again present, and again performed, except indeed that my part in the drama was of a more studied and perfect cast. For I was conscious of much that might have been finely expressed and dexterously achieved; and to introduce all this, I indulged in imaginary scenes. There was a long interview between myself and Musæus, most harrowing; a logomachy between myself and the chief of the faction, most pungent. I became so excited, that I could no longer restrain the outward expression of my strong feeling. My voice broke into impassioned tones; I audibly uttered the scornful jest. My countenance was in harmony with my speech; my action lent a more powerful meaning to my words.

And suddenly there was a great change whose order I cannot trace. For Musæus, though he looked upon me, was not Musæus, but a youth in a distant land, and I was there in a sumptuous dress, with a brilliant star; and we were friends. And a beautiful woman rose up, a blending of Christiana and Egeria. Both of us loved her, and she yielded herself to me, and Musæus fled for aid. And there came a king with a great power, and as I looked upon his dazzling crown, lo! it encircled the brow of my late antagonist.

And I beheld and felt all this growing and expanding life with a bliss so keen, so ravishing, that I can compare it to nothing but to joys, which I was then too young even to participate. My brain seemed to melt into a liquid, rushing stream; my blood quickened into action, too quick even to recognise pulsation, fiery and fleet, yet delicate and soft. With difficulty I breathed, yet the oppression was delicious. But in vain I endeavour to paint the refined excitement of this first struggle of my young creation.

The drama went on, nor was it now in my power to restrain it. At length, oppressed with the vitality of the beings I had formed, dazzled with the shifting brilliancy of the scenes in which they moved, exhausted with the marvellous action of my shadowy self, who figured before me in endless exploit, now struggling, now triumphing, now pouring forth his soul in sentences of burning love, now breathing a withering blast of proud defiance, I sought for means to lay the wild ghosts that I had unconsciously raised.

I lifted my hand to my face, that had been gazing all this time, in fixed abstraction, upon a crimson cloud. There was a violent struggle, which I did not comprehend. Every thing was chaos, but soon, as it were, a mystic music came rising out of the incongruous mass, a mighty secret was revealed to me, all was harmony, and order, and repose, and beauty. The whirling scene no longer changed; there was universal stillness; and the wild beings ceased their fierce action, and bending down before me in humility, proffered their homage to their creator.

"Am I then," I exclaimed, looking around with an astonished and vacant air, "am I then, after all, a poet?"

I sprang up—I paced up and down before the tree, but not in thought. The perspiration ran down my forehead—I trembled—I panted—I was lost. I was not conscious of my existence. My memory deserted me—the rudder of my mind broke away.

My thought came back—I threw myself upon the ground. "Yes," I exclaimed, "beautiful beings, I will release you from the prison-house of my brain. I will give you to freedom and to light. You shall exist not only for me—you shall go forth to the world to delight and to conquer."

And this was the first time in my life that the idea of literary creation occurred to me. For I disliked poetry, of which indeed I had read little except plays, and although I took infinite delight in prose fiction, it was only because the romance, or the novel, offered to me a life more congenial to my feelings, than the world in which I lived. But the conviction of this day threw light upon my past existence. My imaginary deeds of conquest, my heroic aspirations, my long, dazzling dreams of fanciful adventure, were perhaps but sources of ideal action; that stream of eloquent and choice expression that seemed ever flowing in my ear was probably intended to be directed in a different channel than human assemblies, and might melt, or kindle the passions of mankind in silence. And the visions of beauty and the vows of love—were they too to glitter and glow only in imagination.

XI.

I REPAIRED the next day to my favourite tree, armed with a pencil and a paper book. My mind was, as I thought, teeming with ideas. I had composed the first sentence of my work in schooltime—it seemed full of music. I had repeated it a thousand times—I was enchanted with its euphony. It was now written, fairly written. With rapture I perceived it placed in its destined position. But what followed?—Nothing. In vain I rubbed my forehead; in vain I summoned my fancies. The traitors would not listen. My mind seemed full to the very brink, but not a drop of the rich stream overflowed. I became anxious, nervous, fretful. I walked about; I reseated myself. Again I threw down the pencil. I was like a man disenchanted. I could scarcely recall the visions of yesterday, and if, with an effort, I succeeded, they appeared cold, tame, dull, lifeless. Nothing can describe my blank despair.

They know not, they cannot tell—the cold, dull world—they cannot even remotely conceive the agony of doubt and despair which is the doom of youthful genius. To sigh for Fame in obscurity is like sighing in a dungeon for light. Yet the votary and the captive share an equal hope. But to feel the strong necessity of fame, and to be conscious without intellectual excellence life must be insupportable, to feel all this with no simultaneous faith in your own power—these are moments of despondency for which no immortality can compensate.

As for myself, repeated experiments only brought repeated failures. I would not die without a struggle, but I struggled only to be vanquished. One day was too hot; another I fancied too cold. Then again I was not well, or perhaps I was too anxious. I would try only a sentence each day. The trial was most mortifying, for I found when it came to this practical test, that in fact I had nothing to write about. Yet my mind had been so full, and even now a spark, and it would again light up; but the flame never kindled, or if ever I fanned an appearance of heat, I was sure only to extinguish it. Why could I not express what I seemed to feel? All was a mystery.

I was most wretched. I wandered about in very great distress, for my pride was deeply wounded, and I could no longer repose on my mind with confident solace. My spirit was quite broken. Had I fought my great battle now, I should certainly have been beaten. I was distracted with disquietude—I had no point of refuge—hope utterly vanished. It was impossible that I could be any thing. I must always fail. I hated to think of myself. The veriest dunce in the school seemed my superior. I grew meek and dull. I learned my dry lessons—I looked upon a grammar with a feeling of reverence; my lexicon was constantly before me. But I made little advance. I no longer ascribed my ill progress to the uninteresting task, but to my own incapacity. I thought myself, once more, half a fool

XII.

HAD I now been blessed with a philosophic friend, I might have found consolation and assistance. But my instructers, to whom I had a right to look up for this aid, were, of course, wanting. The system which they pursued taught them to consider their pupils as machines, which were to fulfil a certain operation, and this operation was word-learning. They attempted not to discover, or to develope, or to form character. Predisposition was to them a dark oracle: organization, a mystery in which they were not initiated. The human mind was with them always the same soil, and one to which they brought ever the same tillage. And mine was considered a sterile one, for they found that their thistles did not flourish where they should have planted roses.

I was ever considered a lazy, idle boy, because I required ideas instead of words. I never would make any further exertion than would save me from their punishments: their rewards I did not covet. Yet I was ever reading, and in general knowledge was immeasurably superior to all the students—for aught I know, to all the tutors. For indeed in any chance observations in which they might indulge, I could even then perceive that they were individuals of the most limited intelligence. They spoke sometimes of great men, I suppose for our emulation, but their great men were always commentators. They sometimes burst into a eulogium of a great work; you might be sure it was ever a huge bunch of annotations. An unrivalled exploit turned out to be a happy conjecture—a marvellous deed was the lion's skin that covered the ears of a new reading. I was confounded to hear the same epithets applied to their obscure demi-gods that I associated with the names of Cæsar and Socrates, and Pericles, and Cicero. It was perplexing to find that Pharsalia or a Philippic—the groves of Academus or the fanes of the Acropolis, could receive no higher admiration than was lavished upon the unknown exploits of a hunter after syllables.

After my battle, I was never annoyed by my former friends. As time advanced I slightly relaxed in my behaviour, and when it was necessary, we interchanged words, but I never associated with any one. I was however no longer molested. An idea got afloat that I was not exactly in my perfect senses, and on the whole, I was rather feared than disliked.

Reading was my only resource. I seldom indulged in revery. The moment that I perceived my mind wandering, I checked it with a mixed feeling of disgust and terror. I made, however, during this period, more than one attempt to write, and always with signal discomfiture. Neither of the projected subjects in any way grew out of my own character, however they might have led to its delineation, had I proceeded. The first was a theme of heroic life, in which I wished to indulge in the gorgeousness of remote antiquity. I began with a fine description, which again elevated my hopes, but when the scene was fairly painted, my actors would not come on. I flung the sheet into the river, and cursed my repeated idiotism.

After an exposure of this kind, I always instantaneously became practical, and grave, and stupid; as a man, when he recovers from intoxication, vows that he will never again taste wine. Nevertheless, during the vacation, a pretty little German lady one night took it into her head to narrate some of the traditions of her country. Among these I heard, for the first time, the story of the Wild Huntsman of Rodenstein. It was most unlucky. The baroness, who was a fine instrumental musician, but who would never play when I requested her, chanced this night to be indulging us. The mystery and the music combined their damnable spells, and I was again enchanted. Infinite characters and ideas seemed rushing in my mind. I recollected that I had never yet given my vein a trial at home. Here I could command silence, solitude, hours unbroken and undisturbed. I walked up and down the room, once more myself. The music was playful, gay, and joyous. A village dance was before my vision—I marked with delight the smiling peasantry bounding under the clustering vines, the girls crowned with roses—the youth adorned with flowing ribands. Just as a venerable elder advanced, the sounds became melancholy, wild, and ominous. I was in a deep forest, full of doubt and terror—the wind moaned—the big branches heaved—in the distance I heard the baying of a hound. It did not appear, for suddenly the trumpet announced a coming triumph: I felt that a magnificent procession was approaching, that each moment it would appear: each moment the music became louder, and already an advanced and splendid guard appeared in the distance. I caught a flashing glimpse of a sea of waving plumes and glistening arms. The music ceased—the procession vanished—I fell from the clouds, I found myself in a dull drawing-room, a silly boy, very exhausted.

I felt so excessively stupid that I instantly gave up all thoughts of the Hunter of Rodenstein—and went to bed gloomy and without hope; but in the morning when I rose, the sun was shining so softly, the misty trees and the dewy grass were so tender and so bright, the air was so fresh and fragrant, that my first feeling was the desire of composition, and I walked forth into the park cheerful, and moved by a rising faith.

The excited feelings of the evening seemed to return, and when I had sufficiently warmed my mind with revery, I sat down to my table surrounded by every literary luxury that I could remember. Ink enclosed in an ormolu Cupid, clear and brilliant, quires of the softest cream-coloured paper, richly gilt, and a perfect magazine of the finest pens. I was exceedingly nervous, but on the whole not unsuccessful. I described a young traveller arriving at night at a small inn on the borders of a Bohemian forest. I did not allow a single portion of his dress to escape, and even his steed and saddle-bags duly figured. The hostess was founded on our own housekeeper, therefore I was master of my subject. From her ear-rings to her shoe-buckles, all was perfect. I managed to supply my hero with supper, and at length I got him, not to bed, but to his bed-room—for heroes do not get into bed, even when wearied, with the expedition of more commonplace characters. On the contrary, he first opened the window, it was a lattice window, and looked at the moon. I had a very fine moonlight scene. I well remember that the trees were tipped with silver, but O! triumph of art, for the first time in my life, I achieved a simile, and the evening breeze came sounding in his ear soft as a lover's sigh!

This last master-touch was too much for me. I was breathless, and indeed exhausted. I read over the chapter. I could scarcely believe its existence possible. I rushed into the park—I hurried to some solitude where, undisturbed by the sight of a human being, I could enjoy my intense existence.

I was so agitated, I was in such a tumult of felicity, that for the rest of the day I could not even think. I could not find even time to determine on my hero's name, or to ascertain the reason for which I had brought him to such a wild scene, and placed him in such exceedingly uncomfortable lodgings. The next morning I had recovered my self-possession. Calm and critical, I reviewed the warm product of brain which had the preceding day so fascinated me. It appeared to me that it had never been my unfortunate fate to read more crude, ragged, silly stuff in the whole course of my experience. The description of costume, which I had considered so perfect, sounded like a catalogue of old clothes. As for the supper, it was very evident that so lifeless a personage could never have an appetite. What he opened the window for I certainly knew not, but certainly if only to look at the moon he must have been disappointed, for in spite of all my asseverations it was very dim indeed, and as for the lover's sigh, at the same time so tame, and so forced, it was absolutely sickening.

I threw away the wretched effusion, the beautiful inkstand, the cream-coloured paper, the fine pens—away they were all crammed in a drawer, which I was ever after ashamed to open. I looked out of the window, and saw the huntsman going out. I called to him, I joined him. I hated field-sports. I hated every bodily exertion except riding, which indeed a scarcely one, but now any thing that was bodily, that was practical, pleased, and I was soon slaughtering birds in the very bowers in which I had loved Egeria.

On the whole, this was a most miserable and wretched year. I was almost always depressed, often felt heartbroken. I entirely lost any confidence in my own energies, and while I was deprived of the sources of pleasure which I had been used to derive from revery, I could acquire no new ones in the pursuits of those around me.

It was in this state of mind that after a long solitary walk I found myself at a village which I had never before visited. On the skirts was a small Gothic building, beautiful and ancient. It was evening. The building was illuminated, the door open. I entered—I found myself in a Catholic church. A Lutheran in a Lutheran country, for a moment I trembled, but the indifference of my father on the subject of religion had prevented me at least from being educated a bigot, and in my Venetian meditations I sometimes would recollect, that my mother must have professed the old faith.

The church was not very full—groups were kneeling in several parts. All was dusk except at the high altar. There, a priest in a flaming vest officiated, and, ever and anon, a kneeling boy, in a scarlet dress, rang a small, and musical, and silver bell. Many tall white candles, in golden sticks, illuminated the sacred table, redolent of perfumes, and adorned with flowers. Six large burnished lamps were suspended above, and threw a magical light upon a magical picture. It was a Magdalen kneeling and weeping in a garden. Her long golden hair was drawn off her ivory forehead, and reached to the ground. Her large blue eyes, full of ecstatic melancholy, pierced to heaven. The heavy tears studded like pearls her wan, but delicate cheek. Her clasped hands embraced a crucifix.

I gazed upon this pictured form with a strange fascination, I came forward, I placed myself near the altar. At that moment, the organ burst forth, as if heaven were opening; clouds of incense rose and wreathed round the rich and vaulted roof, the priest advanced and revealed a God, which I fell down and worshipped. From that moment I became a Catholic.

XIII.

There was a mystery in the secret creed full of delight. Another link too seemed broken in the chain that bound me to the country, which, each day, I more detested. Adoration also was ever a resource teeming with rapture, for a creed is imagination. The Magdalen succeeded to Christiana and to Egeria. Each year my mistress seemed to grow more spiritual. First reality, then fancy, now pure spirit: a beautiful woman, a mystical nymph, a canonized soul. How was this to end? Perhaps I was ultimately designed for angelic intercourse, perhaps I might mount the skies, with the presiding essence of a star.

My great occupations were devout meditation and solitary prayer. I inflicted upon myself many penances. I scrupulously observed every fast. My creative power was exercised in the production of celestial visitants; my thirst for expression gratified in infinite invocation. Wherever I moved, I perceived the flashing of a white wing, the streaming of radiant hair; however I might apparently be employed, I was, in fact, pondering over the music of my next supplication.

One mundane desire alone mingled with these celestial aspirations, and in a degree sprang out of their indulgence. Each day I languished more for Italy. It was a strong longing. Nothing but the liveliness of my faith could have solaced and supported me under the want of its gratification. I pined for the land where the true religion flourished in becoming glory, the land where I should behold temples worthy of the beautiful mysteries which were celebrated within their sumptuous walls, the land which the Vicar of God and the Ruler of Kings honoured and sanctified by his everlasting presence. A pilgrimage to Rome occupied my thoughts.

My favourite retreat now, when at the college, were the ruins of a Gothic abbey, whither an hour's stroll easily carried me. It pleased me much to sit among these beautiful relics, and call back the days when their sanctity was undefiled, and their loveliness unimpaired. As I looked upon the rich framework of the oriel window, my fancy lent perfection to its shattered splendour. I beheld it once more beaming with its saints and martyrs, and radiant with chivalric blazonry. My eye wandered down the mouldering cloisters. I pictured a procession of priests solemnly advancing to the high altar, and blending in sacred melody, with their dark garments and their shining heads, elevating a golden and gigantic crosier, and waving on high a standard of Madonna.

One day, as I was indulging in these soothing visions I heard a shout, and looking around, I observed a man seated at no great distance, who, by his action, had evidently called to me. I arose, and coming out of the ruins, advanced to him. He was seated on a mass of ancient brick-work, and appeared to be sketching. He was a tall man, fair and blue-eyed, but very sunburnt. He was hawk-nosed, with a quick glancing vision, and there was an air of acuteness in his countenance which was very striking. His dress was not the dress of our country, but I was particularly pleased with his cap, which was of crimson cloth, with a broad border of fur, and fell on one side of his head like a cap in a picture.

"My little man," said he, in a brisk, clear voice, "I am sorry to disturb you, but as probably you know this place better than I, you can perhaps tell me whether there be a spring at hand."

"Indeed, sir, a very famous one, for I have often drank its water, which is most sweet, and clear, and cold, and if you will permit me, I will lead you to it."

"With all my heart, and many thanks, my little friend." So saying, he arose, and placing his portfolio under one arm, with the other lifted up a knapsack, which I offered to carry.

"By no means, kind sir," said he, in a most cheerful voice, "I am ever my own servant."

So leading him on round the other side of the abbey, and thence through a small but very fragrant mead, I brought him to the spring of which I had spoken. Over it was built a small, but fair arch, the keystone being formed of a mitred escutcheon, and many parts very much covered with thick ivy

The eye of the stranger kindled with pleasure when he looked upon the arch, and then, sitting down upon the bank, and opening his knapsack, he took out a large loaf and broke it, and, as I was retiring, he said, "Prithee do not go, my little friend, but stay and share my meal. It is rough, but there is plenty. Nay, refuse not, little gentleman, for I wish to prolong our acquaintance. In not more than as many minutes, you have conferred upon me two favours. In this world such characters are rare. You have given me that which I love better than wine, and you have furnished me with a divine sketch, for indeed this arch is of a finer style than any part of the great building, and must have been erected by an abbot of grand taste, I warrant you. Come, little gentleman, eat, prithee, eat."

"Indeed, sir, I am not hungry; but if you would let me look at your drawing of the abbey, I should be most delighted."

"What, dost love art? What! have I stumbled upon a little artist!"

"No, sir, I cannot draw, nor indeed do I understand art, but I love every thing which is beautiful."

"Ah! a comprehensive taste," and he gave me the portfolio.

"O!" I exclaimed, "how beautiful!" for the drawing turned out, not, as I had anticipated, a lean skeleton pencil sketch, but one rapidly and richly coloured. The abbey rose as in reality, only more beautiful, being suffused with a warm light, for he had dashed in a sunset full of sentiment.

"O! sir, how beautiful! I could look at it forever. It seems to me that some one must come forth from the pass of those blue mountains. Cannot you fancy some bright cavalier, sir, with a flowing plume, or even a string of mules, even that would be delicious!"

"Bravo! bravo! my little man," exclaimed the stranger, shooting a sharp, scrutinizing side glance. "You deserve to see sketches. There! undo that strap and open the folio, for there are many others, and some which may please you more."

I opened it as if I were about to enter a sanctuary. I perceived it very full. I culled a drawing which appeared the most richly coloured, as one picks the most glowing fruit. There seemed a river and many marble palaces on each side, and long, thin, gliding boats shooting in every part, and over the stream there sprang a bridge, a bridge with a single arch, an ancient and solemn bridge, covered with buildings. I gazed upon the scene for a moment with breathless interest, a tear of agitating pleasure stole down my cheek, and then I shouted, "Venice! Venice!"

"Little man," said the stranger, "what is the matter?"

"O! sir, I beg your pardon, you must think me very foolish indeed. I am sure I did not mean to call out, but I have been longing all my life to go to Venice, and when I see any thing connected with it, I feel, sir, quite agitated. Your drawing, sir, is so beautiful, that I know not how—I thought for a moment that I was really looking upon these beautiful palaces, and crossing the famous Rialto."

"Never apologize for showing feeling, my friend. Remember that when you do so, you apologize for truth. I too am fond of Venice; nor is there any city where I have made more drawings."

"What, sir, have you been at Venice?"

"Is that so strange a deed? I have been in much stranger places."

"O! sir, how happy you must be! To see Venice, and to travel in the distant countries, I could die at the condition of such enjoyment."

"You know as yet too little of life to think of death," said the stranger.

"Alas! sir," I mournfully sighed, "I have often wished to die."

"But can one so young be unhappy?" asked the stranger.

"O! sir, most, most unhappy. I am alone supported in this world by a fervent persuasion, that the holy Magdalen has condescended to take me under her especial protection."

"The holy Magdalen!" exclaimed the stranger, with an air of great astonishment—"indeed! and what made you unhappy before the holy Magdalen condescended to take you under her especial protection? Do you think, or has anybody told you, that you have committed any sin?"

"No! sir, my life has been, I hope, very innocent; nor do I see indeed how I could commit any sin, for I have never been subject to any temptation. But I have ever been unhappy, because I am perplexed about myself. I feel that I am not like other persons, and that which makes them happy is to me a source of no enjoyment."

"But you have, perhaps, some sources of enjoyment which are peculiar to yourself, and not open to them. Come, tell me how you have passed your life. Indeed, you have excited my curiosity, for I observed to-day, while I was drawing, that you were a good four hours reclined in the same position."

"Four hours, sir! I thought that I had been there but a few minutes."

"Four hours by the sun, as well as by this watch. What were you doing? Were you thinking of the blessed Magdalen?"

"No, sir!" I gravely replied, "not to-day."

"How then?"

"Indeed, sir!" I answered, reddening, "if I tell you, I am afraid, you will think me very foolish."

"Speak out, little man. We are all very foolish; and I have a shrewd suspicion, that if we understood each other better, you might perhaps turn out the least foolish of the two. Open, then, your mind, and fear nothing. For believe me, it is dishonourable to blush when you speak the truth, even if it be to your shame."

There was something in the appearance and manner of the stranger that greatly attracted me. I sought him with the same eagerness with which I always avoided my fellow-creatures. From the first, conversation with him was no shock. His presence seemed to sanctify, instead of outraging my solitude. His voice subdued my sullen spirit, and called out my hidden nature. He inspired me not only with confidence, but even with a degree of fascinating curiosity.

"Indeed, sir," I began, still with a hesitating voice, but a more assured manner—"indeed, sir, I have never spoken of these things to any one, for I feel they could not believe or comprehend what I would wish to express, nor indeed is it delightful to be laughed at. But know that I ever like to be alone, and it is this—that when I am alone, I can indulge in thought, which gives me great pleasure. For I would wish you to comprehend, sir, that I have ever lived in, as it were, two worlds, a public world and a private world. But I should not be unhappy in the private world but for one reason, which is nothing, but I was ever most happy; but in the public world, I am indeed miserable. For you must know, sir, that when I am alone, my mind is full with what seem to me beautiful thoughts, nor indeed are they thoughts alone that make me so happy, but in truth I perform many strange and noble acts, and these too in distant countries, and in unknown places, and other persons appear, and they also act. And we all speak in language more beautiful than common words. And, sir, many other things occur, which it would take long to recount, but which, indeed, I am sure, that is, I think, would make any one very happy."

"But all this is a source of happiness, not of unhappiness," said the stranger. "Am I to comprehend, then, the source has dried up?"

"O! no, sir, for only this morning I had many visions, but I checked them."

"But why check them?"

"Ah! sir," I answered, heaving a deep sigh, "it is this which makes me unhappy; for when I enter into this private world, there arises in the end a desire to express what has taken place in it, which indeed I cannot gratify."

The stranger for a moment mused. Then he suddenly said, "And when you looked upon my sketch of the abbey, there seemed to you a cavalier advancing, I think you said?"

"From the pass of the blue mountains, sir. When ever I look upon pictures, it is thus."

"And when you beheld the Rialto, tell me what occurred then?"

"There was a great rush, sir, in my mind, and when my eye caught that tall young signior who is stepping off the stairs of a palace into a gondola, I wished to write a tale of which he should be the hero."

"It appears to me, my young friend," said the stranger, in a serious tone, and looking at me very keenly—"it appears to me, my young friend, that you are a poet."

"Alas! sir," I exclaimed, extremely agitated and nearly seizing his hand—"alas! alas! sir, I am not. For I once thought so myself, and have often tried to write; and either I have not produced a line, or something so wretchedly flat and dull that even I have felt it intolerable. It is this that makes me so miserable, so miserable that were it not for feeling, in the most marked manner, that I am under the especial protection of the blessed Magdalen, I think I should kill myself."

A gentle smile played upon the lip of the stranger, but it was in an instant suppressed. Then turning to me he said, "Supposing a man were born with a predisposition for painting, as I might have been myself, and that he were enabled to fancy pictures in his eye, do you think that if he took up a brush for the first time, he could transfer these pictures to the canvass?"

"By no means, sir, for the artist must learn his art."

"And is not a poet an artist, and is not writing an art, equally with painting? Words are but chalk and colour. The painter and the poet must follow the same course. Both must study before they execute. Both must alike consult nature and invent the beautiful. Those who delineate imitate nature, and those who describe her must equally study her, if they wish to excel in their own creations; and for man, if the painter study the outward form of the animal, the inward must be equally investigated by the poet. Thus far for the natural; and for the ideal, which is an improvement upon nature, and which you will some day more clearly comprehend, remember this, that the painter and the poet, however assisted by their own organization, must alike perfect their style by the same process—I mean by studying the works themselves of great painters and great poets. See, then, my young friend, how unreasonable you are, that because you cannot be a great artist without studying your art, you are unhappy."

"O! sir, indeed, indeed, I am not. There is no application—there is no exertion, I feel, I feel it strongly, of which I am not capable to gain knowledge. Indeed, sir, you speak to me of great things, and my mind opens to your wisdom, but how am I to study?"

"Be not too rapid. Before we part, which will be in a moment, I will write you some talismanic rules, which have been of great service to myself. I copied them from off an old obelisk amid the ruins of Thebes. They will teach you all that is now necessary."

"O! sir, how good, how kind you are. How different would have been my life, had I been taught by somebody like you."

"Where, then, were you educated?"

"I am a student of the college about two miles off. Perhaps you may have passed it?"

"What, the large house upon the hill, where they learn words?" said the stranger, with a smile.

"Indeed, sir, it is too true. For though it never occurred to me before, I see now why, with an ardent love of knowledge, I have indeed there gained nothing but an ill name."

"And now," said the stranger, rising, "I must away, for the sun will in a few minutes sink, and I have to reach a village which is some miles off for my night's encampment."

I beheld him prepare to depart with a feeling of deep regret. I dropped for a moment into profound abstraction; then rushing to him, I seized his hand, and exclaimed, "O, sir, I am noble, and I am rich, yet let me follow you!"

"By no means," said the stranger, very good-naturedly, "for our professions are different."

"Yet a poet should see all things."

"Assuredly. And you too will wander, but your hour has not yet come."

"And shall I ever see Venice?"

"I doubt not, for when a mind like yours thinks often of a thing it will happen."

"You speak to me of mysteries."

"There is little mystery; there is much ignorance. Some day you will study metaphysics, and you will then understand the nature of volition."

He opened his knapsack and took out two small volumes, in one of which he wrote some lines. "This is the only book," he said, "I have with me, and, as, like myself, you are such a strong Venetian, I will give it you, because you love art and artists, and are a good boy. When we meet again, I hope I may call you a great man.

"Here," he said, giving them to me, "they are full of Venice. Here, you see, is a view of the Rialto. This will delight you. And in the blank leaf I have written all the advice you at present require. Promise me, however, not to read it till you return to your college. And so farewell, my little man—farewell!"

He extended me his hand. I took it, and although it is an awkward thing at all times, and chiefly for a boy, I began telling him my name and condition, but he checked me. "I never wish to know anybody's name. Were I to become acquainted with every being who flits across me in life, the callousness of my heart would be endangered. If your acquaintance be worth preserving, fate or fortune will some day bring us again together."

He departed. I watched his figure until it melted in the rising haze of evening. It was strange the ascendancy that this man exercised over me. When he spoke I seemed listening to an oracle, and now that he had departed, I felt as if some supernatural visitant had disappeared.

I quickened my walk home from the intense anxiety to open the volume in which I was to find the talismanic counsel. When I had arrived, I read written in pencil these words.

"Be patient. Cherish hope. Read more. Ponder less. Nature is more powerful than education. Time will develope every thing. Trust not overmuch in the blessed Magdalen: learn to protect yourself."

XIV.

Indeed I could think of nothing but the stranger. All night his image was before my eyes, and his voice sounded in my ear. I recalled each look, I repeated each expression. When I woke in the morning, the first thing I did was to pronounce from memory his oracular advice. I determined to be patient, I resolved never to despair. Revery was no longer to be endured, and a book was to be ever in my hand.

He had himself enabled me to comply with this last rule. I seized the first opportunity to examine his present. It was the History of Venice in French, by Amelot de la Houssaye—a real history of Venice, not one written years after the extinction of the republic by some solemn sage, full of first principles and dull dissertations upon the vicious constitution—a prophet of the past, trying to shuffle off his commonplace deductions for authentic inspiration—but a history of Venice written by one who had witnessed the doge sitting on his golden throne, and receiving awe-struck ambassadors in his painted halls.

I read it with an avidity with which I had never devoured any book: some parts of it indeed with absolute rapture. When I came to the chapter upon the nobility, a dimness came over my sight: for a moment I could not proceed. I saw them all; I marked all the divisions; the great magnificoes, who ranked with crowned heads, the nobles of the war of Candia, and the third, and still inferior class. I was so excited, that for a moment I did not observe that the name of Contarini did not appear. I looked for it with anxiety. But when I read that there were yet four families of such preeminent ancestry, that they were placed even above the magnificoes, being credited descendants of Roman consular families, and that of these the unrivalled house of Contarini was the chief, I dashed down the book in a paroxysm of nervous exultation, and rushed into the woods.

I ran about like a madman for some time, cutting down the underwood that opposed my way with a sharp stick, leaping trenches, hallooing, spouting, shouting, dashing, through pools of water. At length I arrived at a more open part of the wood. At a slight distance was a hill. I rushed on up the hill, and never stopped till I had gained the summit. That steep ascent a little tamed me. I found myself upon a great ridge, and a vast savage view opened upon all sides. I felt now more at ease, for the extent of the prospect harmonized with the largeness and swell of my soul.

"Ha! ha!" I cried, like a wild horse. I snorted in the air, my eyes sparkled, my crest rose. waved my proud arm. "Ha! ha! have I found it out at last! I knew there was something. Nature whispered it to me, and time has revealed it. He said truly; time has developed every thing. But shall these feelings subside into poetry? Away! give me a sword, give me a sword! My consular blood demands a sword. Give me a sword, ye winds, ye trees, ye mighty hills, ye deep cold waters, give me a sword. I will fight! by heavens, I will fight! I will conquer. Why am I not a doge? A curse upon the tyranny of man, why is she not free? why am I not a doge? By the God of heaven, I will be a doge! O! thou fair and melancholy saint," I continued, falling on my knees, "who in thy infinite goodness condescended, as it were, to come down from heaven to call me back to the true and holy faith of Venice, and to take me under thy especial protection, blessed and beautiful Mary Magdalene, look down from thy glorious seat above, and smile upon thy elected and favourite child!"

I rose up refreshed by this short prayer, calmer and cooler, and began to meditate upon what was now fitting to be done. That Contarini Fleming must with all possible despatch cease to be a schoolboy was indeed evident, necessary, and indispensable. The very idea of the great house upon the hill, where they teach words, was ludicrous. Nor indeed would it become me ever again, under any pretence whatever, to acknowledge a master, or, as it would appear, to be subject to any laws, save the old laws of Venice, for I claimed for myself the rights and attributes of a Venetian noble of the highest class, and they were those pertaining to blood royal. But when I called to my recollection the cold, worldly, practical character of my father, the vast quantity of dull, lowering, entangling ties that formed the great domestic mesh, and bound me to a country which I detested, covered me with a climate which killed me, surrounded me with manners with which I could not sympathize, and duties which nature impelled me not to fulfil, I felt that, to ensure my emancipation, it was necessary at once to dissolve all ties of blood and affection, and to break away from those links which chained me as a citizen to a country which I abhorred. I resolved therefore immediately to set out for Venice. I was, for the moment, I conceived, sufficiently well supplied with money, for I possessed one hundred rix-dollars, more than any five of my fellow-students together. This, with careful husbandry, I counted would carry me to the nearest sea-port, perhaps even secure me a passage. And for the rest, I had a lively conviction that something must always turn up to assist me in any difficulties, for I was convinced that I was a hero, and heroes are never long forlorn.

On the next morning, therefore, long ere the sun had risen, I commenced my adventures. I did not steal away. First I kissed a cross three times, which I carried next to my breast, and then recommending myself to the blessed Magdalen, I walked off proudly and slowly, in a manner becoming Coriolanus or Cæsar, who, after some removes, were both of them, for aught I knew, my great-grandfathers. I carried in a sort of knapsack, which we used for our rambles, a few shirts, my money, a pair of pocket pistols, and some ammunition. Nor did I forget a large loaf of bread—not very heroic food, but classical in my sight, from being the victual of the mysterious stranger. Like him also I determined in future only to drink water.

XV.

I JOURNEYED for some hours without stopping along a road, about which all I knew was, that it was opposite to the one that had first carried me to the college, and consequently, I supposed, did not lead home. I never was so delighted in my life. I had never been up so early in my life. It was like living in a new world. Every thing was still, fresh, fragrant. I wondered how long it would last, how long it would be before the vulgar days, to which I had been used, would begin. At last a soft luminous appearance commenced in the horizon, and gradually gathered in strength and brightness. Then it shivered into brilliant streaks, the clouds were dabbled with rich flaming tints, and the sun rose. I felt grateful when his mild but vivifying warmth fell upon my face, and it seemed to me that I heard the sound of trumpets, when he came forth, like a royal hero, out of his pavilion.

All the birds began singing, and the cocks crowed with renewed pride. I felt as if I myself could sing, my heart was so full of joy and exultation. And now I heard many pleasant rural sounds. A horse neighed, and a whip smacked, there was a whistle, and the sound of a cart-wheel. I came to a large farm-house. I felt as if I were indeed travelling, and seeing the world and its wonders. When I had rambled about before, I had never observed any thing, for I was full of nonsensical ideas. But now I was a practical man, and felt capable, as the stranger said, of protecting myself. Never was I so cheerful.

There was a great barking, and several dogs rushed out at me, all very fierce, but I hit the largest over the nose with my stick, and it retreated yelping into the yard, where it again barked most furiously behind the gate; the lesser dogs were so frightened that they slunk away immediately through different hedges, nor did they bark again till I passed the gate; but I heard them then, though very feeble, and rather snappish than fierce.

The farmer was coming out of the gate, and saluted me. I returned him the salute with a firm voice and a manly air. He spoke then of the weather, and I differed with him to show that I was a thinking being, and capable of protecting myself. I made some inquiries respecting the distance of certain places, and I acquired from him much information. The nearest town was fifteen miles off. This I wished to reach by night, as there was no great village, and this I doubted not to do.

When the heat increased, and I felt a little fatigued, I stopped at a beautiful spring, and taking my loaf out of my knapsack like the stranger, I ate with a keen relish, and slaked my slight thirst in the running water. It was the coldest and purest water that I had ever tasted. I felt quite happy, and was full of confidence and self-gratulation at my prosperous progress. I reposed here till noon, and as the day, though near midsummer, became cloudy, I then recommenced my journey without dread of the heat.

On I went, full of hope. The remembrance of the cut that I had given the great dog over the nose had wonderfully inflamed my courage. I longed to knock down a man. Every step was charming. Every flower, every tree gave me delight, which they had not before yielded. Sometimes, yet seldom, for it was an unfrequented road, I met a traveller, and always prepared myself for an adventure. It did not come, but there was yet time. Every person I saw, and every place I observed, seemed strange and new: I felt in a far land. And for adventures, my own consciousness was surely a sufficient one, for was I not a nobleman incognito, going on a pilgrimage to Venice? To say nothing of the adventures that might then occur, here were materials for the novelist! Pah! my accursed fancy was again wandering. I forgot that I was no longer a poet, but something which, though difficult to ascertain, I doubted not in the end all would agree to be infinitely greater.

As the afternoon advanced, the thin gray clouds melted away, the sun mildly shone in the warm, light-blue sky. This was again fortunate, and instead of losing my gay heart with the decline of day, I felt inspired with fresh vigour, and shot on joyous and full of cheerfulness. The road now ran through the skirts of a forest. It was still less like a commonplace journey. On each side was a large plot of turf, green and sweet. Seated on this at some little distance I perceived a group of men and women. My heart beat at the prospect of an incident. I soon observed them with more advantage. Two young women were seated together repairing a bright garment, which greatly excited my wonder. It seemed of very fine stuff, and richly embroidered with gold and silver. Greatly it contrasted with their own attire and that of their companions, which was plain, and indeed shabby. As they worked, one burst into repeated fits of laughter, but the other was more sedulous, and looking grave, seemed to reprove her. A man was feeding with sticks a fire, over which boiled a great pot; a middle-aged woman was stirring its contents. A young man was lying asleep upon the grass; an older one was furbishing up a sword. A lightly built but large wagon was on the other side of the road, the unharnessed horses feeding on the grass.

A little dog shrilly barked when I came up, but I was not afraid of dogs. I flourished my stick, and the laughing girl called out "Harlequin," and the cur ran to her. I stopped and inquired of the fire-lighter the distance to the town where I hoped to sleep. Not only did he not answer me, but he did not even raise up his head. It was the first time in my life that I had not obtained an answer. I was astonished at his insolence. "Sir," I said, in a tone of offended dignity, "how long is it since you have learned not to answer the inquiry of a gentleman?"

The laughing girl burst into a renewed fit. All stopped their pursuits. The fire-lighter looked up with a puzzled sour face, the old woman stared with her mouth open, and the furbisher ran up to us with his naked weapon. He had the oddest and most comical face that I had ever seen. It was like that of a seal, but full of ludicrous mobility. He came rushing up, saying, with an air and voice of mock heroism, "To arms to arms!"

I was astonished, and caught the eye of the laughing girl. She was very fair, with a small nose, and round cheeks breaking into most charming dimples. When I caught her eye, she made a wild grimace at me, and I also laughed. Although I was trudging along with a knapsack, my dress did not befit my assumed character, and in a moment of surprise, I had given way to a manner which still less became my situation. Women are quicker than men in judging of strangers. The two girls were evidently my friends from the first, and the fair laugher beckoned me to come and sit down by her. This gay wench had wonderfully touched my fancy. I complied with her courteous offer without hesitation. I threw away my knapsack and my stick, and stretched my legs with the air of a fine gentleman. I was already ashamed of my appearance, and forgot every thing in the desire to figure to the best advantage to my new friend. "This is the first time," I drawled out, with a languid air, and looking in her face, "this is the first time in life that I ever walked, and I am heartily sick of it."

"And why have you walked, and where have you come from, and where are you going to?" eagerly she demanded.

"I was tired to death of riding every day of my life," I rejoined, with the tone of a man who had exhausted pleasure. "I am not going anywhere, and I forget where I came from."

"O! you odd thing!" said the wench, and she gave me a pinch.

The other girl, who was handsome, but dark, and of a more serious beauty, at this moment rose, and went and spoke to the crusty fire-lighter. When she returned, she seated herself on my other side, so I was now between both, but as she seated herself, though doubtless unconsciously, she pressed my hand in a very sentimental manner.

"And what is your name?" asked the laughing girl.

"Theodora! how can you be so rude?" remarked the serious beauty.

"Do you know," said the laughing girl, whispering in my ear, "I think you must be a little count."

I only smiled in answer, but it was a smile which complimented her penetration.

"And now, may I ask who you may be, and whither you may be going?"

"We are going to the next town," replied the serious beauty, "where, if we find the public taste not disinclined, we hope to entertain them with some representations."

"You are actors, then. O! what a charming profession. How I love the theatre. When I am at home I go in my father's box every night. I have often wished to be an actor."

"Be one," said the serious beauty, pressing my hand.

"Join us," said the laughing girl, pinching my elbow.

"Why not?" I replied, and almost thought. "Youth must be passed in adventure."

The fairy nymph produced a box of sugarplums, and taking out a white almond, kissed it, and pushed it into my mouth. While I laughed at her wild kitten-like action, the dark girl drew a deep-coloured rose from her bosom, and pressed it to my nose. I was nearly stifled with their joint sweets and kindness. Neither of them would take away their hands. The dark girl pressed her rose with increased force; the sugarplum melted away, but I found in my mouth the tip of a little finger scarcely larger, and as white and sweet. There was giggling without end; I sank down upon my back. The dark girl snatched a hasty embrace, her companion fell down by my side, and bit my cheek.

"You funny little count!" said the fair beauty.

"I shall keep these in remembrance of a happy moment," said her friend, with a sentimental air, and she glanced at me with her flashing eye. So saying, she picked up the scattered leaves of the rose.

"And I! am I to have nothing?" exclaimed the blue-eyed girl with an air of mock sadness, and she crossed her arms upon her lap with a drooping head.

I took a light iron chain from my neck, and threw it over hers. "There," I said, "Miss Sugarplum, that is for you."

She jumped up from the ground, and bounded about as if she were the happiest of creatures, laughing without end, and kissing the slight gift. The dark girl rose and began to dance full of grace and expression: Sugarplum joined her, and they fell into one of their stage figures. The serious beauty strove to excel, and indeed was the greater artist of the two, but there was a wild grace about her companion which pleased me most.

"Can you dance, little count?" she cried.

"I am too tired," I answered.

"Nay, then, another day, for it is pleasant to look forward to frolic."

The man with the odd face now advanced towards me. He fell into the most ridiculous attitudes. I thought that he would never have finished his multiplied reverences. Every time he bowed he saluted me with a new form of visage. It was the most ludicrous medley of pomposity, and awkwardness, and humour. I thought that I had never seen such a droll person, and was myself a little impregnated with his oddity. I also made him a bow with assumed dignity, and then he became more subdued.

"Sir," said he, placing his huge hand upon his breast, and bowing nearly to the ground, "I assure you, sir, indeed, sir, the greatest honour, sir, your company, sir, a very great honour indeed."

"I am equally sensible of the honour," I replied, "and think myself most fortunate to have found so many and such agreeable friends."

"The greatest honour, sir, the greatest honour, indeed, sir, very sensible, sir, always sensible, sir."

He stopped, and I again returned his reverence, but this time without speaking.

"The greatest liberty, sir, the greatest liberty indeed, sir, never take liberties, sir, but fear you will consider it a very great liberty, a very great liberty indeed, sir."

"Indeed, I shall esteem myself very fortunate to comply with any wish that you can express."

"O! sir, you are too kind, sir, too kind, indeed, sir, always are kind, have no doubt, no doubt at all, sir, but our meal, sir, our humble meal, very humble indeed, we venture to request the honour, very great honour indeed, sir, your company, sir," and he pronounced the last and often-repeated monosyllable with a musical shake, and renewed reverence.

"Indeed I fear that I have already too much, and too long intruded."

"O come, pray come!" and each girl seized an arm and led me to their banquet.

I sat down between my two friends. The fire-lighter, who was the manager, and indeed proprietor of the whole concern, now received me with great courtesy. When they were all seated, they called several times, "Frederick, Frederick," and then the young man who was on the ground jumped up, and seated himself. He was not ill-looking, but I did not like the expression of his face. His countenance and his manner seemed to me vulgar. I took rather a prejudice against him. Nor indeed did my appearance seem much to please him, for he stared at me not very courteously, and when the manager mentioned that I was a young gentleman travelling, who had done them the honour to join their repast, he said nothing.

The repast was not very humble. There was plenty to eat. While the manager helped the soup, they sat very quiet and demure; perhaps my presence slightly restrained them. Even the laughing girl was, for a moment, calm. I had a keen appetite, and though I at first, from shame, restrained it, I played my part well. The droll carved a great joint of boiled meat. I thought I should have died; he seldom spoke, but his look made us all full of merriment. Even the young man sometimes smiled.

"We prefer living in this way to sojourning in dirty inns," said the manager, with an air of dignity.

"You are quite right," I replied. "I desire nothing better than to live always so."

"Inns are indeed wretched things," said the old mother. "How extravagantly they charge for what costs them in a manner nothing!"

Wine was now produced. The manager filled a cup, and handed it to me. I was just going to observe, that I drank only water, when Sugarplum, first touching it with her lips, placed it in my hand, and pledging them all, I drank it off.

"You are eating rough fare," said the old mother, "but you are welcome."

"I never enjoyed any thing so much in my life," I truly replied. "How I envy you all the happy life you lead!"

"Before you style it happy you should have experienced it," remarked Frederick.

"What you say is in part true. But if a person have imagination, experience appears to me of little use, since both are means by which we can equally arrive at knowledge."

"I know nothing about imagination," said the young man, "but what I know, I owe to experience. It may not have taught me as much as imagination has taught you."

"Experience is every thing," said the old mother, shaking her head.

"It sometimes costs dear," said the manager.

"Terrible, terrible," observed the droll with a most sad and solemn shake of the head, and lifting up his hands. I burst into a fit of laughter, and poured down another draught of wine.

Conversation now became more brisk, and I took more than my share of it, but I being new, they all wished me to talk. I got very much excited by my elocution as much as by the wine. I discussed upon acting, which I pronounced to be one of the first and finest of arts. I treated this subject indeed very deeply, and in a spirit of æsthetical criticism, with which they seemed unacquainted, and a little surprised.

"Should we place it," I asked, "before painting?"

"Before scene-painting, certainly," said the droll, in a hoarse thick voice, "for it naturally takes its place there."

"I never knew but one painter," said the old mother, "and therefore cannot give an opinion." The manager was quite silent.

"All employments are equally disgusting," said the young man.

"On further reflection," I continued, "it appears to me that if we examine"—but here the white girl pinched me so severely under the table, that I could not contain myself, and was obliged to call out. All stared, and she looked quite demure, as if nothing had happened.

After this all was merriment, fun, and frolic. The girls pelted the droll with plums, and he unfurled an umbrella to protect himself. I assisted them in the attack. The young man lighted his pipe and walked off. The old mother in vain proclaimed silence. I had taken too much wine, and for the first time in my life. All of a sudden I felt the trees dancing and whirling round. I took another bumper to set myself right. In a few minutes I fell down quite flat, and remember nothing more

XVI.

"I MUST get out. I am so hot."

"You shall not," said Thalia.

"I must, I must. I am so very hot."

"Will you desert me?" exclaimed Melpomene.

"O! how hot I am. Pray let me out."

"No one can get out at night," said the dark girl, earnestly, and in a significant voice, which intimated to her companion to take up the parable.

"No, indeed," said her friend.

"Why not?" I asked.

"Because it is a rule. The manager will not permit it."

"Confound the manager! What is he to me? I will get out."

"O! what a regular little count," said Thalia.

"Let me out, let me out. I never was so hot in my life."

"Hush! hush! hush! or you will wake them."

"If you do not let me out, I will scream."

The manager and the droll were in the fore part of the wagon affecting to drive, but they were both asleep. The old mother was snoring behind them. They had put me in the back part of the wagon with my two friends.

"Let him out, Theodora," for the other was afraid of a contention.

"Never," said Theodora, and she embraced me with increased energy. My legs were in the other girl's lap. I began to kick and struggle.

"O! you naughty little count," said one.

"Is this the return for all our love!" exclaimed the other.

"I will get out, and there is an end of it. I must have some air. I must stretch my legs. Let me out at once, or I will wake them all."

"Let him out, Theodora."

"He is certainly the wickedest little count,—but promise you will come back in five minutes."

"Any thing, I will promise any thing; only let me out."

They unbolted the back of the wagon, the fresh air came in. They shivered, but I felt it delightful.

"Farewell, dearest," exclaimed Melpomene, "one parting embrace. How heavily will the moments roll until we again meet!"

"Adieu, count," said Thalia, "and remember you are to come back in five minutes."

I jumped into the road. It was a clear, sharp night, the stars shining very brightly. The young man was walking behind, wrapped up in a great-coat, and smoking his pipe. He came up and assisted me in shutting the door with more courtesy than he had hitherto shown, and asked me if I would try a cigar.

I declined this offer, and for some little way we walked on in silence. I felt unwell, my head ached, my mouth was parched. I was conscious that I had exposed myself. I had commenced the morning by vowing that I would only drink water, and, for the first time in my life, I had got tipsy with wine. I had committed many other follies, and altogether felt much less like a hero. I recalled all my petty vanity and childish weaknesses with remorse. Imagination was certainly not such a sure guide as experience. Was it possible that one who had already got into such scrapes, could really achieve his great purpose! My conduct and my situation were assuredly neither of them Roman.

As I walked on, the fresh air did its kind office. My head was revived by my improved circulation, my companion furnished me with an excellent draught of water. Hope did not quite desert my invigorated frame. I began to turn in my mind how I might yet prosper.

"I feel better," I said to my companion, with a feeling of gratitude.

"Ay! ay! that wagon is enough to make any one ill, at least any one accustomed to a more decent conveyance. I never enter it. To say nothing of their wine, which is indeed intolerable to those who may have tasted a fair glass in the course of this sad life."

"You find life, then, sad?" I inquired, with a mixed feeling of curiosity and sympathy.

"He who knows life will hardly style it joyous."

"Ah! ah!" I thought to myself, "here is some chance of philosophical conversation. Perhaps I have found another stranger, who can assist me in self-knowledge." I began to think that I was exceedingly wrong in entertaining a prejudice against this young man, and in a few minutes I had settled that his sullen conduct was the mark of a very superior mind, and that he himself must be a very interesting personage.

"I have found life very gloomy myself," I rejoined; "but I think it arises from our faulty education. We are taught words and not ideas."

"There is something in that," said the young man, thoughtfully.

"After all, perhaps, the best is to be patient, and cherish hope."

"Doubtless," said the young man.

"And I think it equally true, that we should read more and ponder less.

"O! curse reading," said my friend, "I never could read."

"You have, like myself, then, indulged in your own thoughts?

"Always," he affirmed.

"Ah! indeed, my dear friend, there is, after all, nothing like it. Let them say what they will, but give me the glorious pleasure of my private world, and all the jarring horror of a public one I leave without regret to those more fitted to struggle with them."

"I believe that most public men are scoundrels," said the young man.

"It is their education," I rejoined, although I did not clearly detect the connexion of his remark. "What can we expect?"

"No, sir, it is corruption," he replied, in a firm tone.

"Pray," said I, leading back the conversation to a point which I more fully comprehended, "is it your opinion that nature is stronger than education?"

"Why," said my friend, taking a good many whiffs of his pipe, "there is a great deal to be said on both sides."

"One of the wisest and most extraordinary men I ever knew, however, was of a decided opinion that nature would ultimately prevail."

"Who might he be?" asked my companion.

"Why, really, his name—but it is a most extraordinary adventure, and to this hour I cannot help half believing that he was a supernatural being—but the truth is, I do not know his name, for I met him casually, and under very peculiar circumstances, and though we conversed much and of very high matters, he did not, unfortunately, favour me with his name."

"That certainly looks odd," said Mr. Frederick, "for when a man sheers off giving his name, I, for one, never think him better than he should be."

"Had he not spoken of the blessed Magdalen in a way which can scarcely reconcile with his other sentiments, I should certainly have considered him a messenger from that holy personage, for I have the best reason for believing that I am under her especial protection."

"If he abused her, that could scarcely be," remarked Frederick.

"No. Certainly I think he must have been only a man. For he presented me with a gift before his departure—"

"That was handsome."

"And I can hardly believe that he was really deputed—though I really do not know. Every thing seems mysterious, although I believe, after all, there is little mystery, but, on the contrary, much ignorance."

"No doubt: though they are opening schools now in every parish. And how much did he give you?" continued Frederick.

"How much! I do not understand you."

"I mean what did he give you?"

"A most delightful book, to me particularly interesting."

"A book!"

"A book which I shall no doubt find of great use in my travels."

"I have myself some thoughts of travelling," said Frederick, "for I am sick of this life, which is ill-suited to my former habits, but one gets into scrapes without thinking of it."

"One does in a most surprising manner." I never made an observation in a tone of greater sincerity.

"You have led a very different sort of life, then?" I asked—"To tell you the truth, I thought so. You could not disguise from me that you were superior to your appearance. I suppose, like myself, you are incog.?"

"That is the exact truth."

"Good heavens! how lucky it is that we have met. Do not you think that we could contrive to travel together? What are your plans?"

"Why, to say truth, I care little where I go. It is necessary that I should travel about for some time, and see the world, until my father, the count, is reconciled."

"You have quarrelled with your father?"

"Do not speak of it. It is a sad affair. But I hope that it will end well. Time will show."

"Time indeed developes every thing."

"I hope every thing from my mother the countess's influence—but I cannot bear speaking about it. I am supported now by my sister Lady Caroline, out of her own allowance too, poor creature. There is nothing like those sisters."—And he raised his hand to his face, and would have brushed away the tear that nearly started from his manly eye.

I was quite affected. I respected his griefs, and would not press him for details. I exhorted him to take courage.

"Ay! ay! it is very easy talking, but when a man accustomed to the society and enjoyments I have been, finds himself wandering about the world in this manner—it is very easy to talk—but, curse it—do not let us speak of it. And now where do you intend to go?"

"I am thinking of Venice."

"Venice! just the place I should long to see. But that requires funds. You are very welcome to share mine as far as they will last—but have you any thing yourself?"

"I have one hundred rix-dollars," I replied, "not too much, certainly, but I quitted home without notice; you understand?"

"O, yes! I have done these things myself. I was just such a fellow as you are at your age. A hundred rix-dollars?—not too much, to be sure, but with what I have got, it will do. I scorn to leave a companion in distress like you. Let me be shivered, if I would not share the last farthing with the fellow I liked."

"You shall never repent, sir, your kindness to me; of that feel assured. The time may come, when I may be enabled to yield you assistance, nor shall it be wanting."

We now began seriously to consult over our plans. He recommended an immediate departure even that night, or else, as he justly remarked, I should get perhaps entangled with these girls. I objected to quitting so unceremoniously, and without thanking my kind friends for their hospitality, and making some little present to the worthy manager, but he said that that worthy manager already owed him a year's salary, and therefore I need not be anxious on his account. Hamburgh, according to him, was the port to which we must work our way, and indeed our departure must not be postponed an hour, for, luckily for us, the next turning was the route to Hamburgh. I was delighted to find for a friend such a complete man of the world, and doubted not, under his auspices, most prosperously to achieve my great object.

XVII.

"Here is your knapsack. I woke the girls getting it. They thought it was you, and would have given me more kind words and kisses than I care for. Theodora laughed heartily when she found out her mistake, but Æmilia was in a great rage."

"Good-natured lasses! I think I must give them a parting embrace."

"Pooh! pooh! that will spoil all. Think of Venice. I cannot get at my portmanteau. Never mind, it matters little. I always carry my money about me. We must make some sacrifices, and we shall get on the better for it, for I can now carry provisions; and yet my riband of the order of the Fox is there—pah! I will not think of it. See! here runs the Hamburgh road. Cheerily, boy, and good-bye to the old wagon."

He hurried me along. I had no time to speak.

We pushed on with great spirit. The road again entered the forest, on the skirts of which I had been the whole day journeying.

"I know this country well," said Frederick, "for in old days I have often hunted here with my father's hounds. I can make many a short cut that will save us much. Come along down this glade. We are making fine way."

We continued in this forest several hours, walking with great speed. I was full of hope, and confidence, and self-congratulation, that I had found such a friend. He took the whole management upon himself, always decided upon our course, never lost his readiness. I had no care. The brisk exercise prevented me from feeling wearied. We never stopped.

The morning broke and gave me fresh courage. The sun rose. It was agreeable to think that I was still nearer Venice. We came to a pleasant piece of turf, fresh from the course of a sparkling rivulet.

"We have gone as good as thirty miles," said Frederick. "Had we kept the common road, we should have got through barely half."

"Have we, indeed!" I said. "This is indeed progress: but there is nothing like willing hearts. May we get on as well each day."

"Here I propose to rest a while," said my companion, "a few hours repose will bring us quite round. You must not forget that you rather debauched yesterday."

Now that I had stopped, I indeed felt wearied and exceedingly sleepy. My companion kindly plucked some fern, and made me an excellent bed under a branching tree.

"This is indeed a life of adventure," I said. "How very kind you are. Such a bed in such a scene would alone repay me for all our fatigue."

He produced some bread and a bottle, and gathered some cresses; but I felt no desire to eat or drink, and before he had finished his meal, I had sunk into a deep slumber.

I must have slept many hours, for when I woke it was much past noon. I woke wonderfully refreshed. I looked round for Frederick, but, to my surprise, he was not there. I jumped up, I called his name. No answer. I became alarmed. I ran about the vicinity of our encampment shouting "Frederick!" There was still no answer. Suddenly I observed that my knapsack also was gone. A terrible feeling of doubt, or rather dismay, came over me. I sank down and buried my face in my hands, and it was some minutes before I could even think.

"Can it be! It is impossible! Infamous knave, or rather miserable ass! Have I been deceived, entrapped, plundered! O, Contarini, Contarini, you are at length punished for all your foolery! Frederick, Frederick! he cannot surely have left me? He is joking, he is trying to frighten me. I will not believe that I have been deceived. I will not appear frightened. I will not shout the least. Ah! I think I see him behind that tree." I jumped up again and ran to the tree, but there was no Frederick. I ran about in turn shouting his name, execrating my idiotism, confiding in his good faith, proclaiming him a knave. An hour, a heavy but agitating hour, rolled away before I was convinced of the triumph of experience over imagination.

I was hungry, I was destitute, I was in a wild and unknown solitude, I might be starved, I might be murdered, I might die. I could think of nothing but horrible events. I felt for the first time in my life like a victim. I could not bear to recall my old feelings. They were at once maddening and mortifying. I felt myself, at the same time, the most miserable and the most contemptible of beings. I entirely lost all my energy. I believed that all men were villains. I sank upon the ground and gave myself up to despair. In a word, I was fairly frightened.

I heard a rustling in a neighbouring copse. I darted up. I thought it was Frederick. It was not Frederick, but it was a human being. An ancient woodman came forth from a grove of oaks, a comely and venerable man. His white hair, his fresh hale face, his still keen eye, and the placid, benignant expression of his countenance, gave me hope. I saluted him, I told him my story. My appearance, my streaming eyes, my visible emotion, were not lost upon him. Sharply he scrutinized me, many were the questions he asked, but he finally credited my tale. I learned from him, that during the night I had advanced far into the interior of the forest, that he himself lived in a cottage on its skirts some miles off, that he was about to return from his daily labour, and that I should accompany him. As for the road to Hamburgh, that was a complete invention. I also collected, that home as well as the college were very distant.

We proceeded together along a turf road, with his donkey laden with the day's spoils. I entirely regained my cheerfulness, and was very much interested by my new companion. Never had I seen any one so kind, and calm, and so truly venerable. We talked a great deal about trees. He appeared to be entirely master of his calling. I began to long to be a woodman, to pass a quiet, and contemplative, and virtuous life, amid the deep silence and beautiful scenery of forests—exercising all the primitive virtues which became so unsophisticated a career.

His dog darted on before us with joyful speed. We had arrived at his cottage. It was ancient, and neat, and well ordered as himself. His wife, attentive to the welcome bark, was ready at the gate. She saluted me, and her husband, shortly telling my tale, spoke of me in kind terms. Never had I been treated with greater kindness, never was I more grateful for it. The twilight was dying away, the door was locked and the lamp lighted, a blazing log thrown upon the fire, and the round table covered with a plenteous and pleasant meal. I felt quite happy, and indeed to be happy yourself, you must live among the happy.

The good woman did not join us in our meal. She sat by the fireside, under the lamp, watching us with a fond smile. Her appearance delighted me, and seemed like a picture.

"Now does not the young gentleman remind you of Peter?" said the dame. "For that is just where he used to sit, God bless him. I wonder when we shall hear of him again?"

"She speaks of our son, young master," said my host, turning to me in explanation.

"A boy as has been seldom seen among people of our condition, sir, I can well say," continued the old woman, speaking with great animation. "O! why should he have ever left home! Young people are ever full of fancies, but will they ever find friends in the world they think so much of, like the father who gives them bread, and the mother who gives them milk?"

"My father brought me up at home, and I have ever lived at home," observed Peter. "I have ever lived in this old forest. Many is the tree that is my forest brother, and that is sixty-eight years come Martinmas. I saw my father happy and wished no more. Nor had I ever a heavy hour till Peter began to take these fancies in his head, and that indeed was from a boy this high, for he was ever full of them, and never would do any thing with the axe. I am sure I do not know how they got there. The day will come he will wish he had never left home, and perhaps we may yet see him."

"Too late, too late," said the old woman; "he might have been the prop of our old age. Many is the girl that would have given her eyes for Peter. Our grandchildren might have been running this moment about the room. God bless them, whom we shall never bless. And the old man now must work for the old woman as if it were his wedding year."

"Pooh! pooh! as for that, say nothing," rejoined Peter; "for I praise God my arms and legs are hearty yet. And indeed were they not, we cannot say that our poor boy has ever forgotten us."

"Indeed it is true. He is our own son. But where does the money come from? that is the question. I am sure I think what I dare not say, and pray God to forgive me. How can a poor woodman's son, who never works, gain wherewith to support himself, much more to give away? I fear that if all had their rights, we should have better means to succour Peter, than Peter us."

"Nay, nay, say not that, Mary," said her husband, reprovingly, "for it is in a manner tempting the devil."

"The devil perhaps sent the thought, but it often comes," answered the old woman, firmly.

"And where is your son, sir?" I asked.

"God, who knows all, can tell, not I," said the old man; "but wherever he be, I pray God to bless him."

"Has he left you long, sir?"

"Fifteen years last September; but he ran away once before, when he was barely your height, but that was not for long."

"Indeed," I said, reddening.

"I believe he is a good lad," said the father, "and will never believe harm against him till I hear it. He was a kind boy, though strong-tempered, and even now every year he sends us something, and sometimes writes a line, but never tells us where he is, only that he is very happy, if we are. But for my part, I rather think he is in foreign parts."

"That is certain," interrupted Dame Mary. "I dare say he has got among the French."

"He was ever a wrong headed, queer chap," continued the father, in an under-tone, to me: "sometimes he wanted to be a soldier, then a painter, then he was all for travelling about, and I used to say, 'Peter, my boy, do you know what you are?' And when I sent him into the woods to work, when he came home at night, I found he had been painting the trees!"

The conversation had taken a turn which induced meditation. I was silent, and thoughtful; the dame busied herself with work, the old man resumed his unfinished meal. Suddenly there was a loud shouting at the garden gate. All stared and started. The dog jumped up and barked. The shouting was repeated, and was evidently addressed to the inmates of the cottage. The old woodman seized his rifle, and opened the casement.

"Who calls," he demanded, "and what want you?"

"Dwelleth Peter Winter here?" was inquired.

"He speaks to you," was the reply.

"Open the door, then," said the shouter.

"Tell me first who you are."

"My name has been already mentioned," answered the shouter, with a laugh.

"What mean you?"

"Why, that my name is Peter Winter."

The old woman screamed, a strange feeling also was my lot, the woodman dropped the loaded rifle. I prevented it from going off—neither of them could move. At last I opened the door, and the stranger of the abbey entered.

XVIII.

There was some embracing, much blessing, the old woman never ceased crying, and the eyes of the father were full of tears. The son was calm, and imperturbable, and smiling.

"Are you indeed Peter?" exclaimed the old woman, sobbing with joy.

"I never heard so from any one but you," answered the son.

"And am I blessed with a sight of you before my death?" continued the mother.

"Death! why you look ten years younger than when I last saw you!"

"O! dear, no, Peter. And why did not you tell us where you were?" she continued.

"Because I never knew."

"O! my dear, dear son, how tall you have grown! and pray how have you managed to live? honestly, I am sure: your face says so."

"As for that, it does not become me to praise myself, but you see I nave saved my neck."

"And what would you like to eat?"

"Any thing."

The father could not speak for silent joy. I had reured to the remotest corner of the room.

"The old cottage, pretty as ever. I have got a drawing of it in my portfolio—always kept it, and your portrait too, mother, and my father cutting down Schinkel's oak, do you remember?"

"Do I remember! Why what a memory the child has got, and only think of its keeping its poor old mother's head in its pocketbook, and the picture of the cottage, and father cutting down Schinkel's oak. Do I remember!—Why, I remember—"

"Come, my dear old lady, give me something to eat, and, father, your hand again. You flourisn like one of your foster brothers. A shower of blessings on you both."

"Ah! what do we want more than to see our dear Peter!" said the old woman, bustling about the supper. "And as for working, I warrant you, you shall be plagued no more about working; shall be as idle as it pleases, that's for it. For old Peter was only saying this evening, that he could do more work now, and more easily, than when he first married—Ay! he will make old bones, I warrant him."

"I said, Mary—"

"Pooh! pooh! never mind what you said, but get the brandy bottle, and give our dear Peter a sup. He shall be plagued no more about working, and that's for it. But Lord bless us, where is the young master all the time, for I want him to help me get the things."

I advanced forward and caught the eye of the son.—"What," he exclaimed, "my little embryo poet—and how came you here, in the name of the holy Magdalen?"

"It is a long story," I said.

"O! then, pray, do not tell it," he replied.

Supper soon appeared. He ate heartily, talking between each mouthful, and full of jests. The father could not speak, but the mother was never silent. He asked many questions about old acquaintances, and I fancied he asked them with little real interest, and only to gratify his mother, who, at each query, burst into fresh admiration of his memory, and his kind-heartedness. At length, after much talk, he said, "Come, old people, to bed, to bed; these hours are not for gray hairs. We shall have you all knocked up to-morrow, instead of fresh and joyful."

"I am sure I cannot sleep," said the dame. "I am in such a taking."

"Pooh! you must sleep, mother—good-night to you, good-night," and kissing her, he pushed her into the next room—"Good-night, dear father," he added, in a soft and serious tone, as he pressed the honest woodman's hand.

"And now, little man, you may tell me your story, and we will try to talk each other to sleep." So saying, he flung a fresh log on the fire, and stretched his legs in his father's ancient seat.

XIX.

It was settled that I should remain at the cottage for a few days, and then that, accompanying Winter, I should repair to the capital. Hither he was bound—and for myself, both from his advice, and his own impulse, I had resolved to return home.

On the next morning the woodman went not to his usual labour, but remained with his son. They strolled out together, but in a short time returned. The mother bustled about preparing a good dinner. For her, this was full employment, but time hung heavy on the old man. At last he took his axe, and fairly set at work at an old tree near his dwelling, which he had long condemned, and never found time to execute. His son and he had few ideas to exchange, and he enjoyed his happiness more while he was employed. Winter proposed to me a ramble, and I joined him.

He was very gay, but would not talk about himself, which I wished. I longed to know what he exactly was, but deemed a direct inquiry indelicate. He delighted to find out places he had known when he was young, and laughed at me very much about my adventures.

"You see what it is to impart knowledge to youth like you. In eight-and-forty hours all these valuable secrets are given to Master Frederick, who will perhaps now turn out a great poet."

I bore his rallying as good-humouredly as he could wish, and tried to lead our conversation to subjects which interested me. "Ask me no more questions," he said, "about yourself—I have told you every thing. All that I can recommend you now is to practise self-forgetfulness."

We rested ourselves on a bank, and talked about foreign countries, of which, though he himself never figured in his tales, he spoke without reserve. My keen attention proved with what curiosity and delight I caught each word. Whenever he paused, I led him by a question to fresh narrative. I could not withstand expressing how I was charmed by such conversation. "All that I tell you," he said, "and much more, may be found in books. Those that cannot themselves observe, can at least acquire the observation of others. These are indeed shadows, but by watching these shadows we learn that there are substances. Little man, you should read more. At your time of life, you can do nothing better than read good books of travellers."

"But is it not better myself to travel?"

"Have I not told you that your wandering days have not yet come? Do you wish to meet another Mr. Frederick? You are much too young. Travel is the great source of true wisdom, but to travel with profit, you must have such a thing as previous knowledge. Do you comprehend?"

"Ah! sir! I fear me much that I am doomed to be unhappy."

"Pooh! pooh! Clear your head of all such nonsense. There is no such thing as unhappiness."

"No such thing as unhappiness, sir? How may this be, for all men believe—"

"All men believe many things which are not true; but remember what I say, and when you have lived as long as I have, you will perhaps discover that it is not a paradox. In the mean time it is nonsense talking about it, and I have got an enormous appetite. A fine dinner to-day for us, I warrant you."

So we returned home at a brisk pace. The old woman looked out at the door when she heard our steps, and nodding to her son with a smile of fondness, "You must walk in the garden a while, Peter," she said, "for I am busy getting the room ready. Now, I dare say, you are thinking of the dinner, but you cannot tell me what there is for Peter, that you cannot. But I'll tell you, for if you fret yourself with guessing, mayhap it will hurt your relish. Do you remember crying once for a pig, Peter, and father saying a woodman's boy must not expect to live like the forest farmer's son? Well, he may say what he likes, Peter, there *is* a pig."

The father joined us cleanly shaved, and in his Sunday raiment. I never saw any one look so truly respectable as did this worthy old peasant in his long blue coat with large silver buttons, deep waistcoat covered with huge pink flowers and small green leaves, blue stockings, and massy buckles.

The three days at the woodman's cottage flew away most pleasantly. I was grieved when they were gone, and in spite of my natural courage, which was confirmed by meditation, and heightened by my constantly trying it in ideal conjectures, I thought of my appearance at home with a little anxiety.

We were to perform our journey on foot. The morning of the third day was to light us into the city. All was prepared. I parted with my kind friends with many good wishes, hearty shakes of the hand, and frequent promises of another visit. Peter was coming to them again very shortly. They hoped I might again be his companion. The father walked on with us some little way. The mother stood in the cottage door till we were out of sight, smiling through her tears, and waving her hand with many blessings.

"I must take care of my knapsack," said the younger Winter; "evil habits are catching."

"Nevertheless, I hope you will sometimes let me carry it. At any rate, give me your portfolio."

"No, no, you are not to be trusted, and so come on."

XX.

"But, my dear friend, you have lodged, you have fed, you have befriended, you have supported me. If my father were to know that we parted thus, he would never forgive me. Pray, pray, tell me."

"Prithee, no more. You have told me your name, which is against my rules; you know mine, no one of my fellow-travellers ever did before; and yet you are not contented. You grow unreasonable Did I not say that if our acquaintance were worth maintaining, we should meet again. Well! I say the same thing now—and so good-bye."

"Dear sir, pray, pray—"

"This is my direction—your course lies over that bridge—look sharp about you, and do not enter into your private world, for the odds are, you may find your friend Count Frederick picking a pocket. Good morning, little man."

We parted. I crossed the bridge. The stir of man seemed strange after the silence of the woods. I did not feel quite at my ease; my heart a little misgave me. I soon reached the street in which my father resided. I thought of the woodman's cottage, and the careless days I had spent under that simple roof. I wished myself once more by Schinkel's oak, talking of Arabia the Blessed with that strange man with whom my acquaintance, although so recent, seemed now only a dream. Did he really exist—were they all real beings with whom I seemed lately to have consorted? Or had I indeed been all this time plunged in one of my incurable reveries! I thought of the laughing girl, and her dark sentimental friend. I felt for the chain which I always wore round my neck. It was gone. No doubt, then, it must all be true.

I had reached the gate. I uttered an involuntary sigh. I took up the knocker. It was for a moment suspended. I thought of the Contarinis, and my feeble knock hurried into a sharp rap. .. entered. "'Tis a nervous business," thought I, "there is no concealing it. 'Tis flat rebellion—'tis desertion—'tis an outrage of all parental orders—'tis a viola tion of the law of nature and of nations." I sighed again. "Yet these are all bug-bears, for what can they do to me? Is there any punishment that they can inflict that I care for? Certainly not, and 'tis likely it will all blow over. Yet the explanations, and the vile excuses, and the petty examinations, there is something pitiful, and contemptible, and undignified in the whole process. What is it that so annoys me? 'Tis not fear. I think it is the disgust of being accountable to any human being."

I went up stairs. My father, I felt sure, was away. I found the baroness alone. She started when I entered, and looked sullen. Her countenance, she flattered herself, was a happy mixture of the anxiety which became both a spouse and a mother, pity for my father, pity for me, and decided indignation at my very improper conduct.

"How do you do, madam?" I inquired, in as quiet a tone as I could command. "My father is, I suppose, at his office."

"I am sure I cannot tell," she replied, speaking in a very subdued, serious tone, as if there were death in the house. "I believe he *has* gone out to-day. He has been very agitated indeed, and I think is extremely unwell. We have all been extremely agitated and alarmed. I have kept myself as quiet as I can, but can bear no noise whatever. The baron has received a fine letter from your tutor," she continued, in a brisker and rather malignant tone, "but your father will speak to you. I know nothing about these things, I wished to have said something to soothe him, but I know I never interfere for any good."

"Well," I observed, with a dogged, desperate tone, speaking through my teeth, "well! all I can say is, that if my father has been prejudiced against me by a parcel of infamous falsehoods, as it appears by your account, I know how to protect myself. I see how the ground lies; I see that I have already been judged, and am now to be punished without a trial. But I will not submit any longer to such persecution. Kindness in this house I never expect, but justice is a right enjoyed by a common woodman, and denied only to me."

"Dear me, Contarini, how violent you are! I never said your father was even angry. I only said I thought he was a little unwell—a little bilious, I think. My dear Contarini, you are always so very violent. I am sure I said I was confident you would never have left college without a very good cause indeed. I have no doubt you will explain every thing in the most satisfactory manner possible. I do not know what you mean always by talking of not expecting kindness in this house. I am sure I never interfered with you. I make it a rule always, when your interest is in the least concerned, never to give an opinion. I am sure I wish you were quite happy and less violent. As for judging and punishing without a trial, you know your father never punishes any one, nor has he decided any thing, for all he knows is from the letter of your tutor, and that is merely a line, merely saying you had quitted the college without leave, and, as they supposed, had gone home. They said, too, that they were the more surprised, as your general behaviour was quite unexceptionable. Not at all against you the letter was, not at all, I assure you. I pointed out to your father more than once, that the letter was, if any thing, rather in your favour, because I had no doubt that you would explain the step in the most satisfactory manner; and they said, you see, that your conduct, otherwise, was perfectly unexceptionable."

"Well, my dear madam, I am very sorry if I have offended you. How are my brothers?"

"I am very willing to forget it. You may say and think what you please, Contarini, as long as you are not violent. The children are pretty well. Ernest quite ready to go to college, and now there is no one to take care of him. I always thought of your being there with quite a feeling of satisfaction, for I was sure that you would not refuse to do what you could for him among the boys. As it is, I have no doubt he will be killed the first half year, or, at least, have a limb broken, for, poor dear boy, he is so delicate, he cannot fight."

"Well, my dear madam, if I be not there, I can recommend him to some one who will take care of him. Make yourself quite easy. A little rough life will do him no harm, and I will answer he is not killed, and even have not a limb broken. Now, what do you recommend me to do about my father? Shall I walk down to him?"

"I certainly think not. You know that he will certainly be at home this afternoon, though, to be sure, he will be engaged, but to-morrow, or the day after, I have no doubt he will find half an hour to speak to you. You know he is so very busy."

I immediately resolved to walk down to him. I had no idea of having a scene impending over me in this manner for days. My father at this time filled the office of Secretary of State for Foreign Affairs. He had been appointed to this post recently, and I had never yet visited him at his new office. I repaired to it immediately. It was at some distance from his house. His horses were waiting at the door, therefore I was sure that he was to be found. When I entered, I found myself in a hall. A porter was loitering in a large chair. I asked him for Baron Fleming. He did not deign to answer me, but pointed to a mahogany door. I entered, and found myself in a large well-furnished room, fitted up with desks. At the end, two young men were fencing. Another, seated at a round table covered with papers, was copying music, and occasionally trying a note on his guitar. A fourth was throwing himself into attitudes before a pier-glass; and the fifth, who was the only one whose employment was in any degree of a political nature, was seated at his desk, reading the newspaper.

No one noticed my entrance. I looked in vain for my father, and with some astonishment at those I found in his place. Then I inquired for Baron Fleming, and, for the second time in one day, I did not receive any answer. I repeated my query in a more audible tone, and the young gentleman who was reading the newspaper, without taking his eyes off the columns, demanded, in a curt voice, what I wanted with him.

"What is that to you?" I ingenuously asked.

This unusual reply excited attention. They all looked at me, and when they had looked at me, they looked at each other, and smiled. My appearance indeed, of which, till I had seen myself in the pier-glass, I was not sensible, was indeed well calculated to excite a smile, and to attract a stare. My clothes were not untattered, and were very much soiled, being covered with shreds of moss and blades of grass, and stuck over with thistle-tops; my boots had not been cleaned for a week, my shirt frill, which fell over my shoulders, was torn and dirtied, my dishevelled and unbrushed locks reached my neck, and could scarcely be said to be covered by the small forester's cap, which I always wore at school, and in which I had decamped. Animate the countenance of this strange figure with that glow of health which can only be obtained by the pedestrian, and which seemed to shock the nerves of this company of dapper youths.

"If you want Baron Fleming, then you must go up stairs," said the student of the newspaper in a peevish voice.

As I shut the door, I heard the burst of laughter, I mounted up the great staircase and came into an antechamber.

"What do you want, sir, what do you want, sir? You must not come here," said a couple of pompous messengers, nearly pushing me out.

"I shall not go away," I replied; "I want Baron Fleming."

"Engaged, young gentleman, engaged—can't see any one—impossible."

"I shall wait, then."

"No use waiting, young gentleman; better go."

"It is not such an easy matter, I perceive, to see one's father," I thought to myself.

I did not know which was his room, otherwise I would have gone in: but turning round, I detected written on a door, "Under Secretary's Office," and I ran to it.

"Stop, sir, stop," said the messengers.

But I had hold of the lock. They pulled me, I kicked the door, and out came the private secretary of the under secretary.

"What is all this, what is all this?" asked the private secretary. He was a fit companion for the young gentlemen I had left down stairs.

"I want Baron Fleming," I replied, "and these men will not tell me where he is, and therefore I come to the under secretary to ask." So saying, I most indignantly freed my arm from the capture of one of the messengers, and kicked the shin of the other.

"May I ask who you are?" demanded the private secretary.

"I am Baron Contarini Fleming," I replied.

"Pray sit down," said the private secretary, "I will be with you in a moment."

The two messengers darted back, and continued bowing without turning their backs, until they unexpectedly reached the end of the room.

The private secretary returned with the under secretary. The under secretary told me that my father was engaged with the chancellor, and that his door was locked, but that the moment the door was unlocked, and the chancellor departed, he would take care that he was informed of my arrival. In the mean time, as he himself had a deputation to receive in his room, who were to come today to complain in form of what they had for months been complaining informally, he begged that I would have the kindness to accompany his private secretary to the room down stairs.

The room down stairs I again entered. The private secretary introduced me. All looked very confused, and the young gentleman who was still reading the newspaper immediately handed it to me. I had never read a newspaper in my life, but I accepted his offer to show my importance. As I did not understand politics, I turned the back of the sheet, where there is generally an article on the fine arts, or a review of a new book. My wandering eye fixed upon a memoir of the Chevalier de Winter. I was equally agitated and astonished. My eye quivered over the page. I saw in an instant enough to convince me it was my friend, and that my friend was styled "a great ornament to the country," and the Northmen were congratulated on at length producing an artist whom the Italians themselves acknowledged unrivalled among the living. I learned how he was the son of a peasant: how his genius for painting early developed itself; how he had led four years an eccentric and wandering life; how he had returned to Rome, and at once produced a master-piece: how he had gained prizes in academies: how he was esteemed and honoured by foreign princes; how his own illustrious monarch, ever alive to the patronage of the fine arts, had honoured him with two commissions; how he had returned to his native country with these magnificent pictures, which were daily exhibiting at the Royal Academy of Arts; how the king had conferred on him the collar of a high order and offered him a great pension; how he had refused the pension, and requested only that a competency might be settled on his parents.

I was bewildered, I fell into a deep revery, the paper dropped from my hand, the door opened, and the private secretary summoned me to the presence of my father.

XXI.

It is time you should know something of my father. You must remember that he was little more than a score of years my senior. Imagine then a man about four-and-thirty years of age, tall and thin, slightly bald, handsome and elegant, pensive and pale. His clear broad brow, his aquiline, but delicately-chiselled nose, his gray, deep-set, and penetrating eye, and his compressed lips, altogether formed a countenance which enchanted women, and awed men.

His character is more difficult to delineate. It was perhaps inscrutable. I will attempt to sketch it, as it might then have appeared to those who considered themselves qualified to speculate upon human nature.

His talents were of a high order, and their exercise alone had occasioned his rise in a country in which he had no interest and no connexions. He had succeeded in every thing he had undertaken. As an orator, as a negotiator, and in all the details of domestic administration he was alike eminent, and his luminous interpretation of national law had elevated the character of his monarch in the opinion of Europe, and had converted a second-rate power into the mediator between the highest.

The minister of a free people, he was the personal as well as the political pupil of Metternich. Yet, he respected the institutions of his country, because they existed, and because experience proved that, under their influence, the natives had become more powerful machines.

His practice of politics was compressed in two words—subtelty and force. The minister of an emperor, he would have maintained his system by armies; in the cabinet of a small kingdom, he compensated for his deficiency by intrigue.

His perfection of human nature was a practical man. He looked upon a theorist either with alarm or with contempt. Proud in his own energies, and conscious that he owed every thing to his own dexterity, he believed all to depend upon the influence of individual character. He required men not to think but to act, not to examine but to obey, and animating their brute force with his own intelligence, he found the success which he believed could never be achieved by the rational conduct of an enlightened people.

Out of the cabinet, the change of his manner might perplex the superficial. The moment that he entered society, his thoughtful face would break into a fascinating smile, and he listened with interest to the tales of levity, and joined with readiness in each frivolous pursuit. He was sumptuous in his habits, and was said to be even voluptuous. Perhaps he affected gallantry because he was deeply impressed with the influence of women, both upon public and upon private opinion. With them he was a universal favourite; and as you beheld him assenting with conviction to their gay or serious nonsense, and waving, with studied grace, his perfumed handkerchief in his delicately-white and jewelled hand, you might have supposed him for a moment a consummate lord-chamberlain—but only for a moment,—for had you caught his eye, you would have withdrawn your gaze with precipitation, and perhaps with awe. For the rest, he spoke all languages, never lost his self-possession, and never in my recollection, had displayed a spark of strong feeling.

I loved my father deeply, but my love was mixed with more than reverence; it was blended with fear. He was the only person before whom I ever quailed. To me he had been universally kind. I could not recall, in the whole period of my existence, a single harsh word directed to myself that had ever escaped him. Whenever he saw me, he smiled and nodded; and sometimes, in early days, when I requested an embrace, he had pressed my lips. As I grew in years, every thing was arranged that could conduce to my happiness. Whatever I desired was granted, whatever wish I expressed was gratified. Yet with all this, by some means or other which I could not comprehend, the intercourse between my father and myself seemed never to advance. I was still to him as much an infant as if I were yet a subject of the nursery, and the impending and important interview might be considered the first time that it was ever my fortune to engage with him in serious converse.

The door was opened, my heart palpitated, the private secretary withdrew, I entered the lofty room. My father was writing. He did not look up as I came in. I stood at his table a second. He raised his eyes, stared at my odd appearance, and then pointing to a chair, he said, "How do you do, Contarini? I have been expecting you some days." Then he resumed his writing.

I was rather surprised, but my entrance had so agitated me that I was not sorry to gain time. A clock was opposite to me, and I employed myself in watching the hands. They advanced over one, two, three minutes very slowly and solemnly; still my father wrote; even five minutes disappeared, and my father continued writing. I thought five minutes had never gone so slowly; I began to think of what I should say, and to warm up my courage by an imaginary conversation. Suddenly I observed that ten minutes had flown, and these last five had scudded in a most surprising manner. Still my father was employed. At length he rang his bell. One of my friends the messengers entered. My father sent for Mr. Strelamb, and before Mr. Strelamb, who was his private secretary, appeared, he had finished his letter and given it to the other messenger. Then Mr. Strelamb came in and seated himself opposite to my father, and took many notes with an attention and quickness which appeared to me quite marvellous, and then my father, looking at the clock, said he had an appointment with the Prussian ambassador at his palace; but, while Mr. Strelamb was getting some papers in order for him, he sent for the under secretary and gave him so many directions, that I thought the under secretary must have the most wonderful memory in the world. At length my father left the room, saying, as he quitted it, "Rest you here, Contarini."

I was consoled for his neglect by the consciousness that my father was a very great man indeed. I had no idea of such a great man. I was filled with awe. I looked out of the window to see him mount his horse, but just as he had one foot in his stirrup, a carriage dashed up to the door, my father withdrew his foot, and saluting the person in the carriage, entered it. It was the Austrian ambassador. In ten minutes he came out, but just as the steps were rattled up, and the chasseur had closed the door with his best air, my father returned to the carriage, but he remained only a minute, and then, mounting his horse, galloped off.

"This is indeed a great man," I thought, "and I am his son." I began to muse upon this idea of political greatness. The simple woodman, and his decorous cottage, and his free forest life recurred to my mind, unaccompanied by that feeling of satisfaction which I had hitherto associated with them, and were pictured in faded and rather insipid colours. Poetry, and philosophy, and the delights of solitude, and the beauty of truth, and the rapture of creation—I know not how it was, they certainly did not figure in such paramount beauty and colossal importance as I had previously viewed them. I thought of my harassing hours of doubt and diffidence with disgust, I sickened at the time wasted over imperfect efforts, at what, when perfect, seemed somehow of questionable importance. I was dissatisfied with my past life. Ambassadors, and chancellors, under secretaries, and private secretaries, and public messengers, flitted across my vision. I was sensibly struck at the contrast between all this greatness achieved, and moving before me in its quick and proud reality, and my weak meditations of unexecuted purposes and dreamy visions of imaginary grandeur. I threw myself in my father's chair, took up a pen, and, insensibly to myself, while I indulged in these reflections, scribbled Contarini Fleming over every paper that afforded itself for my signature.

My father was a long while away. I fell into a profound revery. He entered the room. I did not observe him, I was entirely lost. I was engaged in a conversation with both the Prussian and Austrian ambassadors together. My father called me; I did not hear him. My eyes were fixed on vacancy, but I was listening with the greatest attention to their excellencies. My father approached, lifted me gently from his seat, and placed me in my original chair. I stared, looked up, and shook myself like a man awakened. He slightly smiled, and then seating himself, shrugging up his shoulders at my labours, and arranging his papers, he said, at the same time,

"Now, Contarini, I wish you to tell me why you have left your college?"

This was a home query, and entirely brought me to myself. With the greatest astonishment, I found that I had no answer. I did not speak, and my father commenced writing. In two or three instances he said, "Well can you answer my question?"

"Yes, sir," I replied, to gain time.

"Well! tell me."

"Because, sir, because it was no use staying there."

"Why?"

"Because I learned nothing!"

"Were you the first boy in the school, or the last? had you learned every thing that they could teach you, or nothing?"

"I was neither first nor last. Not that I should be ashamed of being last where I considered it no honour to be first."

"Why not?"

"Because I do not think that it is an enviable situation to be the first among the learners of words."

My father gave me a sharp glance, and then said, "Did you leave college because you considered that they taught you only words?"

"Yes, sir, and because I wished to learn ideas."

"Some silly book has filled your head, Contarini, with these ridiculous notions about the respective importance of words and ideas. Few ideas are correct ones, and what are correct no one can ascertain. But with words we govern men."

This observation completely knocked up all my philosophy, and I was without an answer.

"I tell you what, Contarini: I suspect that there must be some other reason for this step of yours. I wish you to tell it to me. If you were not making there that progress which every intelligent youth desires, such a circumstance might be a very good reason for your representing your state to your parent, and submitting it to his consideration, but you—you have never complained to me upon the subject. You said nothing of the kind when you were last with me, you never communicated it by letter. I never heard of a boy running away from school because they did not teach him sufficient, or sufficiently well. Your instructers do not complain of your conduct, except with regard to this step. There must be some other reason which induced you to adopt a measure which, I flatter myself, you have already learned to consider as both extremely unauthorized and very injudicious."

I had a good mind to pour it all out. I had a good mind to dash Venice in his teeth, and let him chew it as he could. I was on the point of asking a thousand questions, which I had been burning all my life to know, but the force of early impressions was too strong. I shunned the fatal word, and remained silent with a clouded brow, and my eyes fixed upon the ground.

"Answer me, Contarini," he continued; "you know that all I ask is only for your good. Answer me, Contarini; I request that you answer me. Were you uncomfortable? Were you unhappy?"

"I am always unhappy," I replied, in a gloomy tone.

My father moved round his chair. "You astonish me, Contarini. Unhappy! always unhappy! Why are you unhappy? I should have thought you the happiest boy of my acquaintance. I am sure I cannot conceive what makes you unhappy. Pray tell me. Is there any thing you want? Have you done, has anybody done any thing to annoy you? Have you any thing upon your mind?"

I did not answer, my eyes were still fixed upon the ground, the tears stealing down my cheek, tears not of tenderness, but rage.

"My dear Contarini," continued my father, "I must indeed earnestly request you to answer me. Throughout life you have never disobeyed me. Do not let to-day be an epoch of rebellion. Speak to me frankly. Tell me why you are unhappy."

"Because I have no one I love, because there is no one who loves me, because I hate this country, because I hate every thing and everybody, because I hate myself." I rose from my seat and stamped about the room.

My father was perfectly astounded. He had thought that I might possibly have got into debt, or had a silly quarrel, but he did not lose his self-command.

"Sit down, Contarini," he said very calmly, "never give way to your feelings. Explain to me quietly what all this means. What book have you been reading to fill your head with all this nonsense? What could have so suddenly altered your character?"

"I have read no book, my character is what I always was, and I have only expressed to-day, for the first time, what I have ever felt. Life is intolerable to me, and I wish to die."

"What can you mean by persons not loving you?" resumed my father, "I am sure the baroness—"

"The baroness!" I enterrupted him in a sharp tone; "what is the baroness to me? Always this wretched nursery view of life—always considered an insignificant, unmeaning child—What is the baroness, and her petty persecutions to me?—Pah!"

I grew bold. The truth is, my vanity was flattered by finding the man, who was insensible to all, and before whom all trembled, yield his sympathy and his time to me. I began to get interested in the interview. I was excited by this first conversation with a parent. My suppressed character began unconsciously to develope itself, and I unintentionally gave way to my mind, as if I were in one of my own scenes.

"I should be sorry if there were even petty persecutions," said my father, "and equally so, if you were insensible to them; but I hope that you speak only under excited feelings. For your father, Contarini, I can at least answer, that his conscience cannot accuse him of a deficiency in love for one who has such strong claims upon a father's affection. I can indeed say that I have taken no important step in life which had not for its ulterior purpose your benefit; and what, think you, can sweeten this all-engrossing and perhaps fatal labour, to which I am devoted, but the thought that I am toiling for the future happiness of my child? You are young, Contarini. Some day you will become acquainted with the feelings of a father, and you will then blush with shame and remorse that you have ever accused me of insensibility."

While he spoke I was greatly softened. The tears stole down my cheek. I leaned my arm upon the table, and tried to shade my face with my hand. My father rose from his seat, turned the key of the door, and resumed his place

"Occupied with affairs," he resumed, "which do not always allow me sleep, I have never found time for those slight parental offices which I do not think less delightful because it has been my misfortune not to fulfil, or to enjoy them. But you, Contarini, have never been absent from my thoughts, and I had considered that I had made such arrangements as must secure you the gratification of every innocent desire. But to-day I find, for the first time, that I have been mistaken for years. I regret it: I wish, if possible, to compensate for my unhappy neglect, or rather unfortunate ignorance. Tell me, Contarini, what do you wish me to do?"

"Nothing, nothing," I sobbed and sighed.

"But if necessity have hitherto brought us less together than I could wish, you are now, Contarini, fast advancing to that period of life, to which I looked forward as a consolatory recompense for this deplorable estrangement, I hoped to find in you a constant companion. I hoped that I might have the high gratification of forming you into a great and good man—that I might find in my son, not merely a being to be cherished, but a friend, a counsellor, a colleague—yes! Contarini, perhaps a successor."

I clasped my hands in agony, but restrained a cry.

"And now," he continued, "I am suddenly told, and by himself, that I have never loved him; but still more painful, still more heart-rending, is the accompanying declaration, which indeed is what I could not be prepared for. Misconception on his part, however improbable, might have accounted for his crediting my coldness, but alas! I have no room for hope or doubt; his plain avowal can never be misconstrued. I must then yield to the terrible conviction that I am an object of abhorrence to my child."

I flung myself at his feet, I seized his hand, I kissed it, and bathed it with my tears.

"Spare me, O! spare me," I faintly muttered. "Henceforth I will be all you wish!" I clung upon his hand, I would not rise till he pardoned me. "Pardon me," I said, "pardon me, I beseech you, father, for I spoke in madness! Pardon me, pardon me, dear father! It was in madness, for indeed there is something which comes over me sometimes like madness, but now it will never come, because you love me. Only tell me that you love me, and I will always do every thing. I am most grieved for what I said about the baroness. She is too good! I will never give you again an uneasy moment, not a single uneasy moment. Now that I know that you love me, you may depend upon me, you may indeed. You may depend upon me forever."

He smiled, and raised me from the ground, and kissed my forehead. "Compose yourself, dearest boy! Strelamb must soon come in. Try more to repress your feelings. There, sit down and calm yourself."

He resumed his writing directly, and I sat sobbing myself into composure. In about a quarter of an hour, he said, "I *must* send for Strelamb now, love. If you go into the next room, you can wash your face."

When I returned, my father said, "Come! come! you look quite blooming. By-the-by, are you aware what a very strange figure you are, Contarini? After being closeted all the morning with me, they will think, from your costume, that you are a foreign ambassador. Now, go home, and dress, for I have a large dinner-party to-day, and I wish you to dine with me. There are several persons whom you should know. And, if you like, you may take my horses, for I had rather walk home."

XXII.

I WAS so very happy that, for some time, I did not think of the appalling effort that awaited me. It was not till I had fairly commenced dressing, that I remembered, that in the course of an hour, for the first time in my life, I was to enter a room full of strangers, conducting themselves with ease in all that etiquette of society in which I was entirely unpractised. My heart misgave me. I wished myself again in the forest. I procrastinated my toilet to the last possible moment. Ignorant of the art of dress, I found myself making a thousand experiments, all of which failed. The more I consulted my glass, the less favourable was the impression. I brushed my hair out of curl. I confined my neck for the first time in a cravat. Each instant my appearance became more awkward, more formal, and ineffective. At last I was obliged to go down, and less at my ease, and conscious of appearing worse than I ever did in my life, at the only moment of that life in which appearance had been of the slightest consequence, and had ever occupied my thoughts, I entered the room at the side door. It was very full, as I had expected. I stole in, without being observed, which a little reanimated my courage. I looked round in vain for a person I knew; I crept to a corner. All seemed at their ease. All were smiling, all exchanging words, if not ideas. The women all appeared beautiful, the men all elegant. I painfully felt my wretched inferiority. I watched the baroness, magnificently attired, and sparkling with diamonds, wreathed with smiles, and scattering, without effort, phrases which seemed to diffuse universal pleasure. This woman, whom I had presumed to despise, and dared to insult, became to me an object of admiration and of envy. She even seemed to me beautiful. I was bewildered.

Suddenly a gentleman approached me. It was the under secretary. I was delighted by his notice. I answered his many uninteresting questions about every school pastime, which I detested, as if I felt the greatest interest in their recollection. All that I desired was, that he would not leave me, that I might at least appear to be doing what the others were, and might be supposed to be charmed, although I was in torture. At length he walked off to another group, and I found myself once more alone, apparently without a single chance of keeping up the ball. I felt as if every one were watching with wonder, the strange, awkward, ugly, silent boy. I coined my cheek into a base smile, but I found that it would not pass. I caught the eye of the baroness; she beckoned me to come to her. I joined her without delay. She introduced me to a lady who was sitting at her side. This lady had a son at the college, and asked me many questions. I answered in the most nervous, rapid manner, as if her son were my most intimate friend, gave the anxious mother a complete detail of all his occupations, and praised the institution up to the seventh heaven. I was astonished at the tone of affection with which the baroness addressed me, at the inte rest which she took in every thing which concerned me. It was ever "Contarini, dear"—"Contarini, my love"—"You have been riding to-day. Where have you been? I have hardly had time to speak to you. He only came home to-day. He is looking vastly well—very well indeed—very much grown—O! amazingly—quite a beau for you, baroness—O! yes, quite delightful."

What amiable people, I thought, and what would I give to be once more in old Winter's cottage!

The door opened, the Chevalier de Winter was announced. My fellow-traveller entered the room, though I could scarcely recognise him in his rich, and even fanciful dress, and adorned with his brilliant order. I was struck with his fine person, his noble carriage, and his highly-polished manner.. Except my father, I had never seen so true a nobleman. The baron went forward to receive him with his most courteous air, and most fascinating smile. I withdrew as he led him to my mother. I watched the baroness as she rose to greet him. I was surprised at the warmth of her welcome, and the tone of consideration with which she received him. Some of the guests, who were the highest nobles in the country, requested my father to present them to him: with others Winter was already acquainted, and they seemed honoured by his recognition.

"This also is a great man," I exclaimed, "but of a different order." Old feelings began to boil up from the abyss in which I had plunged them. I sympathized with this great and triumphant artist. In a few days it seemed that the history of genius had been acted before me for my instruction, and for my encouragement. A combination of circumstances had allowed me to trace this man from his first hopeless obscurity. I had seen all—the strong predisposition, the stubborn opposition of fortune, the first efforts, the first doubts, the paramount conviction, the long struggle, the violated ties, the repeated flights, the deep studies, the sharp discipline, the great creation, and the glorious triumph.

My father, crossing the room, saw me. "Contarini," he said, "where have you been all this time? I have been often looking for you. Come with me, and I will introduce you to the Chevalier de Winter, one of the first painters in the world, and who has just come from Rome. You must go and see his pictures; every one is talking of them. Always know eminent men, and always be master of the subject of the day. Chevalier," for we had now come up to him, "my son desires your acquaintance."

"Ah! fellow-traveller, welcome, welcome—I told you we should soon meet again," and he pressed my hand with warmth.

"Sir, I had a prescience that I had been the companion of a great man."

This was pretty well said for a bashful youth, but it was really not a compliment. The moment I addressed Winter, I resumed unconsciously my natural tone, and, reminded by his presence that higher accomplishments and qualities existed than a mere acquaintance with etiquette, and the vivacity which could enliven the passages of ordinary conversation, I began to feel a little more at my ease.

Dinner was announced. The table was round. I sat between the under secretary and the lady to whom I had been introduced. The scene was a very novel one, and I was astonished at observing a magnificent repast, which all seemed to pique themselves upon tasting as little as possible. They evidently assembled here, then, I thought, for the sake of conversation, yet how many are silent, and what is said might be omitted. But I was then ignorant of the purposes for which human beings are brought together. My female companion, who was a little wearied by a great general, who, although a hero and a strategist, was soon beaten and bewildered in a campaign of repartee, turned round to amuse herself with her other supporter. Her terrific child was again introduced. I had drank a glass or two of wine, and altogether had, in a great degree, recovered my self-possession. I could support her tattle no longer. I assured the astonished mother that I had never even heard of her son; that, if really at college, he must be in a different part of the establishment; and that I had never met him, that I did not even know the name, that the college was a very bad college indeed, that nobody learned any thing there, that I abhorred it, and that I hoped I should never return, and then I asked her to do me the honour of taking wine.

XXIII.

The day after the party, I went with the baroness to see the great pictures of Winter in the Royal Academy of Arts. They both of them seemed to me magnificent, but one, which was a national subject, and depicted the emancipating exploits of one of the heroic monarchs, was the most popular. I did not feel so much interested with this. I did not sympathize with the gloomy, savage scene, the black pine forests, the rough mountains, the feudal forms and dresses; but the other, which was of a very different character, afforded me exquisite delight. It represented a procession going up to sacrifice at a temple in a Grecian isle. The brilliant colouring, the beautiful and beautifully-clad forms, the Ionian fane, seated on a soft acclivity covered with sunny trees, the classical and lovely background, the deep-blue sea, broken by a tall white scudding sail, and backed by undulating and azure mountains—I stood before it in a trance, a crowd of ideas swiftly gathered in my mind. It was a poem.

After this, I called upon Winter, and found him in his studio. Many persons were there, and of high degree. It was the first time I had ever been in the studio of an artist. I was charmed with all I saw; the infinite sketches, the rough studies, the unfinished pictures, the lay figure, the beautiful cast, and here and there some choice relic of antiquity, a torso, a bust, or a gem. I remained here the whole morning examining his Venetian sketches: and a day seldom passed over that I did not drop in to pay my devotions at this delighttul temple.

I was indeed so much at home, that if he were engaged, I resumed my portfolio without notice, so that in time I knew perhaps more about Venice than many persons who had passed their whole lives there.

When I had been at home a fortnight, my father one day invited me to take a ride with him, and began conversing with me on my plans. He said that he did not wish me to return to college, but that he thought me at least a year too young to repair to the university, whither, on every account.

he desired me to go. "We should consider, then," he continued, "how this interval can be turned to the greatest advantage. I wish you to mix as much as is convenient with society. I apprehend that you have, perhaps, hitherto indulged a little too much in lonely habits. Young men are apt to get a little abstracted, and occasionally to think that there is something singular in their nature, when the fact is, if they were better acquainted with their fellow-creatures, they would find they were mistaken. This is a common error, indeed the commonest. I am not at all surprised that you have fallen into it. All have. The most practical business-like men that exist have many of them, when children, conceived themselves totally disqualified to struggle in the world. You may rest assured of this. I could mention many remarkable instances. All persons, when young, are fond of solitude, and when they are beginning to think, are sometimes surprised at their own thoughts. There is nothing to be deplored, scarcely to be feared, in this. It almost always wears off; but sometimes it happens, that they have not judicious friends by them to explain, that the habits which they think peculiar are universal, and, if unreasonably indulged, can ultimately only turn them into indolent, insignificant members of society, and occasion them lasting unhappiness."

I made no reply, but gave up all idea of writing a tale, which was to embrace both Venice and Greece, and which I had been for some days meditating.

"But to enter society with pleasure, Contarini, you must be qualified for it. I think it quite time for you to make yourself master of some accomplishments. Decidedly, you should make yourself a good dancer. Without dancing, you can never attain a perfectly graceful carriage, which is of the highest importance in life, and should be every man's ambition. You are yet too young fully to comprehend how much in life depends upon manner. Whenever you see a man who is successful in society, try to discover what makes him pleasing, and, if possible, adopt his system. You should learn to fence. For languages, at present, French will be sufficient. You speak it fairly—try to speak it elegantly. Read French authors. Read Rochefoucault. The French writers are the finest in the world, for they clear our heads of all ridiculous ideas. Study precision.

"Do not talk too much at present—do not *try* to talk. But, whenever you speak, speak with self-possession. Speak in a subdued tone, and always look at the person whom you are addressing. Before one can engage in general conversation with any effect, there is a certain acquaintance with trifling, but amusing subjects, which must be first attained. You will soon pick up sufficient by listening and observing. Never argue. In society nothing must be discussed—give only results. If any person differ with you—bow, and turn the conversation. In society, never think—always be on the watch, or you will miss many opportunities, and say many disagreeable things.

"Talk to women—talk to women as much as you can. This is the best school. This is the way to gain fluency—because you need not care what you say, and had better not be sensible. They, too, will rally you on many points, and, as they are women, you will not be offended. Nothing is of so much importance, and of so much use, to a young man entering life, as to be well criticised by women. It is impossible to get rid of those bad habits which we pick up in boyhood without this supervision. Unfortunately, you have no sisters. But never be offended if a woman rally you. Encourage her. Otherwise, you will never be free from your awkwardness, or any little oddities, and certainly never learn to dress.

"You ride pretty well, but you had better go through the manège. Every gentleman should be a perfect cavalier. You shall have your own groom and horses, and I wish you to ride regularly every day.

"As you are to be at home for so short a time, and for other reasons, I think it better that you should not have a tutor in the house. Parcel out your morning, then, for your separate masters. Rise early and regularly, and read for three hours. Read the memoirs of the Cardinal de Retz—the life of Richelieu—every thing about Napoleon—read works of that kind. Strelamb will prepare you a list. Read no history—nothing but biography, for that is life without theory. Then fence. Talk an hour with your French master, but do not throw the burden of the conversation upon him. Give him an account of something. Describe to him the events of yesterday, or give him a detailed account of the constitution. You will have then sufficiently rested yourself for your dancing. And, after that, ride and amuse yourself as much as you can. Amusement to an observing mind is study."

I pursued the system which my father had pointed out with exactness, and soon with pleasure. I sacredly observed my hours of reading, and devoted myself to the study of the lives of what my father considered really great men—that is to say, men of great energies and violent volition, who look upon their fellow-creatures as mere tools, with which they can build up a pedestal for their solitary statue, and who sacrifice every feeling, which should sway humanity, and every high work which genius should really achieve, to the short-sighted gratification of an irrational and outrageous selfism. As for my manners, I flattered myself that they had advanced in measure with my mind, although I already emulated Napoleon. I soon overcame the fear which attended my first experiments in society, and by scrupulously observing the paternal maxims, I soon became very self-satisfied. I listened to men with a delightful mixture of deference and self-confidence: were they old, and did I differ with them, I contented myself by positively stating my opinion in a most subdued voice, and then either turning the subject or turning upon my heel. But as for women, it is astonishing how well I got on. The nervous rapidity of my first rattle soon subsided into a continuous flow of easy nonsense. Impertinent and flippant, I was universally hailed an original and a wit But the most remarkable incident was, that the baroness and myself became the greatest friends. I was her constant attendant, and rehearsed to her flattered ear all my evening performance. She was the person with whom I practised, and as she had a taste in dress, I encouraged her opinions. Unconscious that she was at once my lay figure and my mirror, she loaded me with presents, and announced to all her coterie, that I was the most delightful young man of her acquaintance.

From all this, it may easily be suspected that, at

the age of fifteen, I had unexpectedly become one of the most affected, conceited, and intolerable atoms that ever peopled the sunbeam of society.

A few days before I quitted home for the university, I paid a farewell visit to Winter, who was himself on the point of returning to Rome.

"Well, my dear chevalier," I said, seizing his hand, and speaking in a voice of affected interest, "I could not think of leaving town without seeing you. I am off to-morrow, and you—you, too, are going. But what a difference—a Gothic university and immortal Rome! Pity me, my dear chevalier," and I shrugged my shoulders.

"O! yes, certainly—I think you are to be pitied."

"And how does the great work go on? Your name is everywhere. I assure you, Prince Besborodsko was speaking to me last night of nothing else. By-the-by, shall you be at the opera to-night?"

"I do not know."

"O! you must go. I am sorry I have not a box to offer you. But the baroness's, I am sure, is always at your service."

"You are vastly kind."

"'Tis the most charming opera. I think his master-piece. That divine air—I hum it all day. I do indeed. What a genius! I can bear no one else. Decidedly the greatest composer that ever existed."

"He is certainly very great, and you are, no doubt, an excellent judge of his style; but the air you meant to hum is an introduction, and by Pacini."

"Is it, indeed? Ah! Italy is the land of music. We men of the north must not speak of it."

"Why is Italy the land of music? Why not Germany?"

"Perhaps music is more cultivated in Germany at present, but do not you think that it is, as it were, more indigenous in Italy?"

"No."

As I never argued, I twirled my cane, and asked his opinion of a new Casino.

"Ah! by-the-by, is it true, chevalier, that you have at last agreed to paint the princess-royal? I tell you what I recommend you seriously to do—most seriously, I assure you—most decidedly it is my opinion—most important thing, indeed—should not be neglected a day. Certainly, I should not think of going to Italy without doing it."

"Well, well!"

"Countess Arnfeldt, chevalier. By heavens, she is divine! What a neck, and what a hand! A perfect study."

"Poh!"

"Don't you think so, really? Well, I see I am terribly breaking into your morning. Adieu! Let us hope we may soon meet again. Perhaps at Rome—who knows? *Au revoir, au revoir.*"

I kissed my hand, and tripped out of the room in all the charming fulness of a perfectly graceful manner.

PART THE SECOND.

I.

Our schoolboy days are looked back to by all with fondness. Oppressed with the cares of life, we contrast our worn and harassed existence with that sweet prime, free from anxiety, and fragrant with innocence. I cannot share these feelings. I was a most miserable child, and school I detested more than I ever abhorred the world in the darkest moments of my experienced manhood. But the university—this new life yielded me different feelings, and still commands a grateful reminiscence.

My father, who studied to foster in me every worldly feeling, sought all means which might tend to make me enamoured of that world to which he was devoted. An extravagant allowance, a lavish establishment, many servants, numerous horses were forced upon, rather than solicited by me. According to his system, he acted dexterously. My youthful brain could not be insensible to the brilliant position in which I was placed. I was now, indeed, my own master, and every thing around me announced that I could command a career flattering to the rising passions of my youth. I well remember the extreme self-complacency with which I surveyed my new apartments, how instantataneously I was wrapped up in all the mysteries of furniture, and how I seemed to have no other purpose in life than to play the honoured and honourable part of an elegant and accomplished host.

My birth, my fortune, my convivial habits, rallied around me the noble and the gay, the flower of our society. Joyously flew our careless hours, while we mimicked the magnificence of men. I had no thought but for the present moment. I discoursed only of dogs and horses, of fanciful habiliments and curious repasts. I astonished them by a new fashion, and decided upon the exaggerated charms of some ordinary female. How long the novelty of my life would have been productive of interest, I know not. An incident occurred which changed my habits.

A new professor arrived in the university. He was by birth a German. I attended, by an accident, his preliminary lecture on Grecian history. I had been hunting, and had suddenly returned home. Throwing my gown over my forest frock, I strolled, for the sake of change, into the theatre. I nodded, with a smile, to some of my acquaintance, I glanced with listlessness at their instructer. His abstracted look, the massiness of his scull, his large luminous eye, his long gray hair, his earnest and impassioned manner, struck me. He discoursed on that early portion of Grecian history which is entirely unknown. I was astonished at the fulness of his knowledge. That which to a common student appears but an inexplicable or barren tradition, became, in his magical mould, a record teeming with deep knowledge and picturesque interest. Hordes, who hitherto were only dimly distinguished wandering over the deserts of antiquity, now figured as great nations, multiplying in beautiful cities, and moving in the grand and progressive march of civilization; and I listened to animated narratives of their creeds, their customs, their manners, their philosophy, and their arts. I was deeply impressed with this mystical creation of a critical spirit. I was charmed with the blended profundity and imagination. I revelled in the sagacious audacity of his revolutionary theories. I yielded to the full spell of his archaic eloquence. The curtain was removed from the sacred shrine of antique ages, and an inspired prophet, ministering in the sanctuary, expounded the mysteries which had perplexed the imperfect intelligence of their remote posterity.

The lecture ceased; I was the first who broke into plaudits; I advanced, I offered to our master my congratulations and my homage. Now that his office had finished, I found him the meekest, the most modest, and nervous being that ever trembled in society. With difficulty he would receive the respectful compliments even of his pupils. He bowed, and blushed, and disappeared. His reserve only the more interested me. I returned to my rooms, musing on the high matters of his discourse. Upon my table was a letter from one of my companions, full of ribald jests. I glanced at its uncongenial lines, and tossed it away unread. I fell into a revery of Arcadian loveliness. A beautiful temple rose up in my mind like the temple in the picture of Winter. The door opened, a band of loose revellers burst into their accustomed gathering room. I was silent, reserved, cold, moody. Their inane observations amazed me. I shrunk from their hollow tattle, and the gibberish of their foul slang. Their unmeaning, idiotic shouts of laughter tortured me. I knew not how to rid myself of their infernal presence. At length one offered me a bet. I rushed out of the chamber.

I did not stop until I reached the room of the professor. I found him buried in his books. He stared at my entrance. I apologized, I told him all I felt, all I wanted; the wretched life I was leading, my deep sympathy with his character, my infinite disgust at my own career, my unbounded love of knowledge, and admiration of himself.

The simplicity of the professor's character was not shocked by my frank enthusiasm. Had he been a man of the world, he would have been alarmed, lest my strong feeling and unusual conduct should have placed us both in a ridiculous position. On the contrary, without a moment's hesitation, he threw aside his papers, and opened his heart to all my wants. My imperfect knowledge of the Greek language was too apparent. Nothing could be done until I mastered it. He explained to me a novel and philosophical mode of acquiring a full acquaintance with it. As we proceeded in our conversation, he occasionally indicated the outlines of his grand system of metaphysics. I was fascinated by the gorgeous prospect of comprehending the unintelligible. The professor was gratified by the effect that his first effusion had produced. He was interested by the ardour of my mind. He was flattered in finding an enthusiastic votary in one whose mode of life had hitherto promised any thing but study, and whose position in society was perhaps an apology, if not a reason, for an irrational career.

I announced to my companions that I was going to read. They stared, they pitied me. Some deemed the avowal affectation, and trusted that increased frolic would repay them for the abstinence of a week of application. Fleming and his books was only a fresh instance of his studied eccentricity. But they were disappointed. I worked at Greek for nearly fourteen hours a-day, and at the end of a month I had gained a very ample acquaintance with the construction of the language, and a still fuller one of its signification. So much can be done by an ardent and willing spirit. I had been for six or seven years nominally a Greek student, and had learned nothing, and how many persons waste even six or seven more, and only find themselves in the same position!

I was amply rewarded for my toilsome effort. I felt the ennobling pride of learning. It is a fine thing to know that which is unknown to others, it is still more dignified to remember that we have gained it by our own energies. The struggle after knowledge too is full of delight. The intellectual chase, not less than the material one, brings fresh vigour to our pulses, and infinite palpitations of strange and sweet suspense. The idea that is gained with effort affords far greater satisfaction than that which is acquired with dangerous facility. We dwell with more fondness on the perfume of the flower that we have ourselves tended, than on the odour which we cull with carelessness, and cast away without remorse. The strength and sweetness of our knowledge depend upon the impression which it makes upon our own minds. It is the liveliness of the ideas that it affords, which renders research so fascinating, so that a trifling fact or deduction, when discovered or worked out by our own brain, affords us infinitely greater pleasure than a more important truth obtained by the exertions of another.

I thought only of my books; I was happy, I was quite emancipated from my painful selfism. My days passed in unremitting study. My love of composition unconsciously developed itself. My note-books speedily filled, and my annotations soon swelled into treatises. Insensibly I had become an author. I wrote with facility, for I was master of my subject. I was fascinated with the expanding of my own mind. I resolved to become a great historical writer. Without intention, I fixed upon subjects in which imagination might assist erudition. I formed gigantic schemes which many lives could not have accomplished: yet I was sanguine I should achieve all. I mused over an original style which was to blend profound philosophy, and deep learning, and brilliant eloquence. The nature of man, and the origin of nations, were to be expounded in glowing sentences of oracular majesty.

Suddenly the university announced a gold medal for the writer of the ablest treatise upon the Dorian people. The subject delighted me. Similar ones had already engaged my notice. I determined to be a candidate.

I shut myself up from all human beings; I collected all the variety of information that I could glean from the most ancient authors, and the rarest modern treatises. I moulded the crude matter into luminous order. A theory sprang out of the confused mass like light out of chaos. The moment of composition commenced. I wrote the first sentence while in chapel, and under the influence of music. It sounded like the organ that inspired it. The whole was composed in my head before I committed it to paper,—composed in my daily rides, and while pacing my chamber at midnight. The action of my body seemed to lend vitality to my mind.

Never shall I forget the moment when I finished the last sentence of my fair copy, and, sealing it, consigned it with a motto to the principal. It was finished, and at the very instant, my mind seemed exhausted, my power vanished. The excitement had ceased. I dashed into the forest, and throwing myself under a tree, passed the first of many days that flew away in perfect indolence, and vague and unmeaning revery.

In spite of my great plans, which demanded the devotion of a life, and were to command the admiration of a grateful and enlightened world, I was so anxious about the fate of my prize essay, that all my occupations suddenly ceased. I could do nothing. I could only think of sentences which might have been more musical, and deductions which might have been more logically true. Now that it was finished, I felt its imperfectness. Week after week I grew more desponding, and the very morning of the decision I had entirely discarded all hope.

It was announced: the medal was awarded,—and to me. Amid the plaudits of a crowded theatre, I recited my triumphant essay. Full of victory, my confident voice lent additional euphony to the flowing sentence, and my bright, firm eye added to the acuteness of my reasoning, and enforced the justice of my theory. I was entirely satisfied. No passage seemed weak. Noble, wealthy, the son of the minister, congratulations came thick upon me. The seniors complimented each other on such an example to the students. I was the idol of the university. The essay was printed, lavishly praised in all the journals, and its author, full of youth and promise, anticipated as the future ornament of his country. I returned to my father in a blaze of glory.

II.

I addressed him with the confidence that I was now a man, and a distinguished one. My awe of his character had greatly worn off. I was most cordial to the baroness, but a slight strain of condescension was infused into my courtesy. I had long ceased to view her with dislike: on the contrary, I had even become her protegé. That was now over. We were not less warm, but I was now the protector, and if there was a slight indication of pique, or a chance ebullition of temper, instead of their calling forth any simultaneous sentiments on my side, I only bowed with deference to her charms, or mildly smiled on the engaging weaknesses of the inferior sex. I was not less self-conceited or less affected than before, but my self-conceit and my affectation were of a nobler nature. I did not consider myself a less finished member of society, but I was also equally proud of being the historiographer of the Dorians. I was never gloomy. I was never in repose. Self-satisfaction sparkled on my countenance, and my carriage was agitated with the earnestness and the excitement with which I busied myself with the trivial and the trite. My father smiled, half with delight and half with humour, upon my growing consciousness of importance, and introduced me to his friends with increased satisfaction. He even listened to me while, one day after dinner, I disserted upon the Pelasgi, but when he found that I believed in innate ideas, he thought my self-delusion began to grow serious.

As he was one of those men who believe that directly to oppose a person in his opinions is a certain mode of confirming him in his error, he attacked me by a masked battery. Affecting no want of interest in my pursuits, he said to me one day, in a very careless tone, "Contarini, I am no great friend to reading, but as you have a taste that way, if I were you, during the vacation, I would turn over Voltaire."

Now I had never read any thing of Voltaire's. The truth is, I had no very great opinion of the philosopher of Ferney, for my friend the professor assured me that Voltaire knew nothing of the Dorians, that his Hebrew also was invariably incorrect, and that he was altogether a very superficial person,—but I chanced to follow my father's counsel.

I stood before the hundred volumes; I glanced with indifference upon the wondrous and witching shelf. History, poetry, philosophy, the lucid narrative, and the wild invention, and the unimpassioned truth—they were all before me, and with my ancient weakness for romance I drew out Zadig. Never shall I forget the effect this work produced on me. What I had been long seeking offered itself. This strange mixture of brilliant fantasy and poignant truth, this unrivalled blending of ideal creation and worldly wisdom—it all seemed to speak to my two natures. I wandered a poet in the streets of Babylon, or on the banks of the Tigris. A philosopher and a statesman, I moralized over the condition of man and the nature of government. The style enchanted me. I delivered myself up to the full abandonment of its wild and brilliant grace.

I devoured them all, volume after volume. Morning, and night, and noon, a volume was ever my companion. I ran to it after my meals, it reposed under my pillow. As I read, I roared, I laughed, I shouted with wonder and admiration, I trembled with indignation at the fortunes of my race, my bitter smile sympathized with searching ridicule and withering mockery.

Pedants, and priests, and tyrants, the folios of dunces, the fires of inquisitors, and the dungeons of kings, and the long, dull system of imposture and misrule, that had sat like a gloating incubus on the fair neck of nature, and all our ignorance, and all our weakness, and all our folly, and all our infinite imperfection—I looked round—I thought of the dissertation of the Dorians, and I considered myself the most contemptible of my wretched species.

I returned to the university: I rallied round me my old companions, whom I had discarded in a fit of disgusting pedantry. But not now merely to hold high revels. The goblet indeed still encircled, but a bust of the author of "Candide" over the head of the president, warned us, with a smile of prophetic derision, not to debase ourselves, and if we drank deep, our potations were perhaps necessary to refresh the inexperienced efforts of such novices in philosophy. Yet we made way: even the least literary read the romances, or parts of the Philosophical Dictionary; the emancipation of our minds was rapidly effecting, we entirely disembarrassed ourselves of prejudice, we tried every thing by the test of first principles, and finally we resolved ourselves into a Secret Union for the Amelioration of Society.

Of this institution I had the honour of being elected president by acclamation. My rooms were the point of meeting. The members were in number twelve, chiefly my equals in rank and fortune. One or two of them were youths of talents, and not wholly untinctured by letters; the rest were ardent, delighted with the novelty of what they did and heard, and, adopting our thoughts, arrived at conclusions the truth of which they did not doubt

My great reputation at the university long prevented these meetings from being viewed with sus picion, and when the revolutionary nature of our opinions occasionally developed itself in a disregard for the authorities by some of our society, who perhaps considered such license as the most delightful portion of the new philosophy, my interest often succeeded in stifling a public explosion. In course of time, however, the altered tenor of my own conduct could no longer be concealed. My absence from lectures had long been overlooked, from the conviction that the time thus gained was devoted to the profundity of private study; but the systematic assembly at my rooms of those who were most eminent for their disregard of discipline, and their neglect of study, could no longer be treated with inattention, and after several intimations from inferior officers, I was summoned to the presence of the High Principal.

This great personage was a clear-headed, cold-minded, unmanageable individual. I could not cloud his intellect, or control his purpose. My ever-successful sophistry, and my ever-fluent speech failed. At the end of every appeal, he recurred to his determination to maintain the discipline of the university, and repeated with firmness that this was the last time our violation of it should be privately noticed. I returned to my rooms in a dark rage. My natural impatience of control and hatred of responsibility, which had been kept off of late years by the fondness of society, which developed itself with my growing passions, came back upon me. I cursed authority, I paced my room like Cataline.

At this moment my accustomed companions assembled. They were ignorant of what had passed, but they seemed to me to look like conspirators. Moody and ferocious, I headed the table, and filling a bumper, I drank confusion to all government. They were surprised at such a novel commencement, for, in general, we only arrived at this great result by the growing and triumphant truths of a long evening, but they received my proposition, as indeed they ever did, with a shout.

The wine warmed me. I told them all. I even exaggerated in my rage the annoying intelligence. I described our pleasant meetings about to cease for ever. I denounced the iniquitous system which would tear us from the pursuit of real knowledge and ennobling truths—knowledge that illuminated, and truths that should support the destinies of existing man—to the deplorable and disgusting study of a small collection of imperfect volumes, written by Greeks, and preserved by Goths. It was bitter to think that we must part. Surely society, cruel society, would too soon sever the sweet and agreeable ties that bound our youth. Why should we be parted ever? Why, in pursuance of an unnatural system, abhorred by all of us—why were we to be dispersed and sent forth to delude the world in monstrous disguises of priests, and soldiers, and statesmen? Out upon such hypocrisy! A curse light upon the craven knave who would not struggle for his salvation from such a monotonous and degrading doom. The world was before us. Let us seize it in our prime. Let us hasten away—let us form a society in some inviolate solitude founded upon the eternal principles of truth and justice. Let us fly from the feudal system. Nobles and wealthy, let us cast our titles to the winds, and our dross to the earth which produced it. Let us pride ourselves only on the gifts of nature, and exist only on her beneficence.

I ceased, and three loud rounds of cheering announced to the High Principal and all his slaves that we had not yet yielded.

We drank deep. A proposition came forth with the wine of every glass. We all talked of America Already we viewed ourselves in a primeval forest, existing by the chase, to which many of us were devoted. The very necessary toil of life seemed, in such an existence, to consist of what, in this worn-out world, was considered the choicest pastime and the highest pleasure. And the rich climate, and the simple manners, and the intelligible laws, and the fair aborigines, who must be attracted by such interesting strangers—all hearts responded to the glowing vision. I alone was grave and thoughtful. The remembrance of Master Frederick and the Venetian expedition, although now looked back to as a childish scrape, rendered me nevertheless the most practical of the party. I saw immediately the invincible difficulty of our reaching with success such a distant land. I lamented the glorious times when the forests of our own northern land could afford an asylum to the brave and free.

The young Count de Pahlen was a great hunter. Wild in his life, and daring in his temper, he possessed, at the same time, a lively and not uncultivated intellect. He had a great taste for poetry, and, among other accomplishments, was an excellent actor. He rose up as I spoke, like a volcano out of the sea. "I have it, Fleming, I have it!" he shouted, with a dancing eye and exulting voice. "You know the great forest of Jonsterna. Often have I hunted in it. The forest near us is but, as it were, a huge root of that vast woodland. Nearly in its centre is an ancient and crumbling castle, which, like all old ruins, is of course haunted. No peasant dare approach it. At its very mention the face of the forest-farmer will grow grave and serious. Let us fly to it. Let us become the scaring ghosts whom all avoid. We shall be from man—we shall live only for ourselves—we—" but his proposition was drowned in our excited cheers, and rising together, we all pledged a sacred vow to stand or fall by each other in this great struggle for freedom and for nature.

The night passed in canvassing plans to render this mighty scheme practicable. The first point was to baffle all inquiries after our place of refuge, and to throw all pursuers off the scent. We agreed that on a certain day, in small and separate parties, we should take our way by different routes to the old castle, which we calculated was about sixty miles distant. Each man was to bear with him a rifle, a sword, and pistols, a travelling cloak, his knapsack, and as much ammunition as he could himself carry. Our usual hunting dress afforded an excellent uniform, and those who were without it were immediately to supply themselves. We were to quit the university without notice, and each of us on the same day was to write to his friends, to notify his sudden departure on a pedestrian tour in Norway. Thus we calculated to gain time, and effectually to baffle pursuit.

In spite of our lavish allowances, as it ever happens among young men, money was wanted. All that we possessed was instantly voted a common stock, but several men required rifles, and the fund were deficient. I called for a crucible: I opened a cabinet: I drew out my famous gold medal. I gazed at it for a moment, and the classic cheers amid which it had been awarded seemed to rise upon my ear. I dashed away the recollection, and in a few minutes the splendid reward of my profound researches was melting over the fire, and affording the means of our full equipment.

III.

It was the fourth morning of our journey. My companion was Ulric de Brahe. He was my only junior among the band, delicate of frame and affectionate in disposition, though hasty if excited, but my enthusiastic admirer. He was my great friend, and I was almost as intent to support him under the great fatigue, as about the success of our enterprise. I had bought a donkey in our progress of a farmer, and loaded it with a couple of kegs of the brandy of the country. We had travelled the last two days entirely in the forest, passing many farmhouses, and several villages, and as we believed, were now near our point of rendezvous. I kicked on the donkey before me, and smiled on Ulric. I would have carried his rifle, as well as my own, but his ardent temper and devoted love maintained him, and when I expressed any anxiety about his toil, he only laughed, and redoubled his pace.

We were pushing along an old turf road cut through the thick woods, when suddenly, at the end of a side vista, I beheld the tower of a castle. "Jonsterna!" I shouted, and I ran forward without the donkey. It was more distant than it appeared, but at length we came to a large piece of clear land, and at the other side of it we beheld the long-dreamt-of building. It was a vast structure, rather dilapidated than ruined. With delight I observed a human being moving upon the keep, whom I recognised by his uniform to be one of us, and as we approached nearer we distinguished two or three of our comates stretched upon the turf. They all jumped up and ran forward to welcome us. How heartily we shook hands, and congratulated each other on our reunion! More than half were already assembled. All had contrived, besides their own equipments, to bring something for the common stock. There was plenty of bread, and brandy, and game. Some were already out collecting wood. Before noon the rest arrived, except Pahlen and his comrade. And they came at last, and we received them with a cheer, for the provident vice-president, like an ancient warrior, was seated in a cart. "Do not suppose that I am done up, my boys," said the gay dog, "I have brought gunpowder."

When we had all assembled we rushed into the castle, and, in the true spirit of boyhood, examined every thing. There was a large knights'-hall, covered with tapestry, and tattered banners. This was settled to be our chief apartment. We even found a huge oak table, and some other rude and ancient furniture. We appointed committees of examination. Some surveyed the cellars and dungeons, some the out-buildings. We were not afraid of ghosts, but marvellously fearful that we might have been anticipated by some human beings, as wild and less philosophical than ourselves. It was a perfect solitude. We cleared and cleaned out the hall, lighted an immense fire, arranged our stores, appointed their keeper, made beds with our cloaks, piled our arms, and cooked our dinner. An hour after sunset our first meal was prepared, and the Secret Union for the Amelioration of Society resumed their sittings almost in a savage state.

I shall never forget the scene, and the proud exultation with which I beheld it. The vast and antique hall, the mystic tapestry, moving and moaning with every gust of the windy night—the deep shades of the distant corners, the flickering light flung by the blazing hearth, and the huge pine torches, the shining arms, the rude but plenteous banquet, the picturesque revellers, and I their president, with my sword pressing on a frame ready to dare all things. "This, this is existence," I exclaimed. "O! let us live by our own right arms, and let no law be stronger than our swords!"

I was even surprised by the savage yell of exultation with which my almost unconscious exclamation was received. But we were like young tigers, who, for a moment tamed, had for the first time tasted blood, and rushed back to their own natures. A band of philosophers, we had insensibly placed ourselves in the most antiphilosophical position. Flying from the feudal system, we had, unawares, taken refuge in its favourite haunt. All our artificial theories of universal benevolence vanished. We determined to be what fortune had suddenly made us. We discarded the abstract truths which had in no age of the world ever been practised, and were, of course, therefore impracticable. We smiled at our ignorance of human nature and ourselves. The Secret Union for the Amelioration of Society suddenly turned into a corps of bandits, and their philosophical president was voted their captain.

IV.

It was midnight. They threw themselves upon their rough couches, that they might wake fresh with the morning. Fatigue and brandy in a few minutes made them deep slumberers, but I could not sleep. I flung a log upon the fire, and paced the hall in deep communion with my own thoughts. The rubicon was passed. Farewell my father, farewell my step-country, farewell literary invention, maudlin substitute for a poetic life, farewell effeminate arts of morbid civilization! From this moment I ceased to be a boy. I was surrounded by human beings, bold and trusty, who looked only to my command, and I was to direct them to danger, and guide them through peril. No child's game was this, no ideal play. We were at war, and at war with mankind.

I formed my plans, I organized the whole system. Action must be founded on knowledge. I would have no crude abortive efforts. Our colossal thoughts should not degenerate into a frolic. Before we commenced our career of violence, I was determined that I would have a thorough acquaintance with the country. Every castle and every farmhouse should be catalogued. I longed for a map, that I might muse over it like a general. I looked upon our good arms with complacency. I rejoiced that most of us were cunning of fence. I determined that they should daily exercise with the broadsword, and that each should become a dead shot with his rifle. In the perfection of our warlike accomplishments, I sought a substitute for the weakness of our numbers.

The morning at length broke. I was not the least fatigued. I longed to commence my arrangements. It grew very cold. I slept for an hour. I was the first awake. I determined in future to have a constant guard. I roused Pahlen. He looked fierce in his sleep. I rejoiced in his determined visage. I appointed him my lieutenant. I impressed upon him how much I depended upon his energy. We lighted an immense fire, arranged the chamber, and prepared their meal before any woke. I was determined that their resolution should be supported by the comfort which they found around them. I felt that cold and hunger are great sources of cowardice.

They arose in high spirits. Every thing seemed delightful. The morn appeared only a continuation of the enjoyment of the evening. When they were emboldened by a good meal, I developed to them my plans. I ordered Ulric de Brahe to be first on guard, a duty from which no one was to be exempt but Pahlen and myself. The post was the tower, which had given me the first earnest of their fealty in assembling. No one could now approach the castle without being perceived, and we took measures that the guard should be perfectly concealed. Parties were then ordered out in different directions, who were all to bring their report by the evening banquet. Pahlen alone was to repair to a more distant town, and to be absent four days. He took his cart, and we contrived to dress him as like a peasant as our wardrobe would permit. His purpose was to obtain different costumes, which were necessary for our enterprise. I remained with two of my men, and worked at the interior arrangements of our dwelling.

Thus passed a week, and each day the courage of my band became more inflamed. They panted for action. We were in want of meal. I determined to attack a farmer's grange on the ensuing eve, and I resolved to head the enterprise myself. I took with me Ulric and three others. We arrived an hour before sunset at the devoted settlement. It had been already well reconnoitred. Robberies in this country were unknown. We had to encounter no precautions. We passed the door of the granary, rifled it, stored our cart, and escaped without a dog barking. We returned two hours before midnight, and the excitement of this evening I never shall forget. All were bursting with mad enthusiasm. I alone looked grave, as if every thing depended upon my mind. It was astonishing the influence, that this assumption of seriousness, in the midst of their wild mirth, already produced upon my companions. I was indeed their chief. They placed in me unbounded confidence, and almost viewed me as a being of another order.

I sent off Pahlen the next day in the disguise of a pedlar to a neighbouring village. The robbery was the topic of universal conversation. Everybody was astounded, and no one was suspected. I determined, however, not to hazard in a hurry another enterprise in the neighbourhood. We wanted nothing except wine. Our guns each day procured us meat, and the farmer's meal was a plentiful source of bread. Necessity developes much talent. Already one of our party was pronounced an excellent cook; and the last fellow in the world we should ever have suspected, put an old oven into perfect order, and turned out a most ingenious mechanic.

It was necessary to make a diversion in a distant part of the forest. I sent out my lieutenant with a strong party. They succeeded in driving home from a very rich farm four fine cows in milk. This was a great addition to our luxuries and Pahlen, remaining behind, paid in disguise an observatory visit to another village in the vicinity, and brought us home the gratifying intelligence, that it was settled that the robbers were a party from a town far away on the other side of the forest.

These causes of petty plundering prepared my band for the deeper deeds which I always contemplated. Parties were now out for days together We began to be familiar with every square mile of country. Through this vast forest-land, but much removed from the castle, ran a high road on which there was great traffic. One evening, as Ulric and myself were prowling in this neighbourhood, we perceived a band of horsemen approaching. They were cloth-merchants, returning from a great fair, eight in number, but only one or two armed, and merely with pistols. A cloth-merchant's pistol, that had been probably loaded for years, and was borne, in all likelihood, by a man who would tremble at its own fire, did not appear a very formidable weapon. The idea occurred to both of us simultaneously. We put on our masks, and one of us ran out of each side of the road, and seized the bridle of the foremost horseman. I never saw a man so astonished in my life. He was, perhaps, even more astonished than afraid. But we gave them no time. I can scarcely describe the scene. There was dismounting, and the opening of the saddle-bags, and the clinking of coin. I remember wishing them good-night in the civilest tone possible, and then we were alone.

I stared at Ulric, Ulric stared at me, and then we burst into a loud laugh, and danced about the road. I quite lost my presence of mind, and rejoiced that no one but my favourite friend was present to witness my unheroic conduct. We had a couple of forest ponies, that we had driven home one day from a friendly farmer, tied up in an adjoining wood. We ran to them, jumped on, and scampered away without stopping for five or six hours, at least I think so, for it was an hour after sunset before the robbery was committed, and it was the last hour of the moon before we reached our haunt.

"The captain is come, the captain is come," was a sound that always summoned my band; fresh faggots were thrown on the fire, beakers of wine and brandy placed on the tables. I called for Pahlen and my pipe, flung myself on my seat, and dashing the purses upon the board, "Here," I said, "my boys, here is our first gold."

V.

This affair of the cloth-merchants made us quite mad. Four parties were stopped in as many days. For any of our companions to return without booty, or what was much more prized, without an adventure, was considered flat treason. Our whole band was now seldom assembled. The travellers to the fair were a never-failing source of profit.

Each day we meditated bolder exploits, and understanding that a wedding was about to take place at a neighbouring castle, I resolved to surprise the revellers in their glory, and capture the bride.

One evening, as seated in an obscure corner of the hall, I was maturing my plans for this great achievement, and most of my companions were assembled at their meal, Pahlen unexpectedly returned. He was evidently much fatigued. He panted for breath, he was covered with sweat and dirt, his dress was torn and soiled, he reached the table with staggering steps, and seizing a mighty flask of Rhenish, emptied it at a draught.

"Where is the captain?" he anxiously inquired.

I advanced. He seized me by the arm, and led me out of the chamber.

"A strong party of police and military have entered the forest. They have taken up their quarters at a town not ten miles off. Their orders to discover our band are peremptory. Every spot is to be searched, and the castle will be the first. Not daring to return by our usual route, I have fought my way through the uncut woods. You must decide to-night. What will you do?"

"Their strength?"

"A company of infantry, a party of rangers, and a sufficiently stout body of police. Resistance is impossible."

"It seems so."

"And escape, unless we fly at once. To-morrow we shall be surrounded."

"The devil!"

"I wish to heaven we were once more in your rooms, Fleming!"

"Why, it would be as well! But, for Heaven's sake, be calm. If we quaver, what will the rest do? Let us summon our energies. Is concealment impossible? The dungeons?"

"Every hole will most assuredly be searched."

"An ambush might destroy them. We must fight if they run us to bay."

"Poh!"

"Blow up the castle, then!"

"And ourselves?

"Well?"

"Heavens! what a madman you are! It was all you, Fleming, that got us in this infernal scrape. Why the devil should we become robbers, whom society has evidently intended to be robbed?"

"You are poignant, Pahlen. Come, let us to our friends." I took him by the arm, and we entered the hall together.

"Gentlemen," I said, "my lieutenant brings important intelligence. A strong party of military and police have entered the forest to discover and secure us. They are twenty to one, and therefore too strong for open combat; the castle cannot stand an hour's siege, and ambush, although it might prove successful, and gain us time, will eventually only render our escape more difficult, and our stay here impossible. I propose, therefore, that we should disperse for a few days, and before our departure, take heed that no traces of recent residence are left in this building. If we succeed in baffling their researches, we can again assemble here, or, which I conceive will be more prudent and more practicable, meet once more only to arrange our plans for our departure to another and a more distant country. We have ample funds, we can purchase a ship. Mingling with the crew as amateurs, we shall soon gain sufficient science. A new career is before us. The Baltic leads to the Mediterranean. Think of its blue waters, and beaming skies, its archipelagoes, and picturesque inhabitants. We have been bandits in a northern forest, let us now become pirates on a southern sea!"

No sympathetic cheer followed this eloquent appeal. There was a deep, dull, dead, dismal silence. I watched them narrowly. All looked with fixed eyes upon the table. I stood with folded arms. The foot of Pahlen nervously patting against the ground was the only sound. At length, one by one, each dared to gaze upon another, and tried to read his fellow's thoughts. They could, without difficulty, detect the lurking, but terrible alarm.

"Well, gentlemen," I said, "time presses, I still trust I am your captain?"

"O! Fleming, Fleming," exclaimed the cook, with a broken voice and most piteous aspect, and dropping my title, which hitherto had been scrupulously observed, "How can you go on so! It is quite dreadful!"

There was an assenting murmur.

"I am sure," continued the artiste, whom I always knew was the greatest coward of the set, "I am sure I never thought it would come to this. I thought it was only a frolic. I have got led on, I am sure I do not know how. But you have such a way! What will our fathers think? Robbers! How horrible! And then suppose we are shot! O, Lord! what will our mothers say! And after all we are only a parcel of boys, and did it out of fun. O! what shall I do?"

The grave looks with which this comic ebullition was received, proved that the sentiments, however undignified in their delivery, were congenial to the band. The orator was emboldened by not being laughed at for the first time in his life, and proceeded—

"I am sure I think we had better give ourselves up, and then our families might get us through. We can tell the truth. We can say we only did it for fun, and can give up the money, and as much more as they like. I do not think they would hang us. Do you? Oh!"

"The devil take the hindmost," said the young Count Bornholm, rising, "I am off. It will go hard if they arrest me, because I am out sporting with my gun, and if they do, I will give them my name, and then I should like to see them stop me."

"That will be best," all eagerly exclaimed, and rose. "Let us all disperse, each alone with his gun."

"Let us put out the fire," said the cook; "they may see the light."

"What, without windows?" said Bornholm.

"O! these police see every thing. What shall I do with the kettles? We shall all get detected. To think it should come to this! Shot! perhaps hung! Oh!"

"Throw every thing down the well," said Pahlen, "money and all."

Now I knew it was over. I had waited to hear Pahlen's voice, and I now saw it was all up. I was not sorry. I felt the inextricable difficulties in which we were involved, and what annoyed me most was, that I had hitherto seen no mode of closing my part with dignity.

"Gentlemen," I said, "as long as you are still within these walls, I am still your captain. You desert me, but I will not disgrace you. Fly then, fly to your schools and homes, to your affectionate parents and your dutiful tutors. I should have known with whom I leagued myself. I at least am not a boy, and although now a leader without followers, I will still, for the honour of my race, and of the world in which we breathe, I will still believe that I may find trustier bosoms, and pursue a more eminent career."

Ulric de Brahe rushed forward and placed himself by my side,—"Fleming," he said, "I will never desert you!"

I pressed his hand with the warmth it deserved, but the feeling of solitude had come over me. I wished to be alone. "No, Ulric," I replied, "we must part. I will tie no one to my broken fortunes. And my friends all, let us not part in bitterness. Excuse me if, in a moment of irritation, I said aught that was unkind to those I love, depreciating to those whose conduct I have ever had cause to admire. Some splendid hours we have passed together, some brief moments of gay revel, and glorious daring, and sublime peril. We must part. I will believe that our destiny, and not our will, separates us. My good sword," I exclaimed, and I drew it from my scabbard, "in future you shall belong to the bravest of the brave," and kissing it I presented it to Pahlen. "And now one brimming cup to the past. Pledge me all, and, in spite of every danger, with a merry face."

Each man quaffed the goblet till it was dry, and performed the supernaculum, and then I walked to a distant part of the hall, whispering, as I passed Pahlen, "See that every thing necessary is done."

The castle well was the general receptacle for all our goods and plunder. In a few minutes the old hall presented almost the same appearance as on our arrival. The fire was extinguished. Every thing disappeared. By the light of a solitary torch, each man took his rifle, and his knapsack, and his cloak, and then we were about to disperse. I shook hands with each. Ulric de Brahe lingered behind, and once more whispered his earnest desire to accompany me. But I forbade him, and he quitted me rather irritated.

I was alone. In a few minutes, when I believed that all had gone forth, I came out. Ere I departed, I stopped before the old castle, and gazed upon it in the gray moonlight. The mighty pines rose tall and black into the dark blue air. All was silent. The beauty and the stillness blended with my tumultuous emotions, and in a moment I dashed into poetry. Forgetting the imminent danger in which my presence in this spot, even my voice, might involve me, I poured forth my passionate farewell to the wild scene of my wilder life. I found a fierce solace in this expression of my heart. I discovered a substitute for the excitement of action in the excitement of thought. Deprived of my castle and my followers, I fled to my ideal world for refuge. There I found them—a forest far wilder and more extensive, a castle far more picturesque and awful, a band infinitely more courageous and more true. My imagination supported me under my whelming mortification. Crowds of characters, and incidents, and passionate scenes, clustered to my brain. Again I acted, again I gave the prompt decision, again I supplied the never-failing expedient, again we revelled, fought, and plundered.

It was midnight, when wrapping himself in his cloak, and making a bed of fern, the late Lord of Jonsterna betook himself to his solitary slumber beneath the wide canopy of heaven.

VI.

I ROSE with the sun, and the first thought that occurred to me was to write a tragedy. The castle in the forest, the Protean Pahlen, the tender-hearted Ulric, the craven cook, who was to be the traitor to betray the all-interesting and marvellous hero, myself—here was material. What soliloquies, what action, what variety of character! I threw away my cloak, it wearied me, and walked on, waving my arm, and spouting a scene, I longed for the moment that I could deliver to an imperishable scroll these vivid creations of my fancy. I determined to make my way to the nearest town, and record these strong conceptions, ere the fire of my feelings died away. I was suddenly challenged by the advanced guard of a party of soldiers. They had orders to stop all travellers, and bring them to their commanding officer. I accordingly repaired to their chief.

I had no fear as to the result. I should affect to be a travelling student, and in case of any difficulty, I had determined to confide to the officer my name. But this was unnecessary. I went through my examination with such a confident air that nothing was suspected, and I was permitted to proceed. This was the groundwork for a new incident, and in the third act I instantly introduced a visit in disguise to the camp of the enemy.

I refreshed myself at a farmhouse, where I found some soldiers billetted. I was amused with being the subject of their conversation, and felt my importance. As I thought, however, it was but prudent to extricate myself from the forest without any unnecessary loss of time, I took my way towards its skirts, and continued advancing in that direction for several days, until I found myself in a country with which I was unacquainted. I had now gained the open country. Emerging from the straggling woodland one afternoon, about an hour before sunset, I found myself in a highly cultivated and beautiful land. A small, but finely formed lake spread before me, covered with wild fowl. On its opposite side rose a gentle acclivity, richly wooded, and crowned by a magnificent castle. The declining sun shed a beautiful warm light over the proud building, and its park, and gardens, and the surrounding land, which was covered with orchards, and small fields of tall golden grain.

The contrast of all this civilization and beauty with the recent scene of my savage existence, was very striking. I leaned in thought upon my rifle, and it occurred to me that also, in my dark work, although indeed its characteristic was the terrible, there too should be something sunny, and fresh, and fair. For if in nature, and in life, man finds these changes so delightful, so also should it be in the ideal and the poetic. And the thought of a heroine came into my mind. And while my heart was softened by the remembrance of woman, and the long repressed waters of my passionate affections came gushing through the stern rocks that had so long beat them away, a fanciful and sparkling equipage appeared advancing at a rapid pace to the castle. A light and brilliant carriage, drawn by four beautiful gray horses, and the chasseur in a hussar dress, and the caracoling outriders, announced a personage of distinction. They advanced, the road ran by my feet. As they approached, I perceived that there was only a lady in the carriage. I could not distinguish much, but my heart was prophetic of her charms. The carriage was within five yards of me. Never had I beheld so beautiful and sumptuous a creature. A strange feeling came over me, the carriage and the riders suddenly stopped, and its mistress, starting from her seat, exclaimed almost shouted, "Contarini! surely Contarini!"

VII.

I RUSHED forward, I seized her extended hand, the voice called back the sweetness of the past, my memory struggled through the mist of many years —"Christiana!"

I had seen her once or twice since the golden age of our early loves, but not of late. I had heard too, that she had married, and heard it with a pang. Her husband, Count Norberg, I now learned, was the lord of the castle before us. I gave a hurried explanation of my presence—a walking tour, a sporting excursion, any thing did, while I held her sweet hand, and gazed upon her sparkling face.

I gave my gun and knapsack to an attendant, and jumped into the carriage. So many questions uttered in so kind a voice, I never felt happier. Our drive lasted only a few minutes, yet it was long enough for Christiana to tell me, a thousand times, how rejoiced she was to meet me, and how determined that I should be her guest.

We dashed through the castle gates. We alighted. I led her through the hall, up the lofty staircase, and into a suit of saloons. No one was there. She ran with me up stairs, would herself point out to me my room, and was wild with glee. "I have not time to talk now, Contarini. We dine in an hour. I will dress as fast as I can, and then we shall meet in the drawing-room."

I was alone, I threw myself into a chair, and uttered a deep sigh. It even surprised *me*, for I felt at this moment very happy. The servant entered with my limited wardrobe. I tried to make myself look as much like a man of the world, and as little like a bandit as possible; but I was certainly more picturesque than splendid. When I had dressed, I forgot to descend, and leaned over the mantelpiece, gazing on the empty stove. The remembrance of my boyhood overpowered me. I thought of the garden in which we had first met, of her visit to me in the dark, to solace my despair; I asked myself why, in her presence, every thing seemed beautiful, and I felt happy?

Some one tapped at the door. "Are you ready?" said the voice of voices. I opened the door, and taking her hand, we exchanged looks of joyful love, and descended together.

We entered the saloon; she led me up to a middle-aged but graceful personage; she introduced me to her husband, as the oldest and dearest of her friends. There were several other gentlemen in the room, who had come to enjoy the chase with their host, but no ladies. We dined at a round table, and I was seated by Christiana. The conversation ran almost entirely on the robbers, of whom I heard the most romantic and ridiculous accounts. I asked the countess how she should like to be the wife of a bandit chief?

"I hardly know what I should do," she answered playfully, "were I to meet with some of those interesting ruffians of whom we occasionally read; but I fear in this age of reality, these sentimental heroes would be difficult to discover."

"Yes, I have no doubt," said a young nobleman opposite, "that if we could detect this very captain, of whom we have daily heard such interesting details, we should find him to be nothing better than a decayed innkeeper, or a broken subaltern at the best."

"You think so?" I replied. "In this age we are as prone to disbelieve in the extraordinary, as we were once eager to credit it. I differ with you about the subject of our present discussion, nor do I believe him to be by any means a common character."

My remark attracted general observation. I spoke in a confident, but slow and serious tone. I wished to impress on Christiana that I was no longer a child.

"But may I ask on what grounds you have formed your opinion?" said the count.

"Principally upon my own observation," I replied.

"Your own observation!" exclaimed my host. "What! have you seen him?"

"Yes."

They would have thought me joking had I not looked so grave, but my serious air ill accorded with their smiles.

"I was with him in the forest," I continued, "and had considerable conversation with him. I even accompanied him to his haunt, and witnessed his assembled band."

"Are you serious!" all exclaimed. The countess was visibly interested.

"But were you not very much frightened?" she inquired.

"Why should I be frightened?" I answered; "a solitary student offered but poor prey. He would have passed me unnoticed, had I not sought his acquaintance, and he was a sufficiently good judge of human nature speedily to discover that I was not likely to betray him."

"And what sort of a man is he!" asked the young noble. "Is he young?"

"Very."

"Well! I think this is the most extraordinary incident that ever happened?" observed the count.

"It is most interesting," added the countess.

"Whatever may be his rank or appearance, it is all up with him by this time," remarked an old gentleman.

"I doubt it," I replied, mild, but firm.

"Doubt it! I tell you what, if you were a little older, and knew this forest as well as I do, you would see that his escape is impossible. Never were such arrangements. There is not a square foot of ground that will not be scoured, and stations left on every cross-road. I was with the commanding officer only yesterday. He cannot escape."

"He cannot escape," echoed a hitherto silent guest, who was a great sportsman. "I will bet any sum he is taken before the week is over."

"If it would not shock our fair hostess, Count Prater," I rejoined, "rest assured you should forfeit your stake."

My host and his guests exchanged looks, as if to ask each other who was this very young man who talked with such coolness on such very extraordinary subjects. But they were not cognizant of the secret cause of this exhibition. I wished to introduce myself as a man to the countess. I wished her to associate my name with something of a more exalted nature than our nursery romance. I did not, indeed, desire that she should conceive that I was less sensible to her influence, but I was determined that she should feel her influence was exercised over no ordinary being. I felt that my bold move had already in part succeeded. I more than once caught her eye, and read the blended feelings of astonishment and interest with which she listened to me.

"Well! perhaps he may be taken in a week," said the betting Count Prater; "it would be annoying to lose my wager by an hour."

"Say a fortnight, then," said the young nobleman.

"A fortnight, a year, an age, what you please," observed.

"You will bet, then, that he will not be taken?" asked Count Prater, eagerly.

"I will bet that the expedition retires in despair," I replied.

"Well! what shall it be?" asked the count, feeling he had an excellent bet, and yet fearful, from my youthful appearance, our host might deem it but delicate to insure its being a light one.

"O! what you please," I replied; "I seldom bet, but when I do, I care not how high the stake may be."

"Five, or fifty, or, if you please, five hundred dollars?" suggested the count.

"Five thousand, if you like."

"We are very moderate men here, baron," said our host with a smile, "you university heroes frighten us."

"Well, then," I exclaimed, pointing to the countess's left arm, "you see this ruby bracelet? the loser shall supply its fellow."

"Bravo!" said the young nobleman, and Prater was forced to consent.

A great many questions were now asked about the robbers, as to the nature and situation of their haunt, their numbers, their conduct. To all these queries I replied with as much detail as was safe, but with the air of one who was resolved not in any way to compromise the wild outlaws who had recognised his claim to be considered a man of honour.

In the evening, the count and his friends sat down to cards, and I walked up and down the saloon in conversation with Christiana. I found her manner to me greatly changed since the morning. She was evidently more constrained. Evidently she felt that, in her previous burst of cordiality, she had forgotten that time might have changed me more than it had her. I spoke to her little of home. I did not indulge in the details of domestic tattle. I surprised her by the wild and gloomy tone in which I mentioned myself and my fortunes. I mingled with my reckless prospect of the future, the bitterest sarcasms on my present lot, and when I almost alarmed her by my malignant misanthropy, I darted into a train of gay nonsense, or tender reminiscences, and piqued her by the easy and rapid mode in which my temper seemed to shift from morbid sensibility to callous mockery.

VIII.

I retired to my room, I wrote a letter to my ervant at the university, directing him to repair to Norberg Castle with my horses and wardrobe. The fire blazed brightly, the pen was fresh and brisk, the idea rushed into my head in a moment, and I commenced my tragedy. I had already composed the first scene in my head. The plot was simple, and had been finally arranged while walking up and down the room with the countess. A bandit chief falls in love with the wife of a rich noble, the governor of the province, which is the scene of his ravages. I sat up nearly all night in fervid composition. I wrote with greater facility than before, because my experience of life was so much increased that I had no difficulty in making my characters think and act. There was indeed little art in my creation, but there was much vitality.

I rose very late, and found the chase had long ago called forth my fellow-guests. I could always find amusement in musing over my next scene, and I sauntered forth, almost unconscious of what I did. I found Christiana in a very fanciful flower-garden. She was bending down, tending a favourite plant. My heart beat, my spirit seemed lighter, she heard my step, she raised her smiling face, and gave me a flower.

"Ah! does not this remind you," I said, "of a spot of early days? I should grieve if you had forgotten the scene of our first acquaintance."

"The dear garden-house," exclaimed Christiana, with an arch smile. "Never shall I forget it. O! Contarini, what a little boy you were then!"

We wandered about together till the noon had long passed, talking of old times, and then we entered the castle for rest. She was as gay as a young creature in spring, but I was grave though not gloomy. I listened to her musical voice. I watched the thousand ebullitions of her beaming grace. I could not talk. I could only assent to her cheerful observations, and repose in peaceful silence, full of tranquil joy. The morning died away, the hunters returned, we reassembled again to talk over the day's exploits, and speculate on the result of my bet with Count Prater.

No tidings were heard of the robbers; nearly every observation of yesterday was repeated. It was a fine specimen of rural conversation. They ate keenly, they drank freely, and I rejoiced when they were fairly seated again at their card-table, and I was once more with Christiana.

I was delighted when she quitted the harp, and seated herself at the piano. I care little for a melodious voice, as it gives me no ideas, but instrumental music is a true source of inspiration, and as Christiana executed the magnificent overture of a great German master, I moulded my feelings of the morning into a scene, and when I again found myself in my room, I recorded it with facility, or only with a degree of difficulty with which it was exhilarating to contend.

At the end of three days my servant arrived, and gave me the first information that myself and my recent companions were expelled, for which I cared as little as for their gold medal.

Three weeks flew away, distinguished by no particular incident, except the loss of his gage by Count Prater, and my manifold care that he should redeem it. The robbers could not in any manner be traced, although Jonsterna afforded some indications. The wonder increased, and was universal, and my exploits afforded a subject for a pamphlet, the cheapness of whose price the publisher earnestly impressed upon us could only be justified by its extensive circulation.

Three weeks had flown away, three sweet weeks, and flown away in the almost constant presence of Christiana, or in scarcely less delightful composition. My tragedy was finished. I resolved to return home, I longed to bring my reputation to the test, yet I lingered about Christiana.

I lingered about her as the young bird about the first sunny fruit his inexperienced love dare not touch I was ever with her, and each day grew more silent. I joined her exhausted by composition. In her presence I sought refreshing solace, renewed inspiration. I spoke little, for one feeling alone occupied my being, and even of that I was not cognizant, for its nature to me was indefinite and indistinct, although its power was constant and irresistible. But I avenged myself for this strange silence when I was once more alone, and my fervid page teemed with the imaginary passion, of whose reality my unpractised nature was not yet convinced.

One evening, as we were walking together in the saloon, and she was expressing her wish that I would remain, and her wonder as to the necessity of my returning, which I described as so imperative, suddenly and in the most unpremeditated manner, I made her the confidant of my literary secret. I was charmed with the temper in which she received it, the deep and serious interest which she expressed in my success. "Do you know," she added, "Contarini, you will think it very odd, but I have always believed you were intended for a poet."

My sparkling eye, sparkling with hope and affection, thanked her for her sympathy, and it was agreed that on the morrow I should read to her my production.

I was very nervous when I commenced. This was the first time that my composition had been submitted to a human being, and now this submission was to take place in the presence of the author, through the medium of his voice. As I proceeded, I grew rather more assured. The interest which Christiana really found, or affected to find, encouraged me. If I hesitated, she said, "beautiful!" whenever I paused, she exclaimed, "interesting!" My voice grew firmer, the interest which I myself took banished my false shame. I grew excited, my modulated voice impressed my sentiments, and my action sometimes explained them. The robber scene was considered wonderful, and full of life and nature. Christiana marvelled how I could have invented such extraordinary things and characters. At length I came to my heroine. Her beauty was described in an elaborate, and far too poetic passage. It was a perfect fac-simile of the countess. It was ridiculous. She herself felt it, and looking up, smiled with a faint blush.

I had now advanced into the very heart of the play, and the scenes of sentiment had commenced. I had long since lost my irresolution. The encouragement of Christiana, and the delight which I really felt in my writing, made me more than bold. I really acted before her. She was susceptible. All know how very easy it is for a very indifferent drama, if well performed, to soften even the callous. Her eyes were suffused with tears, my emotion was also visible. I felt like a man brought out of a dungeon, and groping his way in the light. How could I have been so blind when all was so evident? It was not until I had recited to Christiana my fictitious passion, that I had become conscious of my real feelings. I had been ignorant all this time that I had been long fatally in love with her. I threw away my manuscript, and seizing her hand, "O Christiana!" I exclaimed, "what mockery is it thus to veil truth? Before you is the leader of the band of whom you have heard so much. He adores you."

She started, I cannot describe the beautiful consternation of her countenance.

"Contarini," she exclaimed, "are you mad! what can you mean?"

"Mean!" I poured forth, "is it doubtful? Yes! I repeat, I am the leader of that band whose exploits have so recently alarmed you. Cannot you now comprehend the story of my visiting their haunt? Was it probable, was it possible, that I should have been permitted to gain their secret and to retire? The robbers were youth like myself, weary of the dull monotony of our false and wretched life. We have yielded to overwhelming force, but we have baffled all pursuit. For myself, I quit forever the country I abhor. Ere a year has passed, I shall roam a pirate on the far waves of the Ægean. One tie only binds me to this rigid clime. In my life I have loved only one being. I look upon her. Yes! yes! it is you, Christiana. On the very brink of my exile, destiny has brought us once more together. O! let us never part! Be mine,—be mine! Share with me my glory, my liberty, and my love!"

I poured forth this rhapsody with impassionate haste. The countess stared with blank astonishment. She appeared even alarmed. Suddenly she sprang up and ran out of the room.

IX.

I WAS enraged, and I was confused. I do not know whether I felt more shame or more irritation. My vanity impelled me to remain some time with the hope she would return. She did not, and seizing my tragedy, I rushed into the park. I met my servant exercising a horse. I sent him back to the castle alone, jumped on my steed, and in a few minutes was galloping along the high road to the metropolis.

It was about one hundred miles distant. When I arrived home I found that my father and the baroness were in the country. I was not sorry to be alone, as I really had returned without any object, and had not, in any degree, prepared myself to meet my father. After some consideration I enclosed my tragedy to a most eminent publisher, and I sent it him from a quarter whither he could gain no clew as to its source. I pressed him for a reply without unnecessary loss of time, and he, unlike these gentry, who really think themselves far more important personages than those by whose wits they live, was punctual. In the course of a week he returned me my manuscript, with his compliments, and an extract from the letter of his principal critic, in which my effusion was described as a laboured exaggeration of the most unnatural features of the German school. The day I received this my father arrived.

He was alone, and had merely come up to town to transact business. He was surprised to see me, but said nothing of my expulsion, although I felt confident he must be aware of it. We dined together alone. He talked to me at dinner of indifferent subjects, of alterations at his castle, and the state of Europe. As I wished to conciliate him, I affected to take great interest in this latter topic, and I thought he seemed pleased with the earnest readiness with which I interfered in the discussion. After dinner he remarked, very quietly filling his glass, "Had you communicated with me, Contarini, I could perhaps have saved you the disgrace of expulsion."

I was quite taken by surprise, and looked very

confused. At last I said, "I fear, sir, I have occasioned you too often great mortification, but I sometimes cannot refrain from believing that I may yet make a return to you for all your goodness."

"Every thing depends upon yourself, Contarini. You have elected to be your own master. You must take the consequences of your courage, or your rashness. What are your plans? I do not know whether you mean to honour me with your confidence as a friend. I do not even aspire to the authority of a father."

"O! pray, sir, do not say so. I place myself entirely at your disposal. I desire nothing more ardently than to act under your command. I assure you that you will find me a very different personage than you imagine. I am impressed with a most earnest and determined resolution to become a practical man. You must not judge of me by my boyish career. The very feelings that made me revolt at the discipline of schools, will ensure my subordination in the world. I took no interest in their petty pursuits, and their minute legislation interfered with my more extended views."

"What views?" asked my father, with a smile.

I was somewhat puzzled, but I answered, "I wish, sir, to influence men."

"But before you influence others, you must learn to influence yourself. Now those who would judge, perhaps imperfectly, of your temperament, Contarini, would suppose that its characteristic was a nature so headstrong and imprudent that it could not fail of involving its possessor in many dangerous, and sometimes even in very ridiculous positions."

I was silent, with my eyes fixed on the ground.

"I think you have sufficient talents for all that I could reasonably desire, Contarini," continued my father; "I think you have talents indeed for any thing, I mean, that a rational being can desire to attain; but you sadly lack judgment. I think that you are the most imprudent person with whom I ever was acquainted. You have a great enemy, Contarini, a great enemy in yourself. You have a great enemy in your imagination. I think if you could control your imagination, you might be a great man.

"It is a fatal gift, Contarini; for when possessed in its highest quality and strength, what has it ever done for its votaries? What were all those great poets of whom we now talk so much, what were they in their lifetime? The most miserable of their species. Depressed, doubtful, obscure, or involved in petty quarrels and petty precautions, often unappreciated, utterly uninfluential, beggars, flatterers of men unworthy even of their recognition —what a train of disgustful incidents, what a record of degrading circumstances is the life of a great poet? A man of great energies aspires that they should be felt in his lifetime, that his existence should be rendered more intensely vital by the constant consciousness of his multiplied and multiplying power. Is posthumous fame a substitute for all this? Viewed in every light and under every feeling, it is alike a mockery. Nay, even try the greatest by this test, and what is the result? Would you sooner have been Homer or Julius Cæsar, Shakspeare or Napoleon? No one doubts. Moralists may cloud truth with every possible adumbration of cant, but the nature of our being gives the lie to all their assertions. We are active beings, and our sympathy, above all other sympathies is with great action.

"Remember, Contarini, that all this time I am taking for granted that you may be a Homer. Let us now recollect that it is perhaps the most improbable incident that can occur. The high poetic talent,—as if to prove that a poet is only, at the best, a wild, although a beautiful error of nature,—the high poetic talent is the rarest in creation What you have felt is what I have felt myself, is what all men have felt; it is the consequence of our native and inviolate susceptibility. As you advance in life, and become more callous, more acquainted with man, and with yourself, you will find it, even daily, decrease. Mix in society, and I will answer that you lose your poetic feeling; for in you, as in the great majority, it is not a creative faculty originating in a peculiar organization, but simply the consequence of a nervous susceptibility that is common to all."

I suspected very much, that my father had stumbled on the unhappy romance of the "Wild Hunter of Rodenstein," which I had left lying about my drawers, but I said nothing. He proceeded.

"The time has now arrived which may be considered a crisis in your life. You have, although very young, resolved that society should consider you a man. No preparatory situation can now veil your indiscretions. A youth at the university may commit outrages with impunity, which will affix a lasting prejudice on a person of the same age, who has quitted the university. I must ask you again, what are your plans?"

"I have none, sir, except your wishes. I feel acutely the truth of all you have observed. I assure you I am as completely and radically cured of any predisposition that I confess I once conceived I possessed for literary invention, as even you could desire. I will own to you that my ambition is very great. I do not think that I should find life tolerable unless I were in an eminent position, and conscious that I deserved it. Fame, although not posthumous fame, is, I feel, necessary to my felicity. In a word, I wish to devote myself to affairs—I attend only your commands."

"If it meet your wishes, I will appoint you my private secretary. The post, particularly when confirmed by the confidence which must subsist between individuals connected as we are, is the best school for public affairs. It will prepare you for any office."

"I can conceive nothing more delightful. You could not have fixed upon an appointment more congenial to my feelings. To be your constant companion, in the slightest degree to alleviate the burden of your labours, to be considered worthy of your confidence—this is all that I could desire. I only fear that my ignorance of routine may at first inconvenience you, but trust me, dear father, that if devotion, and the constant exertion of any talents I may possess can aid you, they will not be wanting. Indeed, indeed, sir, you never shall repent your goodness."

This same evening I consigned my tragedy to the flames.

X

I devoted myself to my new pursuits with as much fervour as I had done to the study of Greek.

The former secretary initiated me in the mysteries of routine business. My father, although he made no remark, was evidently pleased at the facility and quickness with which I attained this formal, but necessary information. Vattel and Martens were my private studies. I was greatly interested with my novel labours. Foreign policy opened a dazzling vista of splendid incident. It was enchanting to be acquainted with the secrets of European cabinets, and to control or influence their fortunes. A year passed with more satisfaction than any period of my former life. I had become of essential service to my father. My talent for composition found full exercise, and afforded him great aid in drawing up state papers and manifestoes, despatches and decrees. We were always together. I shared his entire confidence. He instructed me in the characters of the public men who surrounded us, and of those who were more distant. I was astonished at the scene of intrigue that opened on me. I found that in some, even of his colleagues, I was only to perceive secret enemies, and in others but necessary tools and tolerated encumbrances. I delighted in the danger, the management, the negotiation, the suspense, the difficult gratification of his high ambition.

Intent as he was to make me a great statesman, he was scarcely less anxious that I should become a finished man of the world. He constantly impressed upon me that society was a politician's great tool, and the paramount necessity of cultivating its good graces. He afforded me an ample allowance. He encouraged me in a lavish expenditure. Above all, he was ever ready to dilate upon the character of women, and while he astonished me by the tone of depreciation in which he habitually spoke of them, he would even magnify their influence, and the necessity of securing it.

I modelled my character upon that of my father. I imbibed his deep worldliness. With my usual impetuosity, I even exaggerated it. I recognised self-interest as the spring of all action. I received it as a truth, that no man was to be trusted, and no woman to be loved. I gloried in secretly believing myself the most callous of men, and that nothing could tempt me to compromise my absorbing selfism. I laid it down as a principle, that all considerations must yield to the gratification of my ambition. The ardour and assiduity with which I fulfilled my duties and prosecuted my studies, had rendered, me, at the end of two years, a very skilful politician. My great fault, as a man of affairs, was, that I was too fond of patronising charlatans, and too ready to give every adventurer credit for great talents. The moment a man started a new idea, my active fancy conjured up all the great results, and conceived that his was equally prophetic. But here my father's severe judgment and sharp experience always interfered for my benefit, and my cure was assisted by hearing a few of my black swans cackle, instead of chant. As a member of society, I was entirely exempt from the unskilful affectation of my boyhood. I was assured, arrogant, and bitter, but easy, and not ungraceful. The men trembled at my sarcasms, and the women repeated with wonderment my fantastic raillery. My position in life, and the exaggerated halo with which, in my case, as in all others, the talents of eminent youth were injudiciously invested, made me courted by all, especially by the daughters of Eve. I was sometimes nearly the victim of hackneyed experience—sometimes I trifled with affections, which my parental instructions taught me never to respect. On the whole, I considered myself as one of the most important personages in the country, possessing the greatest talents, the profoundest knowledge of men and affairs, and the most perfect acquaintance with society. When I look back upon myself at this period, I have difficulty in conceiving a more unamiable character.

XI.

In the third year of my political life, the prime minister suddenly died. Here was a catastrophe! Who was to be his successor? Here was a fruitful theme for speculation and intrigue. Public opinion pointed to my father, who indeed, if qualification for the post were only considered, had no competitor; but Baron Fleming was looked upon by his brother nobles with a jealous eye, and although not unwilling to profit by his labours, they were chary of permitting them too uncontrolled a scope. He was talked of as a new man: he was treated as scarcely national. The state was not to be placed at the disposal of an adventurer. He was not one of themselves. It was a fatal precedent, that the veins of the prime minister should be filled with any other blood but that of their ancient order. Even many of his colleagues did not affect to conceal their hostility to his appointment, and the Count de Moltke, who was supposed to possess every quality that should adorn the character of a first minister, was openly announced as the certain successor to the vacant office. The Count de Moltke was a frivolous old courtier, who had gained his little experience in long service in the household, and, even were he appointed, could only anticipate the practicability of carrying on affairs by implicit confidence in his rival. The Count de Moltke was a tool.

Skilful as my father was in controlling and veilling his emotion, the occasion was too powerful even for his firmness. For the first time in his life he sought a confidant, and, firm in the affection of a son, he confessed to me, with an agitation which was alone sufficient to express his meaning, how entirely he had staked his felicity on this cast. He could not refrain from bitterly dilating on the state of society, in which secret influence, and the prejudices of a bigoted class, should for a moment permit one, who had devoted all the resources of a high intellect to the welfare of his country, to be placed in momentary competition, still more in permanent inferiority with such an ineffable nonentity as the Count de Moltke.

Every feeling in my nature prompted me to energy. I counselled my father to the most active exertions, but although subtle, he was too cautious, and where he was himself concerned, even timorous. I had no compunction, and no fear. I would scruple at no means which could ensure our end. The feeling of society, was in general, in our favour. Even among the highest class, the women were usually on the side of my father. Baroness Engel, who was the evening star that beamed unrivalled in all our assemblies, and who fancied herself a little Dutchess de Longueville, delighted in a political intrigue. I affected to make her our confidante. We resolved together that the only mode was to render our rival ridiculous. I wrote an anonymous pamphlet in favour of the appointment of the Count de Moltke. It took in everybody, until in the last page they read my panegyric of his cream cheeses. It was in vain that the Count de Moltke, and all his friends, protested that his excellency had never made a cream cheese in the whole course of his life. The story was too probable not to be true. He was just the old fool who would make a cream cheese. I secured the channel of our principal journals. Each morning teemed with a diatribe against backstairs influence, the prejudices of a nobility who were behind their age, and indignant histories of the maladministration of court favourites. The evening, by way of change, brought only an epigram, sometimes a song. The fashion took: all the youth were on our side. One day, in imitation of the Tre Giuli, we published a whole volume of epigrams, all on cream cheeses. The baroness was moreover an inimitable caricaturist. The shops were filled with infinite scenes, in which a ludicrous old fribble, such as we might fancy a French marquis before the Revolution, was ever committing something irresistibly ludicrous. In addition to all this, I hired ballad singers, who were always chanting in the public walks, and even under the windows of the palace, the achievements of the unrivalled manufacturer of cream cheeses.

In the mean time my father was not idle. He had discovered that the Count de Bragnaes, one of the most influential nobles in the country, and the great supporter of De Moltke, was ambitious of becoming Secretary for Foreign Affairs, and that De Moltke had hesitated in pledging himself to this arrangement, as he could not perceive how affairs could be carried on if my father was entirely dismissed. My father opened a secret negotiation with De Bragnaes, and shook before his eyes the glittering seals he coveted. De Bragnaes was a dolt, but my father required only tools, and felt himself capable of fulfilling the duties of the whole ministry. This great secret was not concealed from me. I opposed the arrangement, not only because De Bragnaes was absolutely insufficient, but because I wished to introduce into the cabinet Baron Engel.

The post of chief minister had now been three weeks vacant, and the delay was accounted for by the illness of the sovereign, who was nevertheless in perfect health. All this excitement took place at the very season we were all assembled in the capital for the purposes of society. My father was everywhere, and each night visible. I contrasted the smiling indifference of his public appearance with the agonies of ambition, which it was my doom alone to witness.

I was alone with my father in his cabinet when a royal messenger summoned him to the presence. The king was at a palace about ten miles from the city. It did not in any way follow from the invitation that my father was successful: all that we felt assured of was, that the crisis had arrived. We exchanged looks, but not words. Intense as was suspense, business prevented me from attending my father, and waiting in the royal antechamber to hear the great result. He departed.

I had to receive an important deputation, the discussion of whose wishes employed the whole morning. It was with extreme difficulty that I could command my attention. Never in my life had I felt so nervous. Each moment a messenger entered, I believed that he was the important one. No carriage dashed into the court-yard that did not to my fancy bear my father. At last the deputation retired, and then came private interviews and urgent correspondence.

It was twilight. The servant had lit one burner of the lamp, when the door opened, and my father stood before me. I could scarcely refrain from crying out. I pushed out the astonished waiting-man, and locked the door.

My father looked grave, serious, I thought a little depressed. "All is over," thought I, and in an instant I began speculating on the future, and had created much, when my father's voice called me back to the present scene.

"His majesty, Contarini," said my father in a dry, formal manner, as if he were speaking to one who had never witnessed his weakness—"His majesty has been graciously pleased to appoint me to the supreme office of president of his council; and as a further mark of his entire confidence and full approbation of my past services, he has thought fit to advance me to the dignity of count."

Was this frigid form that stood unmoved before me the being whom, but four-and-twenty hours ago, I had watched trembling with his high passions? Was this curt, unimpassioned tone, the voice in which he should have notified the crowning glory of his fortunes to one who had so struggled in their behalf? I could scarcely speak. I hardly congratulated him.

"And your late post, sir?" I at length inquired.

"The seals of this office will be held by the Baron de Bragnaes."

I shrugged my shoulders in silence.

"The king is not less aware than myself that his excellency can bring but a slight portion of intellectual strength to the new cabinet; that he is one indeed about to be placed in a position, to discharge the duties of which he is incapable; but his majesty as well as myself, has unbounded confidence in the perfect knowledge, the energetic assiduity, and the distinguished talents of the individual who will fulfil the duties of under-secretary. He will be the virtual head of this great department. Allow me to be the first to congratulate Count Contarini Fleming on his new dignity, and his entrance into the service of his sovereign."

I rushed forward, I seized his hand. "My dear father," I said, "I am quite overwhelmed. I dreamed not of this. I never thought of myself, I thought only of you."

He pressed my hand, but did not lose his composure. "We dine together to-day alone," he said, "I must now see De Bragnaes. At dinner I will tell you all. Nothing will be announced till to-morrow. Your friend, Engel, is not forgotten."

He quitted the chamber. The moment he disappeared I could no longer refrain from glancing in the mirror. Never had I marked so victorious a visage. An unnatural splendour sparkled in my eye, my lip was impressed with energy, my nostril dilated with triumph. I stood before the tall mirror, and planted my foot, and waved my arm. So much more impressive is reality than imagination! Often, in revery, had I been an Alberoni, a Ripperda, a Richelieu; but never had I felt, when moulding the destinies of the wide globe, a tithe of the triumphant exultation which was afforded by the consciousness of the simple fact that I was an under-secretary of state.

XII.

I HAD achieved by this time what is called a great reputation. I do not know that there was any one more talked of, and more considered in the country, than myself. I was my father's only confidant, and secretly his only counsellor. I managed De Bragnaes admirably, and always suggested to him the opinion, which I at the same time requested. He was a mere cipher. As for the Count de Moltke, he was very rich, with an only daughter, and my father had already hinted at, what I had even turned in my own mind, a union with the wealthy, although not very pleasing, offspring of the maker of cream cheeses.

At this moment, in the zenith of my popularity and power, the Norbergs returned to the capital. I had never seen them since the mad morning which, with all my boasted callousness, I ever blushed to remember, for the count had, immediately after my departure, been appointed to a very important, although distant government. Nor had I ever heard of them. I never wished to. I drove their memory from my mind; but Christiana, who had many correspondents, and among them the baroness, had, of course, heard much of me.

Our family was the first they called upon, and, in spite of the mortifying awkwardness of the meeting, it was impossible to avoid it, and therefore I determined to pay my respects to them immediately. I was careful to call when I knew I could not be admitted, and the first interview finally took place at our own house. Christiana received me with the greatest kindness, although with increased reserve, which might be accounted for by the time that had elapsed since we last met, and the alteration that had since taken place both in my age and station. In all probability, she looked upon my present career as a sufficient guaranty that my head was cleared of the wild fancies of my impetuous boyhood, and rejoicing in this accomplishment, and anticipating our future and agreeable acquaintance, she might fairly congratulate herself on the excellent judgment which had prompted her to pass over in silence my unpardonable indiscretion.

Her manner put me so completely at my ease that, in a moment after my salute, I wondered I could have been so foolish as to have brooded over it. The countess was unaltered, except that she looked perhaps more beautiful. She was a rare creation that time loved to spare. That sweet, and blooming, and radiant face, and that tall, and shapely, and beaming form—not a single bad passion had ever marred their light and grace, all the freshness of an innocent heart had embalmed their perennial loveliness.

The party seemed dull. I, who was usually a great talker, could not speak. I dared not attempt to be alone with Christiana. I watched her only at a distance, and indicated my absorbing mood to others only by my curt and discouraging answers. When all was over, I retired to my own rooms exceedingly gloomy and dispirited.

I was in these days but a wild beast, who thought himself a civilized and human being. I was profoundly ignorant of all that is true and excellent. An unnatural system, like some grand violence of nature, had transformed the teeming and beneficent ocean of my mind into a sandy and arid desert. I had not then discovered even a faint adumbration of the philosophy of our existence. Blessed by nature with a heart that is the very shrine of sensibility, my infamous education had succeeded in rendering me the most selfish of my species.

But nature, as the philosophic Winter impressed upon me, is stronger than education, and the presence of this woman, this sudden appearance, amid my corrupt, and heartless, and artificial life, of so much innocence, and so much love, and so much simplicity, they fell upon my callous heart like the first rains upon a Syrian soil, and the refreshed earth responded to the kindly influence by an instant recurrence to its nature.

I recoiled with disgust from the thought of my present life; I flew back with rapture to my old aspirations. And the beautiful, for which I had so often and so early sighed, and the love that I felt indispensable to my panting frame, and the deep sympathy for all creation that seemed my being, and all the dazzling and extending glory that had hovered, like a halo, round my youthful visions—they returned—they returned in their might and their splendour, and when I remembered what I was, I buried my face in my hands and wept.

I retired to my bed, but I could not sleep. I saw no hope, yet I was not miserable. Christiana could never be mine. I did not wish her to be. I could not contemplate such an incident. I had prided myself on my profligacy, but this night avenged my innate purity. I threw off my factitious passions. It was the innocence of Christiana that exercised over me a spell so potent. Her unsophisticated heart awoke in me a passion for the natural and the pure. She was not made to be the heroine of a hackneyed adventure. To me she was not an individual, but a personification of Nature. I gazed upon her only as I would upon a beautiful landscape, with an admiring sympathy which ennobles my feelings, invigorates my intellect, and calls forth the latent poetry of my being.

The thought darted into my mind in a moment. I cannot tell how it came. It seemed inspiration, but I responded to it with an eager, and even fierce sympathy. Said I that the thought darted into my mind? Let me recall the weak phrase, let me rather say, that a form rose before me in the depth of the dull night, and that form was myself. That form was myself, yet also another. I beheld a youth who, like me, had stifled the breathing forms of his young creation; who, like me, in the cold wilderness of the world, looked back with a mournful glance at the bright gates of the sweet garden of fancy he had forfeited. I felt the deep and agonizing struggle of his genius and his fate; and my prophetic mind, bursting through all the thousand fetters that had been forged so cunningly to bind it in its cell, the inspiration of my nature, that beneficent demon who will not desert those who struggle to be wise and good—tore back the curtain of the future, and I beheld, seated on a glorious throne on a proud Acropolis, one to whom a surrounding and enthusiastic people offered a laurel crown. I laboured to catch the fleeting features and the changing countenance of him who sat upon the throne. Was it the strange youth, or was it indeed myself?

I jumped out of bed. I endeavoured to be calm. I asked myself, soberly, whether I had indeed seen a vision, or whether it were but the invisible phantasm of an ecstatic revery? I looked round me; there was nothing. The moonbeam was stationary on the wall. I opened the window and looked out upon the vast, and cold, and silent street. The bitterness of the night cooled me. The pulsations of my throbbing head subsided. I regained my bed, and instantly sank into a sweet sleep.

The aunt of the Countess Fleming had died, and left to my stepdame the old garden-house, which is not perhaps forgotten. As I had always continued on the best possible terms with the countess, and, indeed, was in all points quite her standard of perfection, she had, with great courtesy, permitted me to make her recently-acquired mansion my habitation, when important business occasionally made me desire for its transaction a spot less subject to constant interruption than my office and my home.

To the garden-house I repaired the next morning at a very early hour. I was so eager that I ordered, as I dismounted, my rapid breakfast, and in a few minutes, this being despatched, I locked myself up in my room, giving orders not to be disturbed, except by a message from my father.

I took up a pen. I held it in the light. I thought to myself what will be its doom, but I said nothing. I began writing some hours before noon, nor did I ever cease. My thoughts, my passion, the rush of my invention, were too quick for my pen. Page followed page; as a sheet was finished I threw it on the floor; I was amazed at the rapid and prolific production, yet I could not stop to wonder. In half a dozen hours I sank back utterly exhausted, with an aching frame. I rang the bell, ordered some refreshment, and walked about the room. The wine invigorated me, and warmed up my sinking fancy, which however required little fuel. I set to again, and it was midnight before I retired to my bed.

The next day I again rose early, and, with a bottle of wine at my side, for I was determined not to be disturbed, I dashed at it again. I was not less successful. This day I finished my first volume.

The third morning I had less inclination to write. I read over and corrected what I had composed. This warmed up my fancy, and in the afternoon I executed several chapters of my second volume.

Each day, although I had not in the least lost my desire of writing, I wrote slower. It was necessary for me each day to read my work from the beginning, before I felt the existence of the characters sufficiently real to invent their actions. Nevertheless, on the morning of the seventh day, the second and last volume was finished.

My book was a rapid sketch of the developement of the poetic character. My hero was a youth whose mind was ever combatting with his situation. Gifted with a highly poetic temperament, it was the office of his education to counteract all its ennobling tendencies. I traced the first indication of his predisposition, the growing consciousness of his powers, his reveries, his loneliness, his doubts, his moody misery, his ignorance of his art, his failures, his despair. I painted his agonizing and ineffectual efforts to exist like those around him. I poured forth my own passion, when I described the fervour of his love.

All this was serious enough, and the most singular thing is that all this time, it never struck me that I was delineating my own character. But now comes the curious part. In depicting the scenes of society in which my hero was forced to move, I suddenly dashed, not only into the most slashing satire, but even into malignant personality. All the bitterness of my heart, occasioned by my wretched existence among their false circles, found its full vent. Never was any thing so imprudent. Everybody figured, and all parties and opinions alike suffered. The same hand that immortalized the cream cheeses of poor Count de Moltke, now avenged his wrongs.

For the work itself, it was altogether a most crude performance, teeming with innumerable faults. It was entirely deficient in art. The principal character, although forcibly conceived, for it was founded on truth, was not sufficiently developed. Of course the others were much less so. The incidents were unnatural, the serious characters exaggerations, the comic ones caricatures; the wit was too often flippant, the philosophy too often forced; yet the vigour was remarkable, the license of an uncurbed imagination not without its charms, and, on the whole, there breathed a freshness which is rarely found, and which, perhaps, with all my art and knowledge, I may never again afford: and indeed when I recall the magnificient enthusiasm, the glorious heat, with which this little work was written, I am convinced that, with all its errors, the spark of true creation animated its fiery page.

Such is the history of "Manstein," a work which exercised a strange influence on my destiny.

XIII.

I PERSONALLY intrusted my novel to the same bookseller to whom I had anonymously submitted my tragedy. He required no persuasion to have the honour of introducing it to the world, and had he hesitated, I would myself have willingly undertaken the charge, for I was resolved to undergo the ordeal. I swore him to the closest secrecy, and, as mystery is part of the craft, I had confidence that his interest would prompt him to maintain his honour.

All now being finished, I suddenly and naturally resumed my obvious and usual character. The pouring forth had relieved my mind, and the strong feelings that prompted it having subsided, I felt a little of the lassitude that succeeds exertion. That reaction, to which ardent and inexperienced minds are subject, now also occurred. I lost my confidence in my effusion. It seemed impossible that any thing I had written could succeed, and I felt that nothing but decided success could justify a person in my position to be an author. I half determined to recall the rash deposite, but a mixture of false shame and lingering hope that I might yet be happily mistaken, dissuaded me. I resolved to think no more or it. It was an inconsiderate venture, but secrecy would preserve me from public shame, and as for my private mortification, I should at least derive from failure a beneficial conviction of my literary incompetency, and increased energy to follow up the path which fortune seemed to destine for my pursuit. Official circumstances occurred also at this moment, which imperatively demanded all my attention, and which indeed interested my feelings in no ordinary degree.

The throne of my royal master had been guaranteed to him by those famous treaties which, at the breaking up of that brilliant vision, the French empire, had been vainly considered by the great European powers as ensuring the permanent settlement of Europe. A change of dynasty had placed the king in a delicate position, but by his sage councils and discreet conduct the last burst of the revolutionary storm passed over without striking his diadem. One of the most distinguished instances of the ministerial dexterity of my father was the discovery of a latent inclination in certain of our powerful allies, to favour the interests of the abdicated dynasty, and ultimately to dispute the succession, which, at the moment, distracted by the multiplicity of important and engrossing interests, they deemed themselves too hastily to have recognised. In this conjuncture, an appeal to arms on our part was idle, and all to which we could trust in bringing about a satisfactory adjustment of this paramount question, was diplomatic ingenuity. For more than three years, secret, but active negotiations had been on foot to attain our end, and circumstances had now occurred which induced us to believe that, by certain combinations, the result might be realized.

I took a very great interest in these negotiations, and was the only person out of the cabinet to whom they were confided. The situation of the prince royal, himself a very accomplished personage, but whose unjust unpopularity offered no obstacle to the views of his enemies, extremely commanded my sympathy: the secrecy, importance, and refined difficulty of the transactions called forth all the play of my invention. Although an affair which, according to etiquette, should have found its place in the Foreign Office, my father, on his promotion, did not think it fitting to transfer a business of so delicate a nature to another functionary, and he contrived to correspond upon it with foreign courts in his character of first minister. As his secretary, I had been privy to all the details, and I continued therefore to assist him in his subsequent proceedings.

My father and myself materially differed as to the course expedient to be pursued. He flattered himself that every thing might be brought about by negotiation, in which he was indeed unrivalled, and he often expatiated to me on the evident impossibility of the king having recourse to any other measures. For myself, when I remembered the time that had already passed without in any way advancing our desires, and believed, which I did most firmly, that the conduct of the great continental powers in this comparatively unimportant affair was only an indication of their resolution to promote the system on which they had based all the European relations—I myself could not refrain from expressing a wish to adopt a very different and far more earnest conduct.

In this state of affairs I was one day desired by my father to attend him at a secret conference with the ambassadors of the great powers. My father flattered himself that he might this day obtain his long-desired end, and so interested was the monarch in the progress, as well as the result, of our conslųtations, that he resolved to be present himself, although incognito.

The scene of the conference was the same palace whither my father had been summoned to receive the notification of his appointment as first minister.

I can well recall the feelings with which, on the morning of the conference, I repaired to the palace with my father. We were muffled up in our pelisses, for the air was very sharp, but the sun was not without influence, and shone with great brilliancy. There are times when I am influenced by a species of what I may term happy audacity, for it is a mixture of recklessness and self-confidence which has a very felicitous effect upon the animal spirits. At these moments, I never calculate consequences, yet every thing seems to go right. I feel in good fortune—the ludicrous side of every thing occurs to me,—I think of nothing but grotesque images,—I astonish people by bursting into laughter, apparently without a cause. Whatever is submitted to me I turn into ridicule. I shrug my shoulders and speak epigrams.

I was in one of these moods to-day. My father could not comprehend me. He was very serious, but instead of sympathizing with all his grave hopes and dull fears, I did nothing but ridicule their excellencies, whom we were going to meet, and perform to him an imaginary conference, in which he also figured.

We arrived at the palace. I became a little sobered. My father went to the king. I entered a large Gothic hall, where the conference was to take place. It was a fine room, hung with trophies, and principally lighted by a large Gothic window. At the farther end, near the fire, and portioned off by a large Indian screen, was a round table, covered with green cloth, and surrounded by seats. The Austrian minister arrived. I walked up and down the hall with him for some minutes, ridiculing diplomacy. He was one of those persons who believe you have a direct object in every thing you say, and my contradictory opinions upon all subjects were to him a fruitful source of puzzled meditation. He thought I was one whose words ought to be marked, and I believe that my nonsense has often occasioned him a sleepless night. The other ministers soon assembled, and in a few minutes, a small door opened at the top of the hall, and the king and my father appeared. We bowed, and took our seats, I, being secretary, seated myself at the desk, to take notes for the drawing up of the protocols.

We believed that the original idea of considering the great treaties as only a guaranty to the individual, and not to his successors, originated at Vienna. Indeed, it was the early acquaintance of my father with the Austrian minister that first assisted him in ascertaining this intention. We believed that the Russian cabinet had heartily entered into this new reading, that Prussia supported it only in deference to the court of St. Petersburgh, and that France was scarcely reconciled to the proposed derangement by the impression that it naturally assisted those principles of government by a recurrence to which the cabinet of Versailles then began to be convinced they could alone maintain themselves.

Such had been our usual view of the state of opinion with respect to this question. It had been the object of my father to induce the French court to join with that of St. James's in a strong demonstration in favour of the present system, and to indicate, in the event of that demonstration being fruitless, the possibility of their entering with the king into a tripartite party treaty, framed in pursuance of the spirit of the invalidated one. He trusted that to-day this demonstration would be made.

We entered into business. The object of our opponents was to deny that the tendency of certain acts, of which we complained, was inimical to the present dynasty, but to refrain from proving their sincerity, by assenting to a new guaranty, on the plea that it was unnecessary, since the treaties must express all that was intended. Hours were wasted in multiplied discussions as to the meaning of particular clauses in particular treaties, and as to precedents to justify particular acts. Hours were wasted, for we did not advance. At length my father recurred to the spirit, rather than the letter of the affair, and in urging the necessity for the peace of Europe and other high causes, that this affair should be settled without delay, he gave an excellent opportunity for the friends he had anticipated to come forward. They spoke, but indeed it was very vague and unsatisfactory. I marked the lip of the Austrian minister curl as if in derision, and the Russian arranged his papers as if all now were finished.

I knew my father well enough by this time to be convinced that, in spite of his apparently unaltered mien, he was bitterly disappointed and annoyed. The king looked gloomy. There was a perfect silence. It was so awkward that the Austrian minister inquired of me the date of a particular treaty, merely to break the dead pause. I did not immediately answer him.

The whole morning my fancy had been busied with the most grotesque images. I had never been a moment impressed with the gravity of the proceedings. The presence of the king alone prevented me from constant raillery. When I recollected the exact nature of the business on which we were assembled, and then called to mind the characters who took part in the discussion, I could scarcely refrain from laughter. "Voltaire would soon settle this," I thought, "and send Messieurs the Austrian, and the Russian, and the Prussian, with their mustachios, and hussar jackets, and furs, to their own country. What business have they to interfere with ours?" I was strongly impressed with the tyrannical injustice and wicked folly of the whole transaction. The great diplomatists appeared to me so many wild beasts ready to devour our innocent lamb of a sovereign, parleying only from jealousy who should first attack him.

The Austrian minister repeated his question as to the treaty. "It matters not," I replied; "let us now proceed to business." He looked a little surprised. "Gentlemen," I continued, "you must be quite aware, that this is the last conference his majesty can permit us to hold upon a subject which ought never to have been discussed. The case is very simple, and demands but little consideration. If the guaranty we justly require be not granted, his majesty must have recourse to a popular appeal. We have no fear about the result. We are prepared for it. His majesty will acquire a new, and, if possible, a stronger title to his crown, and see what you will occasion by your squeamishness to authenticate the right of a sovereign, who, although not the offspring of a dynasty, acquired his throne not by the voice of the people, and has been constantly recognised by all your courts; you will be the direct cause of a most decided democratic demonstration in the election of a king by the people alone. For us, the result has no terrors. Your excellencies are the best judges whether your royal masters possess any territories in our vicinity which may be inoculated with our dangerous example.'

I was astounded by my audacity. Not till I had ceased speaking had I been aware of what I had dared to do. Once I shot a rapid glance at my father. His eyes were fixed on the ground, and I thought a little pale. As I withdrew my glance, I caught the king's fiery eye, but its expression did not discourage me.

It is difficult to convey an idea of the success of my boldness. It could not enter the imagination of the diplomatists that any one could dare to speak, and particularly under such circumstances, without instructions and without authority. They looked upon me only as the mouthpiece of the royal intentions. They were alarmed at our great, and unwonted, and unexpected resolution, at the extreme danger and invisible results of our purposes. The English and French ministers, who watched every turn, made a vehement representation in our favour, and the conference broke up with an expression of irresolution and surprise in the countenances of our antagonists, quite unusual with them; and which promised a speedy attainment of the satisfactory arrangement which shortly afterwards took place.

The conference broke up, my father retired with the king, and desired me to wait for him in the hall. I was alone. I was excited. I felt the triumph of success. I felt that I had done a great action. I felt all my energies. I walked up and down the hall in a frenzy of ambition, and I thirsted for action. There seemed to me no achievement of which I was not capable, and of which I was not ambitious. In imagination I shook thrones and founded empires. I felt myself a being born to breathe in an atmosphere of revolution.

My father came not. Time wore away, and the day died. It was one of those stern sublime sunsets, which is almost the only appearance in the north in which nature enchanted me. I stood at the window gazing at the burnished masses that, for a moment, were suspended, in their fleeting and capricious beauty, on the far horizon. I turned aside and looked on the rich trees suffused with the crimson light, and ever and anon irradiated by the dying shoots of a golden ray. The deer were stealing home to their bowers, and I watched them till their golden and glancing forms gradually lost their lustre in the declining twilight. The glory had now departed, and all grew dim. A solitary star alone was shining in the gray sky, a bright and solitary star.

And as I gazed upon the sunset, and the star, and the dim beauties of the coming eve, my mind grew calm. And all the bravery of my late revery passed away. And I felt indeed a disgust for all the worldliness on which I had been lately pondering. And there arose in my mind a desire to create things beautiful as that golden sun, and that glittering star.

I heard my name. The hall was now darkened. In the distance stood my father. I joined him. He placed his arm affectionately in mine, and said to me, "My son, you will be prime minister of * * * * *; perhaps something greater."

XIV.

As we drove home, every thing seemed changed since the morning. My father was in high spirits, for him, even elated: I, on the contrary, was silent and thoughtful. This evening there was a ball at the palace, which, although little inclined, I felt obliged to attend.

I arrived late; the king was surrounded by a brilliant circle, and conversing with his usual felicitous affability. I would have withdrawn when I had made my obeisance, but his majesty advanced a step, and immediately addressed me. He conversed with me for some time. Few men possess a more captivating address than this sovereign. It was difficult at all times not to feel charmed, and now I was conscious that this mark of his favour recognised no ordinary claims to his confidence. I was the object of admiring envy. That night there were few in those saloons, crowded with the flower of the land, who did not covet my position. I alone was insensible to it. A vision of high mountains and deep blue lakes mingled with all the artificial splendour that dazzled around. I longed to roam amid the solitude of nature, and disburthen a mind teeming with creative sympathy.

I drew near a group which the pretty Baroness Engel was addressing with more than her usual animation. When she caught my eye, she beckoned me to join her, and said, "O! Count Contarini, have you read Manstein?"

"Manstein," I said, in a careless tone, "what is it?"

"O! you must get it directly. The oddest book that ever was written. We are all in it, we are all in it."

"I hope not."

"O, yes! all of us, all of us. I have not had time to make out the characters, I read it so quickly. My man only sent it to me this morning. I must get a key. Now you, who are so clever, make me one."

"I will look at it, if you really recommend me."

"You must look at it. It is the oddest book that was ever written. Immensely clever, I assure you, immensely clever. I cannot exactly make it out."

"That is certainly much in its favour. The obscure, as you know, is a principal ingredient of the sublime."

"How odd you are! But really, now, Count Contarini, get Manstein. Every one must read it. As for your illustrious principal, Baron de Bragnaes —he is really hit off to the life."

"Indeed!" I said, with concealed consternation.

"O! no one can mistake it. I thought I should have died with laughing. But we are all there. I am sure I know the author."

"Who is it? who is it?" eagerly inquired the group.

"I do not *know*, mind," observed the baroness. "It is only conjecture, merely a conjecture. But I always find out everybody."

"O! that you do," said the group.

"Yes, I find them out by the style."

"How clever you are!" exclaimed the group, "but who is it?"

"O, I shall not betray him. Only I am quite convinced I know who it is."

"Pray, pray, tell us," entreated the group.

"You need not look around, Matilda, he is not here. A friend of yours, Contarini. I thought that young Moskoffsky was in a great hurry to run off to St. Petersburg. And he has left us a legacy. We are all in it, I assure you," she exclaimed, to the one nearest, in an under, but decisive tone.

I breathed again. "Young Moskoffsky! To be sure it is," I observed, with an air of thoughtful conviction.

"To be sure it is. Without reading a line, I have no doubt of it. I suspected that he meditated something. I must get Manstein directly, if it be by young Moskoffsky. Any thing that young Moskoffsky writes must be worth reading. What an excellent letter he writes! You are my oracle, Baroness Engel; I have no doubt of your discrimination; but I suspect that a certain correspondence with a brilliant young Muscovite has assisted you in your discovery."

"Be contented," rejoined the baroness, with a smile of affected mystery and pique, "that there is one who can enlighten you, and be not curious as to the source. Ah! there is Countess Norberg—how well she looks to-night!"

I walked away to salute Christiana. As I moved through the elegant crowd, my nervous ear constantly caught half phrases, which often made me linger. "Very satirical—very odd—very personal —very odd, indeed—what can it all be about? Do you know? No, I do not—do you? Baroness Engel—all in it—must get it—very witty—very flippant. Who can it be? Young Moskoffsky. Read it at once without stopping—never read any thing so odd—ran off to St. Petersburgh—always thought him very clever. Who can the Duke of Twaddle mean? Ah! to be sure—I wonder it did not occur to me."

I joined Christiana. I waltzed with her. I was on the point, once or twice, of asking her if she had read "Manstein," but did not dare. After the dance we walked away. Mademoiselle de Moltke, who, although young, was not charming, but very intellectual, and who affected to think me a great genius, because I had pasquinaded her father, stopped us.

"My dear countess, how do you do? You look most delightfully to-night. Count Contarini, have you read Manstein? You never read any thing! How can you say so? but you always say such things. You must read Manstein. Everybody is reading it. It is full of imagination, and very personal—very personal, indeed. Baroness Engel says we are all in it. You are there. You are Horace de Beaufort, who thinks every thing and everybody a bore—exactly like you, count, exactly —what I have always said of you. Adieu! mind you get Manstein, and then come and talk it over with me. Now do, that's a good creature!" And this talkative Titania tripped away.

"You are wearied, Christiana, and these rooms are insufferably hot. You had better sit down."

We seated ourselves in a retired part of the room. I observed an unusual smile upon the face of Christiana. Suddenly she said, with a slight flush, and not without emotion, "I shall not betray you, Contarini, but I am convinced that you are the author of Manstein."

I was very agitated—I could not immediately speak. I was ever different to Christiana to what I was to other people. I could not feign to her. I could not dissemble. My heart always opened to her, and it seemed to me almost blasphemy to address her in any other language but truth.

"You know me better than all others, Christiana. Indeed, you alone know me. But I would sooner hear that any one was considered the author of Manstein than myself."

"You need not fear that I shall be indiscreet, but rest assured it cannot long be a secret."

"Indeed!" I said: "why not?"

"O! Contarini, it is too like."

"Like whom?"

"Nay! you affect ignorance."

"Upon my honour, Christiana, I do not. Have the kindness to believe that there is at least one person in the world to whom I am not affected. If you mean that Manstein is a picture of myself, I can assure you most solemnly that I never less thought of myself than when I drew it. I thought it was an ideal character."

"It is that very circumstance that occasions the resemblance; for you, Contarini, whatever you may appear in this room, you are an ideal character."

"You have read it?" I asked.

"I have read it," she answered, seriously.

"And you do not admire it? I feel you do not. Nay! conceal nothing from me, Christiana. I can bear truth."

"I admire its genius, Contarini. I wish that I could speak with equal approbation of its judgment. It will, I fear, make you many enemies."

"You astonish me, Christiana. I do not care for enemies. I care for nobody but for you. But why should it make me enemies?"

"I hope I am mistaken. It is very possible I am mistaken. I know not why I talk upon such subjects. It is foolish—it is impertinent; but the interest, the deep interest I have always taken in you, Contarini, occasions this conversation, and must excuse it."

"Dear Christiana, how good, how very good you are!"

"And all these people whom you have ridiculed—surely, Contarini, you have enough already who envy you—surely, Contarini, it was most imprudent!"

"People ridiculed! I never meant to ridicule any person in particular. I wrote with rapidity. I wrote of what I had seen and what I felt. There is nothing but truth in it."

"You are not in a position, Contarini, to speak truth."

"Then I must be in a very miserable position, Christiana."

"You are what you are, Contarini. All must admire you. You are in a very envied, I will hope, a very enviable position."

"Alas! Christiana, I am the most miserable fellow that breathes upon this broad world."

She was silent.

"Dearest Christiana," I continued, "I speak to you as I would speak to no other person. Think not that I am one of those who deem it interesting to be considered unhappy. Such trifling I despise. What I say to you I would not confess to another human being. Among these people my vanity would be injured to be considered miserable. But I am unhappy, really unhappy, most desolately wretched. Enviable position! But an hour since I was meditating how I could extricate myself from it! Alas! Christiana, I cannot ask you for counsel, for I know not what I desire, what I could wish; but I feel—each hour I feel more keenly, and never more keenly than when I am with you, that I was not made for this life, nor this life for me."

"I cannot advise you, Contarini. What—what can I advise? But I am unhappy to find that you are. I grieve, I grieve deeply, that one apparently with all that can make him happy, should still miss felicity. You are yet very young, Contarini and I cannot but believe that you will still attain all you desire, and all that you deserve."

"I desire nothing. I know not what I want. All that I know is, that what I possess I abhor."

"Ah! Contarini, beware of your imagination."

XV.

The storm that had been apprehended by the prescient affection of Christiana surely burst. I do not conceive that my publisher betrayed me. I believe internal evidence settled the affair. In a fortnight it was acknowledged by all that I was the author of "Manstein," and all were surprised that this authorship could, for a moment, have been a question. I can give no idea of the outcry. Everybody was in a passion—affected to be painfully sensitive of their neighbours' wrongs. The very personality was ludicrously exaggerated. Everybody took a delight in detecting the originals of my portraits. Various keys were handed about, all different, and not content with recognising the very few decided sketches from life there really were, and which were sufficiently obvious, and not very malignant, they mischievously insisted, that not a human shadow glided over my pages which might not be traced to its substance, and protested that the Austrian minister was the model of an old woman.

Those who were ridiculed insisted that the ridicule called in question the very first principles of society. They talked of confidence violated which never had been shared, and faith broken which never had been pledged. Never was so much nonsense talked about nothing since the days of the schoolmen. But nonsense, when earnest, is impressive, and sometimes takes you in. If you are in a hurry, you occasionally mistake it for sense.

All the people who had read "Manstein," and been very much amused with it, began to think they were quite wrong, and that it was a very improper and wicked book, because this was daily reiterated in their ears by half a dozen bores, who had gained an immortality which they did not deserve. Such conduct, it was universally agreed, must not be encouraged. Where would it end? Everybody was alarmed. Men passed me in the street without notice—I received anonymous letters—and even many of my intimates grew cold. As I abhor explanations, I said nothing; and although I was disgusted with the folly of much that I heard, I contradicted nothing, however ridiculously false, and felt confident that, in time, the world would discover that they had been gulled into fighting the battle of a few individuals whom they despised. I found even a savage delight in being an object, for a moment, of public astonishment, and fear, and indignation. But the affair getting at last troublesome, I fought young De Bragnaes with swords in the Deer Park, and having succeeded in pinking him, it was discovered that I was more amiable. For the rest, out of my immediate circle, the work had been from the first decidedly successful.

In all this not very agreeable affair, I was delighted by the conduct of Christiana. Although she seriously disapproved of what was really objectionable in "Manstein," and although she was of so modest and quiet a temper, that she unwillingly exercised that influence in society to which her rank, and fortune, and rare accomplishments entitled her, she suddenly became my most active and violent partisan, ridiculed the pretended wrongs and mock propriety that echoed around her, and declaring that the author of "Manstein" had only been bold enough to print that which all repeated, rallied them on their hypocrisy. Baroness Engel also was faithful, although a little jealous of the zeal of Christiana, and between them they laughed down the cabal, and so entirely turned the public feeling, that in less than a month it was universally agreed that "Manstein" was a most delightful book, and the satire, as they daintily phrased it, "perfectly allowable."

Amid all this tumult my father was silent. From no look, from no expression of his, could I gain a hint either of his approval or his disapprobation. I could not ascertain even if he had seen the book. The Countess Fleming of course read it immediately, and had not the slightest conception of what it was about. When she heard it was by me, she read it again, and was still more puzzled, but told me she was delighted. When the uproar took place, instead of repeating, which she often did, all the opinions she had caught, she became quite silent, and the volumes disappeared from her table. The storm blew over, and no bolt had shivered me, and the volumes crept forth from their mysterious retirement.

About two months after the publication of "Manstein," appeared a new number of the great critical journal of the north of Europe. One of the works reviewed was my notorious production. I tore open the leaves with a blended feeling of desire and fear, which I can yet remember. I felt prepared for the worst. I felt that such grave censors, however impossible it was to deny the decided genius of the work, and however eager they might be to hail the advent of an original mind,—I felt that it was but reasonable and just that they should disapprove of the temper of the less elevated portions, and somewhat dispute the moral tendency of the more exalted.

With what horror, with what blank despair, with what supreme, appalling astonishment, did I find myself, for the first time in my life, a subject of the most reckless, the most malignant, and the most adroit ridicule. I was scarified—I was scalped. They scarcely condescended to notice my dreadful satire except to remark, in passing, by-the-by, I appeared to be as ill-tempered as I was imbecile. But all my eloquence, and all my fancy, and all the strong expression of my secret feelings—these ushers of the court of Apollo fairly laughed me off Parnassus, and held me up to public scorn, as exhibiting the most lamentable instance of mingled pretension and weakness, and the most ludicrous specimen of literary delusion that it had ever been their unhappy office to castigate, and, as they hoped, to cure.

The criticism fell from my hand. A film floated over my vision, my knees trembled. I felt that sickness of heart that we experience in our first serious scrape. I was ridiculous. It was time to die.

What did it signify? What was authorship to me? What did I care for their flimsy fame,—I, who yet not of age, was an important functionary of the state, and who might look to its highest confidence and honours. It was really too ludicrous. I tried to laugh. I did smile very bitterly. The insolence of these fellows! Why! if I could not write, surely I was not a fool. I had done something. Nobody thought me a fool. On the contrary, everybody thought me a rather extraordinary person. What would they think now? I felt a qualm.

I buried my face in my hands. I summoned my thoughts to their last struggle. I penetrated into my very soul—and I felt the conviction, that literary creation was necessary to my existence, and that for it I was formed. And all the beautiful and dazzling forms that had figured in my youthful visions rose up before me, crowned monarchs, and radiant heroes, and women brighter than day, but their looks were mournful, and they extended their arms with deprecating anguish, as if to entreat me not to desert them. And in the magnificence of my emotions, and the beauty of my visions, the worldly sarcasms that had lately so shaken me, seemed something of another and a lower existence, and I marvelled that, for a moment, this thin, transient cloud could have shadowed the sunshine of my soul. And I arose, and lifted up my arm to heaven, and waved it like a banner, and I swore by the nature that I adored, that in spite of all opposition I would be an author, ay! the greatest of authors, and that far climes and distant ages should respond to the magic of my sympathetic page.

The agony was past. I mused in calmness over the plans that I should pursue. I determined to ride down to my father's castle, and there mature them in solitude. Haunt of my early boyhood, fragrant bower of Egeria, sweet spot where I first scented the bud of my spring-like fancy, willingly would I linger in thy green retreats, no more to be wandered over by one who now feels that he was ungrateful to thy beauty!

Now that I had resolved, at all costs, to quit my country, and to rescue myself from the fatal society in which I was placed, my impartial intelligence, no longer swayed by the conscious impossibility of emancipation, keenly examined and ascertained the precise nature and condition of my character. I perceived myself a being educated in systematic prejudice. I observed that I was the slave of custom, and never viewed any incident in relation to man in general, but only with reference to the particular and limited class of society of which I was a member. I recognised myself as selfish and affected. I was entirely ignorant of the principles of genuine morality, and I deeply felt that there was a total want of nature in every thing connected with me. I had been educated without any regard to my particular, or to my general nature; I had nothing to assist me in my knowledge of myself, and nothing to guide me in my conduct to others. The consequence of my unphilosophical education was my utter wretchedness.

I determined to re-educate myself. Conceiving myself a poet, I resolved to pursue a course which should develope and perfect my poetic power; and never forgetting that I was a man, I was equally earnest in a study of human nature to discover a code of laws which should regulate my intercourse with my fellow-creatures. For both these sublime purposes, it was necessary that I should form a comprehensive acquaintance with nature in all its varieties and conditions; and I resolved therefore to travel. I intended to detail all these feelings to my father, to conceal nothing from him, and request his approbation and assistance. In the event of his opposition, I should depart without his sanction, for to depart I was resolved.

I remained a week at the castle, musing over these projects, and entirely neglecting my duties, in the fulfilment of which, ever since the publication of "Manstein," I had been very remiss. Suddenly, I received a summons from my father to epair to him without a moment's delay.

I hurried up to town, and hastened to his office. He was not there, but expecting me at home. I found him busied with his private secretary, and apparently very much engaged. He dismissed his secretary immediately, and then said, "Contarini, they are rather troublesome in Norway. I leave town instantly for Bergen with the king. I regret it, because we shall not see each other for some little time. His majesty has had the goodness, Contarini, to appoint you secretary of legation at the court of London. Your appointment takes place at once, but I have obtained you leave of absence for a year. You will spend this attached to the legation at Paris. I wish you to be well acquainted with the French people before you join their neighbours. In France and England you will see two great practical nations. It will do you good. I am sorry that I am so deeply engaged now. My chasseur, Lausanne, will travel with you. He is the best travelling servant in the world. He served me when I was your age. He is one of the few people in whom I have unlimited confidence. He is not only clever, but he is judicious. You will write to me as often as you can. Strelamb," and here he rang the bell, "Strelamb has prepared all necessary letters and bills for you." Here the functionary entered: "Mr. Strelamb," said my father, "while you explain those papers to Count Contarini, I will write to the Duke of Montfort."

I did not listen to the private secretary, I was so astonished. My father, in two minutes, had finished his letter. "This may be useful to you, Contarini. It is to an old friend, and a powerful man. I would not lose time about your departure, Contarini. Mr. Strelamb, is there no answer from Baron Engel!"

"My lord, the carriage waits," announced a servant.

"I must go. Adieu! Contarini. Write when you arrive at Paris. Mr. Strelamb, see Baron Engel to-night, and send me off a courier with his answer. Adieu! Contarini."

He extended me his hand. I touched it very slightly. I never spoke. I was thunderstruck.

Suddenly I started up and rang the bell. "Send me Lausanne!" I told the servant.

Lausanne appeared. Had my astonishment not been excited by a greater cause, I might have felt considerable surprise at my father delegating to me his confidential domestic. Lausanne was a Swiss, about my father's age, with a frame of iron, and all the virtues of his mountains. He was, I believe, the only person in whom my father placed implicit trust. But I thought not of this then. "Lausanne, I understand you are now in my service."

He bowed.

"I have no doubt I shall find cause to confirm the confidence which you have enjoyed in our house for more than twenty years. Is every thing ready for my departure?"

"I had no idea that your excellency had any immediate intention to depart."

"I should like to be off to-night, good Lausanne Ay! this very hour. When can I go?"

"Your excellency's wardrobe must be prepared. Your excellency has not given Carl any directions."

"None. I do not mean to take him. I shall travel only with you."

"Your excellency's wardrobe—"

"May be sufficiently prepared in an hour, and Paris must supply the rest. In a word, Lausanne, can I leave this place by daybreak to-morrow? Think only of what is necessary. Show some of your old energy."

"Your excellency may rest assured," said Lausanne, after some reflection, "that every thing will be prepared by that time."

"It is well. Is the countess at home?"

"The Countess quitted town yesterday on a visit to the Countess de Norberg."

"The Countess de Norberg! I should have seen her too. Go, Lausanne, and be punctual. Carl will give you the keys. The Countess de Norberg, Christiana!—Yes! I should have seen *her*. Ah! It is as well. I have no friends, and my adieus are brief, let them not be bitter. Farewell to the father that has no feeling, and thou, too, Scandinavia, stern soil in which I have too long lingered—think of me hereafter as of some exotic bird, who for a moment lost its way in your cold heaven, but now has regained its course, and wings its flight to a more brilliant earth and a brighter sky!"

PART THE THIRD.

I.

On the eighteenth day of August, one thousand eight hundred and twenty-six, I praise the Almighty Giver of all goodness, that, standing upon the height of Mount Jura, I beheld the whole range of the High Alps, with Mont Blanc in the centre, without a cloud: a mighty spectacle rarely beheld, for, on otherwise cloudless days, these sublime elevations are usually veiled.

I accepted this majestic vision as a good omen. It seemed that nature received me in her fullest charms. I was for some time so entranced that I did not observe the spreading and shining scene that opened far beneath me. The mountains, in ranges, gradually diminishing, terminated in isolated masses, whose enormous forms, in deep shade, beautifully contrasted with the glittering glaciers of the higher peaks, and rose out of a plain covered with fair towns and bright chateaux, embosomed in woods of chestnut, and vines festooning in orchards and corn-fields. Through the centre of the plain, a deep blue lake wound its way, which, viewed from the height of Jura, seemed like a purple girdle carelessly thrown upon some imperial robe.

I had remained in Paris only a few days, and, without offering any explanation to our minister, or even signifying my intention to Lausanne, had quitted that city with the determination of reaching Venice without delay. Now that it is probable I may never again cross the mountains, I often regret that I neglected this opportunity of becoming more acquainted with the French people. My head was then full of fantasies, and I looked upon the French as an anti-poetical nation; but I have since often regretted that I neglected this opportunity of becoming acquainted with a race who exercise so powerful an influence over civilization.

I had thought of Switzerland only as of a rude barrier between me and the fair object of my desires. The impression that this extraordinary country made upon me was perhaps increased by my previous thoughts having so little brooded over its idea. It was in Switzerland that I first felt how constantly to contemplate sublime creation developes the poetic power. It was here that I first began to study nature. Those forests of black gigantic pines rising out of the deep snows; those tall white cataracts leaping like headstrong youth into the world, and dashing from their precipices as if allured by the beautiful delusion of their own rainbow mist; those mighty clouds sailing beneath my feet, or clinging to the bosoms of the dark green mountains, or boiling up like a spell from the invisible and unfathomable depths; the fell avalanche, fleet as a spirit of evil, terrific when its sound suddenly breaks upon the almighty silence, scarcely less terrible when we gaze upon its crumbling and pallid frame, varied only by the presence of one or two blasted firs; the head of a mountain loosening from its brother peak, rooting up, in the roar of its rapid rush, a whole forest of pines, and covering the earth for miles with elephantine masses; the supernatural extent of landscape that opens to us new worlds; the strong eagles, and the strange wild birds that suddenly cross you in your path, and stare, and shrieking fly—and all the soft sights of joy and loveliness that mingle with these sublime and savage spectacles, the rich pastures, and the numerous flocks, and the golden bees, and the wild flowers, and the carved and painted cottages, and the simple manners and the primeval grace—wherever I moved, I was in turn appalled or enchanted, but whatever I beheld, new images ever sprang up in my mind, and new feelings ever crowded on my fancy.

There is something magical in the mountain air. My heart is light, my spirits cheerful, every thing is exhilarating. I am in every respect a different being to what I am in lowlands. I cannot even think, I dissolve into a delicious revery, in which every thing occurs to me without effort. Whatever passes before me gives birth in my mind to a new character, a new image, a new train of fancies. I sing, I shout, I compose aloud, but without premeditation, without any attempt to guide my imagination by my reason. How often, after journeying along the wild mule-track, how often, on a sunny day, have I suddenly thrown myself upon the turf, revelled in my existence, and then as hastily jumped up and raised the wild birds with a wilder scream. I think that these involuntary bursts must have been occasioned by the unconscious influence of extreme health. As for myself, when I succeed in faintly recalling the rapture which I have experienced in these solitary rambles, and muse over the flood of fancy which then seemed to pour itself over my whole being, and gush out of every feeling and every object, I contrast with mortification those warm and pregnant hours with this cold record of my maturer age.

I remember that when I first attempted to write, I had a great desire to indulge in simile, and that I never could succeed in gratifying my wish. This inability, more than any other circumstance, convinced me that I was not a poet. Even in "Manstein," which was written in a storm, and without any reflection, there are, I believe, few images, and those probably are all copied from books. That which surprised and gratified me most, when roving about Switzerland, was the sudden developement which took place of the faculty of illustrating my thoughts and feelings. Every object that crossed me in some way associated itself with my moral emotions. Not a mountain, or lake, or river, not a tree, or flower, or bird, that did not blend with some thought, or fancy, or passion, and become the lively personification of conceptions that lie sleeping in abstraction.

It is singular that, with all this, I never felt any desire to write. I never thought of writing. I never thought of the future, or of man, or fame. I was content to exist. I began from this moment to suspect, what I have since learned firmly to believe, that the sense of existence is the greatest happiness, and that deprived of every worldly advantage, which is supposed so necessary to our felicity, life, provided a man be not immured in a dungeon, must nevertheless be inexpressibly delightful. If, in striking the balance of sensation, misery were found to predominate, no human being would permit himself to exist; but however vast may be the wretchedness occasioned to us by the accidents of life, the certain sum of happiness, which is always supplied by our admirably contrived being, ever supports us under the burden. Those who are sufficiently interested with my biography to proceed with it, will find, as they advance, that this is a subject on which I am qualified to offer an opinion.

I returned from these glowing rambles to my head-quarters, which was usually Geneva. I returned like the bees laden with treasure. I mused over all the beautiful images that had occurred to me, and all the new characters that had risen in my mind, and all the observations of nature which hereafter would perhaps permit me to delineate what was beautiful. For the moment that I mingled again with men I wished to influence them. But I had no immediate or definite intention of appealing to their sympathies. Each hour I was more conscious of the long apprenticeship that was necessary in the cunning craft for which, I conceived, I possessed a predisposition. I thought of "Manstein" as of a picture painted by a madman in the dark, and when I remembered that crude performance, and gazed upon the beauty, and the harmony, and the fitting parts of the great creations around me, my cheek has often burned even in solitude.

In these moments rather of humility than despondence, I would fly for consolation to the blue waters of that beautiful lake, whose shores have ever been the favourite haunt of genius, the fair and gentle Leman.

Nor is there indeed in nature a sight more lovely than to watch at decline of day the last embrace of the sun lingering on the rosy glaciers of the White Mountain. Soon, too soon the great luminary dies, the warm peaks subside into purple, and then die into a ghostly white; but soon, ah! not too soon, the moon springs up from behind a mountain, flings over the lake a stream of light, and the sharp glaciers glitter like silver.

I have often passed the whole night upon those enchanted waters, contemplating their beautiful variety; and, indeed, if any thing can console one for the absence of the moon and stars, it would be to watch the lightning, on a dark night, on this superb lake. It is incessant, and sometimes in four or five different places at the same time. In the morning, Leman loses its ultramarine tint, and is covered with the shadows of mountains and chateaux.

In mountain valleys it is very beautiful to watch the effect of the rising and setting of the sun. The high peaks are first illumined, the soft yellow light then tips the lower elevations, and the bright golden showers soon bathe the whole valley, except a dark streak at the bottom, which is often not visited by sunlight. The effect of sunset is perhaps still more lovely. The highest peaks are those which the sun loves most. One by one, the mountains, relatively to their elevations, steal into darkness, and the rosy tint is often suffused over the peaks and glaciers of Mont Blanc, while the whole world below is enveloped in the darkest twilight.

What is it that makes me long to dwell upon these scenes, which, with all their loveliness, I have never again visited? Is it indeed the memory of their extreme beauty, or of the happy hours they afforded me, or is it because I am approaching a period of my life which I sometimes feel I shall never have courage to delineate?

II.

The thunder roared, the flashing lightning revealed only one universal mist, the wind tore up the pines by their roots, and flung them down into the valley, the rain descended in inundating gusts.

When once I had resolved to quit Geneva, my desire to reach Venice returned upon me in all its original force. I had travelled to the foot of the Simplon without a moment's delay, and now I had the mortification to be detained there in a wretched mountain village, intersected by a torrent whose roar was deafening, and with large white clouds sailing about the streets.

The storm had lasted three days; no one had ever heard of such a storm at this time of the year; it was quite impossible to pass; it was quite impossible to say when it would end, or what would happen. The poor people only hoped that no evil was impending over the village of Brigg. As for myself, when, day after day, I awoke only to find the thunder more awful, the lightning more vivid, and the mist more gloomy, I began to believe that my two angels were combatting on the height of Simplon, and that some supernatural, and perhaps beneficent power, would willingly prevent me from entering Italy.

I retired to bed, I flung my cloak upon a chair opposite a blazing wood-fire, and I soon fell asleep. I dreamed that I was in the vast hall of a palace, and that it was full of reverend and bearded men in rich dresses. They were seated at a council table, upon which their eyes were fixed, and I, who had recently entered, stood aside. And suddenly their president raised his head, and observed me, and beckoned to me with much dignity. And I advanced to him, and he extended to me his hand, and said, with a gracious smile, "*You have been long expected.*"

The council broke up, the members dispersed, and by his desire, I followed the president. And we entered another chamber, which was smaller, but covered with pictures, and on one side of the door was a portrait of Julius Cæsar, and on the other one of myself. And my guide turned his head, and pointing to the paintings, said, "*You see you have been long expected. There is a great resemblance between you and your uncle.*"

And my companion suddenly disappeared, and being alone, I walked up to a large window, but I could distinguish nothing, except when the lightning revealed the thick gloom. And the thunder rolled over the palace. And I knelt down and prayed, and suddenly the window was irradiated, and the bright form of a female appeared. Her fair hair reached beneath the waist, her countenance was melancholy, yet seraphic. In her hand she held a crucifix. And I said, "O blessed Magdalen, have you at last returned? I have been long wandering in the wilderness, and methought you had forgotten me. And indeed I am about again to go forth, but Heaven frowns upon my pilgrimage." And she smiled and said, "*Sunshine succeeds to storm. You have been long expected.*" And as she spoke, she vanished, and I looked again through the window, and beheld a beautiful city very fair in the sun. Its marble palaces rose on each side of a broad canal, and a multitude of boats skimmed over the blue water. And I knew where I was. And I descended from the palace to the brink of the canal, and my original guide saluted me, and, in his company, I entered a gondola.

A clap of thunder broke over the very house, and woke me. I jumped up in my bed. I stared. I beheld sitting in my room the same venerable personage in whose presence I had, the moment before, found myself. The embers of the fire shot forth a faint and flickering light. I felt that I had been asleep. I felt that I had dreamed. I even remembered where I was. I was not in any way confused. Yet before me was this mysterious companion, gazing upon me with the same gracious dignity with which he had at first beheld me in the palace. I remained sitting up in my bed, staring with starting eyes, and open mouth. Gradually his image became fainter and fainter. His features melted away, his form also soon dissolved, and I discovered only the empty chair and hanging cloak.

I jumped out of bed. The storm still raged. A bell was tolling. Nothing is more awful than a bell tolling in a storm. It was about three hours past midnight. I called Lausanne.

"Lausanne," I said, "I am resolved to cross the mountain by sunrise, come what come may. Offer any rewards, make what promises you please—but I am resolved to cross—even in the teeth of an avalanche." Although I am a person easily managed in little matters, and especially by servants, I spoke in a tone which Lausanne sufficiently knew me to feel was decisive. He was not one of those men who make or imagine difficulties, but, on the contrary, fruitful in discovering expedients, yet he seemed not a little surprised, and slightly hesitated.

"Lausanne," I said, "if you think it too dangerous to venture, I release you from your duty. But cross the mountain, and in two or three hours, I shall, even if I cross it alone."

He quitted the room. I threw a fresh log upon the fire, and repeated to myself, "*I have been long expected.*"

III.

Before six o'clock, all was prepared. Besides the postilions, Lausanne engaged several guides. I think we must have been about six hours ascend ing, certainly not more, and this does not much exceed the usual course. I had occasion on this, as I have since at many other conjunctures, to observe what an admirable animal is man when thrown upon his own resources in danger. The coolness, the courage, the perseverance, the acuteness, and the kindness with which my companions deported themselves, were as remarkable as they were delightful. As for myself, I could do nothing but lean back in the carriage, and trust to their experience and energy. It was indeed awful. We were almost always enveloped in mist, and if a violent gust, for a moment, dissipated the vapour, it was only to afford a glimpse of the precipices on whose very brink we were making our way. Nothing is more terrific than the near roar of a cataract in the dark. It is horrible. As for myself, I will confess that I was more than once fairly frightened, and when the agitated shouts of my companions indicated the imminence of the impending danger, I felt very much like a man who had raised the devil that he cannot lay.

The storm was only on the lower part of the mountain. As we ascended, it became clearer. The scene was perfect desolation. At length we arrived at a small table-land, surrounded by slight elevations, the whole covered with eternal snows. Cataracts were coursing down these hills in all directions, and the plain was covered with the chaotic forms of crumbled avalanches. The sky was a thick dingy white. My men gave a loud shout of exultation, and welcomed me to the summit of Simplon.

Here I shook hands, and parted with my faithful guides. As I was drinking a glass of brandy, and enveloping myself in my furs, the clouds broke towards Italy, and a beautiful streak of blue sky seemed the harbinger of the Ausonian Heaven. I felt in high spirits, and we dashed down the descent with an ease and rapidity that pleasantly reminded me, by the contrast, of our late labour.

A dashing descent down one of the High Alps is a fine thing. It is very exciting to scamper through one of those sublime tunnels, cut through solid rocks six thousand feet above the ocean,—to whir along those splendid galleries over precipices whose terminations are invisible,—to gallop through passes, as if you were flying from the companions of the avalanches, which are dissolving at your feet,—to spin over bridges spanning a roaring and rushing torrent, and to dash through narrow gorges backed with eternal snows peeping over the nearer and blacker background.

It was a sudden turn. Never shall I forget it. I called to Lausanne to stop, and notwithstanding the difficulty, they clogged the wheels with stones. It was a sudden turn of the road. It came upon me like a spirit. The quick change of scenery around me had disturbed my mind, and prevented me from dwelling upon the idea. So it came upon me unexpectedly, most, most unexpectedly. Ah! why did I not then die! I was too happy. I stood up to gaze for the first time upon Italy, and the tears stole down my cheek.

Yes! yes! I at length gazed upon those beautiful and glittering plains. Yes! yes! I at length beheld those purple mountains, and drank the balmy breath of that fragrant and liquid air. After such longing, after all the dull misery of my melancholy life, was this great boon indeed accorded me! Why, why did I not then die? I was indeed, ind ed too happy!

IV.

I AWOKE. I asked myself, "Am I indeed in Italy?" I could scarcely refrain from shouting with joy. While dressing, I asked many questions of Lausanne, that his answers might assure me of this incredible happiness. When he left the room, I danced about the chamber like a madman.

"Am I indeed in Italy?" My morning's journey was the most satisfactory answer. Although, of late, the business of my life had been only to admire nature, my progress was nevertheless one uninterrupted gaze.

Those azure mountains, those shining lakes, those gardens, and palaces, and statues, those cupolaed convents crowning luxuriant wooded hills, and flanked by a single, but most graceful tree, the undulation of shore, the projecting headland, the receding bay, the roadside uninclosed, yet bounded with walnut, and vine, and fig, and acacia, and almond-trees, bending down under their bursting fruit, the wonderful effect of light and shade, the trunks of every tree looking black as ebony, and their thick foliage, from the excessive light, quite thin and transparent in the sunshine, the white sparkling villages, each with a church with a tall thin tower, the large melons trailing over the marble wall,—and, above all, the extended prospect, so striking after the gloom of Alpine passes, and so different in its sunny light from the reflected, unearthly glare of eternal snows,—yes, yes, this indeed was Italy! I could not doubt my felicity, even if I had not marked, with curious admiration, the black eyes and picturesque forms that were flashing and glancing about me in all directions.

Milan, with its poetic opera, and Verona, gay amid the mingling relics of two thousand years, and Vicenza, with its Palladian palaces and gates of triumph, and pensive Padua, with its studious colonnades, I tore myself from their attractions. Their choicest memorials only accelerated my progress, only made me more anxious to gain the chief seat of the wonderful and romantic people, who had planted in all their marketplaces the winged lion of St. Mark, and raised between Roman amphitheatres and feudal castles, their wild and Saracenic piles.

I was upon the Brenta, upon that river over which I had so often mused beneath the rigour of a Scandinavian heaven; the Brenta was before me with all those villas, which in their number, their variety, and their splendour, form the only modern creation that can be placed with the Baiæ of imperial Rome. I had quitted Padua at a very early hour to reach Venice before sunset. Halfway, the horses jibbed on the sandy road, and the carriage broke a spring. To pass the time while this accident was repairing, Lausanne suggested to me to visit a villa at hand, which was celebrated for the beauty of its architecture and gardens. It was inhabited only by an old domestic, who attended me over the building. The vast suite of chambers, and their splendid, although ancient decorations, were the first evidence I had yet encountered of that domestic magnificence of the Venetians of which I had heard so much. I walked forth into the gardens alone, to rid myself of the garrulous domestic. I proceeded along a majestic terrace, covered with orange trees, at the end of which was a very beautiful chapel. The door was unlocked, and I entered. An immense crucifix of ebony was placed upon the altar, and partly concealed a picture fixed over the holy table. Yet the picture could not escape me. O! no, it could not escape me; for it was the original of that famous Magdalen that had, so many years before, and in so different a place, produced so great a revolution in my feelings. I remained before it some time, and as I gazed upon it, the history of my life was again acted before me. I quitted the chapel, revolving in my mind this strange coincidence, and crossing the lawn I came to a temple which a fanciful possessor had dedicated to his friends. Over the portal was an inscription. I raised my sight, and read, "*Enter; you have been long expected!*"

I started, I looked around, all was silent. I turned pale; I hesitated to go in. I examined the inscription again. My courage rallied, and I found myself in a small, but elegant banqueting-house, furnished, but apparently long disused. I threw myself into a seat at the head of the table, and full of a rising superstition, I almost expected that some of the venerable personages of my dream would enter to share my feast. They came not; half an hour passed away; I rose, and without premeditation, I wrote upon the wall, "*If I have been long expected, I have at length arrived. Be you also obedient to the call.*"

V.

An hour before sunset, I arrived at Fusini, and beheld, four or five miles out at sea, the towers and cupolas of Venice suffused with a rich golden light, and rising out of the bright blue waters. Not an exclamation escaped me. I felt like a man who has achieved a great object. I was full of calm exultation, but the strange incident of the morning made me serious and pensive.

As our gondolas glided over the great Lagune the excitement of the spectacle reanimated me The buildings, that I had so fondly studied in books and pictures, rose up before me. I knew them all; I required no cicerone. One by one, I caught the hooded cupolas of St. Mark, the tall Campanile red in the sun, the Moresco palace of the doges, the deadly Bridge of Sighs, and the dark structure to which it leads. Here my gondola quitted the Lagune, and, turning up a small canal, and passing under a bridge which connected the quays, stopped at the steps of a palace.

I ascended a staircase of marble, I passed through a gallery crowded with statues, I was ushered into spacious apartments, the floors of which were marble, and the hangings satin. The ceilings were painted by Tintoretto and his scholars, and were full of Turkish trophies and triumphs over the Ottomite. The furniture was of the same rich material as the hangings; and the gilding, although of two hundred years duration, as bright and burnished as the costly equipment of a modern palace. From my balcony of blinds, I looked upon the great Lagune. It was one of those glorious sunsets which render Venice, in spite of her degradation, still famous. The sky and sea vied in the brilliant multiplicity of their blended tints. The tall shadows of her Palladian churches flung themselves over the glowing and transparent wave out of which they sprang. The quays were crowded with joyous groups, and the black gondolas flitted, like sea serpents, over the red and rippling waters.

I hastened to the Place of St. Mark. It was crowded and illuminated. Three gorgeous flags waved on the mighty staffs which are opposite the church in all the old drawings, and which once bore the standards of Candia, and Cyprus, and the Morea. The coffee-houses were full, and gay parties, seated on chairs in the open air, listened to the music of military bands, while they refreshed themselves with confectionary so rich and fanciful, that it excites the admiration and the wonder of all travellers, but which I have since discovered in Turkey to be oriental. The variety of costume was also great. The dress of the lower orders in Venice is still unchanged: many of the middle classes yet wear the cap and cloak. The Hungarian and the German military, and the bearded Jew, with his black velvet cap and flowing robes, are observed with curiosity. A few days also before my arrival, the Austrian squadron had carried into Venice a Turkish ship and two Greek vessels, who had violated the neutrality. Their crews now mingled with the crowd. I beheld, for the first time, the haughty and turbaned Ottoman, sitting cross-legged on his carpet under a colonnade, sipping his coffee and smoking a long chiboque, and the Greeks, with their small red caps, their high foreheads, and arched eyebrows.

Can this be modern Venice, I thought? Can this be the silent, and gloomy, and decaying city, over whose dishonourable misery I have so often wept! Could it ever have been more enchanting? Are not these indeed still subjects of a doge, and still the bridegrooms of the ocean? Alas! the brilliant scene was as unusual as unexpected, and was accounted for by its being the feast-day of a favourite saint. Nevertheless, I rejoiced at the unaccustomed appearance of the city at my entrance, and still I recall with pleasure the delusive moments, when strolling about the Place of St. Mark the first evening that I was in Venice, I for a moment mingled in a scene that reminded me of her lost light-heartedness, and of that unrivalled gayety that so long captivated polished Europe.

The moon was now in her pride. I wandered once more to the quay, and heard for the first time a serenade. A juggler was conjuring in a circle under the walls of my hotel, and an itinerant opera was performing on the bridge. It is by moonlight that Venice is indeed an enchanted city. The effect of the floods of silver light upon the twinkling fretwork of the Moresco architecture, the perfect absence of all harsh sounds, the never-ceasing music on the waters, produce an effect upon the mind which cannot be experienced in any other city. As I stood gazing upon the broad track of brilliant light that quivered over the Lagune, a gondolier saluted me. I entered his boat, and desired him to row me to the Grand Canal.

The marble palaces of my ancestors rose on each side, like a series of vast and solemn temples. How sublime were their broad fronts bathed in the mystic light, whose softening tints concealed the ravages of time, and made us dream only of their eternity! And could these great creations ever die! I viewed them with a devotion which I cannot believe could have been surpassed in the most patriotic period of the republic. How willingly would I have given my life to have once more filled their mighty halls with the proud retainers of their free and victorious nobles!

As I proceeded along the canal, and retired from the quarter of St. Mark, the sounds of merriment gradually died away. The light string of a guita.

alone tinkled in the distance, and the lamp of a gondola, swiftly shooting by, indicated some gay, perhaps anxious youth, hastening to the rendezvous of festivity and love. The course of the canal bent, and the moon was hid behind a broad, thick arch, which, black, yet sharply defined, spanned the breadth of the water. I beheld the famous Rialto.

Was it possible? was it true? was I not all this time in a revery gazing upon a drawing in De Winter's studio? Was it not some delicious dream—some delicious dream, from which, perhaps this moment, I was about to be roused to cold, dull life? I struggled not to wake, yet from a nervous desire to move, and put the vision to the test, I ordered the gondolier to row to the side of the canal, jumped out, and hurried to the bridge. Each moment I expected that the arch would tremble and part, and that the surrounding palaces would dissolve into mist, that the lights would be extinguished, and the music cease, and that I should find myself in my old chamber in my father's house.

I hurried along, I was anxious to reach the centre of the bridge before I woke. It seemed like the crowning incident of a dream, which, it is remarkable, never occurs, and which, from the very anxiety it occasions, only succeeds in breaking our magical slumbers.

I stood upon Rialto; I beheld on each side of me, rising out of the waters, which they shadowed with their solemn image, those colossal and gorgeous structures raised from the spoils of the teeming orient, with their pillars of rare marbles, and their costly portals of jasper, and porphyry, and agate; I beheld them ranged in majestic order, and streaming with the liquid moonlight. Within these walls my fathers revelled!

I bowed my head, and covered my face with my hands. I could gaze no more upon that fair, but melancholy vision.

A loud but melodious chorus broke upon the air. I looked up, I marked the tumultuous waving of many torches, and heard the trampling of an approaching multitude. They were at the foot of the bridge. They advanced, they approached. A choir of priests, bearing in triumph the figure of a saint, and followed by a vast crowd carrying lights, and garlands, and banners, and joining in a joyful hymn, swept by me. As they passed, they sang this verse—

"Wave your banners! Sound, sound your voices! for he has come, he has come! Our saint and our lord! He has come, in pride and in glory, to greet with love his Adrian bride."

It is singular, but these words struck me as applicable to myself. The dream at the foot of the Alps, and the inscription in the garden on the Brenta, and the picture in the chapel, there was a connexion in all these strange incidents which indeed harmonized with my early life and feelings. I fully believed myself the object of an omnipotent destiny, over which I had no control. I delivered myself up, without a struggle, to the eventful course of time. I returned home pensive, yet prepared for a great career, and as the drum of the Hungarian guard sounded, as I entered the Lagune, I could not help fancying that its hurried note was ominous of surprise and consternation. I remembered that when a boy, sauntering with Musæus, I believed that I had a predisposition for conspiracies, and I could not forget that, of all places in the world, Venice was the one in which I should most desire to find myself a conspirator.

I returned to the hotel, but as I was little inclined to slumber, I remained walking up and down the gallery, which, on my arrival, amid the excitement of so many distracting objects, I had but slightly noticed. I was struck by its size and its magnificence, and as I looked upon the long row of statues gleaming in the white moonlight, I could not refrain from pondering over the melancholy fortunes of the high race who had lost this sumptuous inheritance, commemorating even in its present base uses, their noble exploits, magnificent tastes, and costly habits.

Lausanne entered. I inquired if he knew to what family of the republic this building had originally belonged?

"This was the Palazzo Contarini, sir."

I was glad that he could not mark my agitation.

"I thought," I rejoined, after a moment's hesitation, "I thought the Palazzo Contarini was on the Grand Canal."

"There is a Palazzo Contarini on the Grand Canal, sir, but this is the original palace of the house. When I travelled with my lord, twenty-five years ago, and was at Venice, the Contarini family still maintained both establishments."

"And now?" I inquired. This was the first time that I had ever held any conversation with Lausanne; for although I was greatly pleased with his talents, and could not be insensible to his ever-watchful care, I had from the first suspected that he was a secret agent of my father, and, although I thought fit to avail myself of his abilities, I had studiously withheld from him my confidence.

"The family of Contarini is, I believe extinct," replied Lausanne.

"Ah!" Then thinking that something should be said to account for my ignorance of that with which apparently I ought to have been well acquainted, I added in a careless voice. "We have never kept up any intercourse with our Italian connexions, which I do not regret, for I shall not enter into society here."

The moment that I had uttered this, I felt the weakness of attempting to mystify Lausanne, who probably knew much more of the reasons of this non-intercourse than myself. He was moving away when I called him back with the intention of speaking to him fully upon this subject of my early speculations. I longed to converse with him about my mother, and my father's youth, about every thing that had happened.

"Lausanne," I said.

He returned. The moon shone brightly upon his imperturbable and inscrutable countenance. I saw only my father's spy. A feeling of false shame prevented me from speaking. I did not like frankly to confess my ignorance upon such delicate subjects to one who would, in all probability, affirm his inability to enlighten me, and I knew enough of him to be convinced that I could not acquire by stratagem that which he would not willingly communicate.

"Lausanne," I said, "take lights into my room. I am going to bed."

VI.

Another sun rose upon Venice, and presented to me the city whose image I had so early acquired. In the heart of a multitude there was stillness. I looked out from the balcony on the crowded quays of yesterday; one or two idle porters were stretched in sleep on the scorching pavement, and a solitary gondola stole over the gleaming waters. This was all.

It was the Villeggiatura, and the absence of the nobility from the city invested it with an aspect even more deserted than it would otherwise have possessed. I cared not for this. For me indeed, Venice, silent and desolate, owned a greater charm than it could have commanded with all its feeble imitation of the worthless bustle of a modern metropolis. I congratulated myself on the choice season of the year in which I had arrived at this enchanting city. I do not think that I could have endured to have been disturbed by the frivolous sights and sounds of society, before I had formed a full acquaintance with all those marvels of art that command our constant admiration, while gliding about the lost capital of the doges, and before I had yielded a free flow to those feelings of poetic melancholy which swell up in the soul as we contemplate this memorable theatre of human action, wherein have been performed so many of man's most famous and most graceful deeds.

If I were to assign the particular quality which conduces to that dreamy and voluptuous existence which men of high imagination experience in Venice, I should describe it as the feeling of abstraction, which is remarkable in that city, and peculiar to it. Venice is the only city which can yield the magical delights of solitude. All is still and silent. No rude sound disturbs your reveries; fancy, therefore is not put to flight. No rude sound distracts your self-consciousness. This renders existence intense. We feel every thing. And we feel thus keenly in a city not only eminently beautiful, not only abounding in wonderful creations of art, but each step of which is hallowed ground, quick with associations, that in their more various nature, their nearer relation to ourselves, and perhaps their more picturesque character, exercise a greater influence over the imagination than the more antique story of Greece and Rome. We feel all this in a city too, which, although her lustre be indeed dimmed, can still count among her daughters maidens fairer than the orient pearls with which her warriors once loved to deck them. Poetry, Tradition, and Love,—these are the graces that have invested with an ever-charming cestus this aphrodite of cities.

As for myself, ere the year drew to a close, I was so captivated with the life of blended contemplation and pleasure that I led in this charming city, that I entirely forgot my great plan of comprehensive travel, that was to induce such important results, and not conceiving that earth could yield me a spot where time could flow on in a more beautiful and tranquil measure, more exempt from worldly anxiety, and more free from vulgar thoughts, I determined to become a Venetian resident. So I quitted the house of my fathers, which its proprietor would not give up to me, and in which, under its present fortune, I could not bear to live, converted Lausanne into a major-domo, and engaged a palace on the Grand Canal

VII.

There is in Venice a very ancient church situate in an obscure quarter of the city, whither I was in the habit of often resorting. It is full of the tombs of Contarinis. Two doges under their fretwork canopies, with their hands crossed over their breasts, and their heads covered with their caps of state, and reposing on pillows, lie on each side of the altar. On the platform before the church, as you ascend the steps from your gondola, is a colossal statue of a Contarini, who defeated the Genoese. It is a small church, built and endowed by the family. To this day there they sing masses for their souls.

One sunshiny afternoon I entered this church, and repaired as was my custom to the altar, which, with its tombs, was partially screened from the body of the building, being lighted by the large window in front, which considerably overtopped the screen. They were singing a mass in the nave, and I placed myself at the extreme side of the altar in the shade of one of the tombs, and gazing upon the other. The sun was nearly setting, the opposite tomb was bathed with the soft, warm light which streamed in from the window. I remained watching the placid and heroic countenance of the old doge, the sunlight playing on it, till it seemed to smile. The melodious voices of the choir, praying for Contarini, came flowing along the roof with so much sentiment and sweetness, that I was soon wrapped in self-oblivion, and although my eye was apparently fixed upon the tomb, my mind wandered in delightful abstraction.

A temporary cessation of the music called me to myself. I looked round, and to my surprise beheld a female figure kneeling before the altar. At this moment, the music recommenced. She evidently did not observe me. She threw over her shoulders the black veil with which her face had hitherto been covered. Her eyes were fixed upon the ground; her hands raised, and pressed together in prayer. I had never beheld so beautiful a creature. She was very young, her countenance perfectly fair, but without colour, or tinted only with the transient flush of devotion. Her features were very delicate, yet sharply defined. I could mark her long eyelashes touching her cheek; and her dark hair, parted on her white brow, fell on each side of her face in tresses of uncommon length and lustre. Altogether she was what I had sometimes fancied as the ideal of a Venetian beauty. As I watched her, her invocation ceased, and she raised her large dark eyes with an expression of melancholy that I never shall forget.

And as I gazed upon her, instead of feeling agitated and excited, a heaviness crept over my frame, and a drowsiness stole over my senses. Enraptured by her presence, anxiously desirous to ascertain who she might be, I felt to my consternation, each moment more difficulty in moving, even in seeing. The tombs, the altar, the kneeling suppliant, moved confusedly together, and mingled into mist, and sinking back on the tomb which supported me, I fell, as I supposed, into a deep slumber.

I dreamed that a long line of Venetian nobles, two by two, passed before me, and, as they passed, they saluted me, and the two doges were there, and as they went by, they smiled and waved their bonnets. And suddenly there appeared my father alone, and he was dressed in a northern dress, the hunting dress I wore in the forest of Jonsterna, and he stopped and looked upon me with great severity, and I withdrew my eye, for I could not bear his glance, and when I looked up again he was not there, but the lady of the altar. She stood before me clinging to a large crucifix, a large crucifix of ebony, the same that I had beheld in the chapel in the gardens on the Brenta. The tears hung quivering on her agitated countenance. I would have rushed forward to console her, but I woke.

I woke, I looked around, I remembered every thing. She was not there. It was twilight, and the tombs were barely perceptible. All was silent, I stepped forth from the altar into the body of the church. A single acolyte was folding up the surplices and placing them in a trunk. I inquired if he had seen any lady go out. He had seen nothing. He stared at my puzzled look, which was the look of a man roused from a very vivid dream. I went forth; one of my gondoliers was lying on the steps: I asked him also if he had seen any lady go out. He assured me that no person had come forth except the priests. Was there any other way? They believed not. I endeavoured to re-enter the church to examine, but it was locked.

VIII.

If ever the science of metaphysics ceases to be a frivolous assemblage of unmeaning phrases, and we attempt to acquire that knowledge of our nature which is doubtless open to us by the assistance of facts instead of words; if ever, in short, the philosophy of the human mind be based on demonstration instead of dogma, the strange incident just related, will perhaps not be considered the wild delusion of a crack-brained visionary. For myself, I have no doubt that the effect produced upon me by the lady in the church was a magnetic influence, and that the slumber which, at the moment, occasioned me so much annoyance, and so much astonishment, was nothing less than a luminous trance.

I knew nothing of these high matters then, and I returned to my palace in a state of absolute confusion. It was so reasonable to believe that I had fallen asleep, and that the whole was a dream. Every thing was thus most satisfactorily accounted for. Nevertheless I could not overcome my strong conviction, that the slumber which I could not deny, was only a secondary incident, and that I had positively, really, absolutely beheld kneeling before the altar that identical and transcendent form, that in my dream or vision I had marked clinging to the cross.

I examined the gondoliers on my return home. I elicited nothing. I examined myself the whole evening. I resolved that I had absolutely seen her. I attended at the church the next day; nothing occurred. I spoke to the priests, I engaged one to keep a constant observation. Nothing ever transpired.

The Villeggiatura was over, the great families returned, the carnival commenced. Venice was full and gay. There were assemblies every evening. The news that a young foreign nobleman had come to reside at Venice, of course, quickly spread. My establishment, my quality, and, above all, my name, ensured me a hospitable reception, although I knew not a single individual, and, of course, had not a single letter. I did not encourage their attentions. I went nowhere, except to the opera, which opened with the carnival. I have a passion for instrumental music, but I admire little the human voice, which appears to me, with all our exertions, a poor instrument. Sense and sentiment too are always sacrificed to dexterity and caprice. A grand orchestra fills my mind with ideas,—I forget every thing in the stream of invention. A prima donna is very ravishing, but while I listen, I am a mere man of the world, or hardly sufficiently well-bred to conceal my weariness.

The effect of music upon the faculty of invention is a subject on which I have long curiously observed, and deeply meditated. It is a finer prelude to creation than to execution. It is well to meditate upon a subject under the influence of music, but to execute, we should be alone, and supported only by our essential and internal strength. Were I writing, music would produce the same effect upon me as wine. I should, for a moment, feel an unnatural energy and fire, but, in a few minutes, I should discover that I shadowed forth only phantoms, my power of expression would die away, and my pen would fall upon the insipid and lifeless page. The greatest advantage that a writer can derive from music is, that it teaches most exquisitely the art of developement. It is in remarking the varying recurrence of a great composer to the same theme, that a poet may learn how to dwell upon the phasis of a passion, how to exhibit a mood of mind under all its alternations, and gradually to pour forth the full tide of feeling.

The last week of the carnival arrived, in which they attempted to compress all the frolic which should be diffused over the rest of the forty days, which, it must be confessed, are dull enough. At Venice, the beauty and the wildness of the carnival still lingered. St. Mark's Place was crowded with masks. It was even more humorous to observe these grotesque forms in repose than in action; to watch a monster with a nose a foot long, and asses' ears, eating an ice, or a mysterious being with a face like a dolphin, refreshing herself with a fan as huge as a parasol. The houses were covered with carpets and tapestry, every place was illuminated, and everybody pelted with sweetmeats and sugarplums. No one ever seemed to go to bed; the water was covered with gondolas, and everybody strummed a guitar.

During the last nights of the carnival, it is the practice to convert the opera-house into a ball-room, and on these occasions, the highest orders are masked. The scene is indeed very gay and amusing. In some boxes, a standing supper is always ready, at which all guests are welcome. But masked you must be. It is even strict etiquette on these occasions for ladies to ramble about the theatre unattended, and the great diversion of course is the extreme piquancy of the incognito conversations, since, in a limited circle, in which few are unknown to each other, it is, of course, not difficult to impregnate this slight parley with a sufficient quantity of Venetian salt.

I went to one of these balls, as I thought something amusing might occur. I went in a domino, and was careful not to enter my box, lest I should be discovered. As I was sauntering along one of the rooms near the stage, a female mask saluted me.

"We did not expect you," she said.

"I only came to meet you," I replied.

"You are more gallant than we supposed you to be."

"The world is seldom charitable," I said

"They say you are in love."

"You are the last person to consider that wonderful."

"Really quite chivalric. Why! they said you were quite a wild man."

"But you, signora, have tamed me."

"But do you know they say you are in love?"

"Well! doubtless with a charming person."

"O! yes, a very charming person. Do you know they say you are Count Narcissus, and in love with yourself?"

"Do they indeed! They seem to say vastly agreeable things, I think. Very witty, upon my honour."

"O! very witty, no doubt of that, and you should be a judge of wit, you know, because you are a poet."

"You seem to know me well."

"I think I do. You are the young gentleman, are you not, who has quarrelled with his papa?"

"That is a very vague description."

"I can give you some further details."

"O! pray spare me, and yourself."

"Do you know I have written your character?"

"Indeed! It is doubtless as accurate as most others."

"O! it is founded upon the best authorities. There is only one part imperfect. I wish to give an account of your works. Will you give me a list?"

"I must have an equivalent, and something more interesting than my own character."

"Meet me to-night at the Countess Malbrizzi's."

"I cannot, I do not know her."

"Do not you know, that in carnival time, a mask may enter any house? After the ball, all will be there. Will you meet me? I am now engaged."

This seemed the opening of an adventure which youth is not inclined to shun. I assented, and the mask glided away, leaving me in great confusion and amazement at her evident familiarity with my history.

IX.

I ARRIVED at the steps of the Malbrizzi palace amid a crowd of gondolas. I ascended without any announcement into the saloons, which were full of guests. I found, to my great annoyance, that I was the only mask present. I felt that I had been fairly taken in. I perceived that I was an object of universal attention. I had a great inclination to make a precipitate retreat. But on reflection, I determined to take a rapid survey before my departure, and then retire with dignity. Leaning against a pillar, I flattered myself I appeared quite at my ease.

A lady, whom I had already conjectured to be the mistress of the mansion, advanced and addressed me. Time had not yet flown away with her charms.

"Signor Mask," she said, "ever welcome, and doubly welcome, if a friend."

"I fear I have no title to admission within these walls, except the privilege of the season."

"I should have thought otherwise," said the lady, "if you be one for whom many have inquired."

"You must mistake me for another. It is not probable that any one would inquire after *me*."

"Shall I tell you your name?"

"Some one has pretended to give me that unnecessary information already to-night."

"Well! I will not betray you, but I am silent in the hope that you will, ere midnight, reward me for my discretion by rendering it unnecessary. We trust that the ice of the north will melt beneath our Venetian sun. You understand me?" So saying, she glided away.

I could not doubt that this lady was the Countess Malbrizzi, and that she was the female mask who had addressed me in the opera-house. She evidently knew me. I had not long to seek for the source whence she attained this knowledge. The son of the Austrian minister at our court, and who had himself been attached to the legation, passed by me. His uncle was Governor of Venice. Every thing was explained.

I moved away, intending to retire. A group, in the room I entered, attracted my attention. Several men were standing round a lady apparently entreating her, with the usual compliments and gesticulations, to play upon the guitar. Her face was concealed from me; one of her suite turned aside, and notwithstanding the difference of her rich dress, I instantly recognised the kneeling lady of the church. I was extremely agitated. I felt the inexplicable sensation that I had experienced on the tomb. I was fearful that it might end in as mortifying a catastrophe. I struggled against the feeling, and struggled successfully. As I thus wrestled with my mind, I could not refrain from gazing intently upon the cause of my emotion. I felt an overwhelming desire to ascertain who she might be. I could not take my eyes from her. She impressed me with so deep an interest, that I entirely forgot that any other human beings were present. It was fortunate that I was masked. My fixed stare must have excited great curiosity.

As I stood thus gazing upon her, and as each moment her image seemed mere vividly impressed upon my brain, a chain round her neck snapped in twain, and a diamond cross suspended to it fell to the ground. The surrounding cavaliers were instantly busied in seeking for the fallen jewel. I beheld, for the first time, her tall and complete figure. Our eyes met.

To my astonishment, she suddenly grew pale, she ceased conversing, she trembled, and sank into a chair. A gentleman extended to her the cross she received it, her colour returned, a smile played upon her features, and she rose from her seat.

The countess passed me. I saluted her. "I now wish you to tell me," I said, "not my own name, but the name of another person. Will you be kind?"

"Speak."

"That lady," I said, pointing to the group, "I have a very great wish to know who that lady may be."

"Indeed!" said the countess, "I have a great wish also that your curiosity should be gratified That is Signora Alceste Contarini."

"Contarini!" I exclaimed, "how wonderful! I mean to say, how singular! that is, I did not know—"

"That there were any other Contarinis but your excellency, I suppose."

"It is idle to wear this disguise," I said, taking off my mask, and letting my domino slip to the ground. "I have ever heard that it was impossible to escape the penetration of the Countess Malbrizzi."

"My penetration has not been much exercised to-night, count; but I assure you I feel gratified to have been the means of inducing you to enter a society, of which the Baroness Fleming was once the brightest ornament. Your mother was my friend."

"You have, indeed, the strongest claim then to the respect of her son. But this young lady—"

"Is your cousin, an orphan, and the last of the Contarinis. You should become acquainted. Permit me to introduce you." I accompanied her. "Alceste, my love," continued the countess, "those should not be unknown to each other whom nature has intended to be friends. Your cousin, Count Contarini Fleming, claims your acquaintance."

"I have not so many relations that I know not how to value them," said Alceste, as she extended me her hand. The surrounding gentlemen moved away. We were alone. "I arrived so unexpectedly at Venice, that I owe to a chance my introduction to one whose acquaintance I should have claimed in a more formal manner."

"You are merely, then, a passing visiter? We heard it was your intention to become a resident."

"I have become one. It has been too difficult for me to gain this long-desired haven, again to quit it without a very strong cause. But when I departed from my country, it was for the understood purpose of making a very different course. My father is not so violent a Venetian as myself, and, for aught I know, conceives me now in France or England. In short, I have played truant, but I hope you will pardon me."

"To love Venice is with me so great a virtue," she replied, with a smile, "that, I fear, instead of feeling all the impropriety of your conduct, I sympathize too much with this violation of duty."

"Of course you could not know my father. You may have heard of him. It has always been to me a source of deep regret that he did not maintain his connexion with my mother's family. I inherit something even more Venetian than her name. But the past is too painful for my father to love to recall it. My mother, you know—"

"I am an orphan, and can feel all your misfortune. I think our house is doomed."

"I cannot think so when I see you."

She faintly smiled, but her features settled again into an expression of deep melancholy, that reminded me of her countenance in the church.

"I think," I observed, "this is not the first time I have had the pleasure of seeing you."

"Indeed! I am not aware of our having before met."

"I may be wrong. I dare say you will think me very strange. But I cannot believe it was a dream, though certainly I was—but really it is too ridiculous. You know the church where are the tombs of our family?"

"Yes!" Her voice was low, but quick. I fancied she was not quite at ease.

"Well! I cannot help believing that we were once together before that altar."

"Indeed! I have returned to Venice a week. I have not visited the church since we came back."

"O! this must have been a month ago. It certainly is very strange; I suppose it must have been a dream; I have sometimes odd dreams, and yet—it is in consequence of that supposed meeting in the church that I recognised you this evening, and immediately sought an introduction."

"I know the church well. To me—I may say to us," she added, with a gentle inclination of the head, "it is, of course, a spot very interesting."

"I am entirely Venetian. I have no thought for any other country. This is not a new sentiment excited by the genius of the place. It was as strong amid the forests and snows of the north, as strong, I may truly say, when a child, as at this moment, when I would peril my life and fortunes in her service."

"You are indeed enthusiastic. Alas! enthusiasm is little considered here. We are, at least, still light-hearted, but what cause we have for gayety, the smilers perhaps know. It is my misfortune not to be one of them. And yet resignation is all that is left us, and—"

"And what?" I asked, for she hesitated.

"Nothing," she replied, "nothing. I believe I was going to add, it is better to forget."

"Never! The recollection of the past is still glory. I would sooner be a Contarini amid our falling palaces, than the mightiest noble of the most flourishing of modern empires."

"What will your father say to such romance?"

"I have no father. I have no friend, no relative in the world, except yourself. I have disclaimed my parentage, my country, my allotted career, and all their rights, and honours, and privileges, and fame, and fortune. I have, at least, sacrificed all these for Venice; for, trifling as the circumstances may be, I can assure you this, merely to find myself a visitant of that enchanting city, I have thrown to the winds all the duties and connexions of my past existence."

"But why bind your lot to the fallen and the irredeemable? I have no choice but to die where I was born, and no wish to quit a country from which spring all my associations; but you—you have a real country, full of real interests to engage your affections and exercise your duties. In the north you are a man—your career may be active, intelligent and useful; but the life of a Venetian is a dream, and you must pass your days like a ghost gliding about a city fading in a vision."

"It is this very character that interests me. I have no sympathy with reality. What vanity is all the empty bustle of common life! It brings to me no gratification; on the contrary, most degrading annoyance. It developes all the lowering attributes of my nature. In the world, I am never happy but in solitude; and in solitude so beautiful and so peculiar as Venice, my days are indeed a dream, but a dream of long delight. I gaze upon the beautiful, and my mind responds to the inspiration, for my thoughts are as lovely as my visions."

"Your imagination supports you. It is a choice gift. I feel too keenly my reality."

"At least, I cannot imagine that you should either feel, or give rise to, any other feelings but those that are enchanting."

"Nay! a truce to compliments. Let me hear something worthier from you."

"Indeed," I said, seriously, "I was not thinking of compliments, nor am I in a mood for such frivolities. Yet I wish not to conceal, that in meeting you this evening, I have experienced the most gratifying incident of my life."

"I am happy to have met you—if, indeed, it be possible to be happy about any thing."

"Dear Alceste—may I call you Alceste?—why should so fair a brow be clouded?"

"It is not unusually gloomy—my heaven is never serene. But, see! the rooms are nearly empty, and I am waited for."

"But we shall soon meet again?"

"I shall be here to-morrow. I reside with my maternal uncle, Count Delfini. I go out but little, but to-morrow I shall certainly be here."

"I shall not exist until we again meet. I entreat you, fail not."

"O! I shall certainly be here; and, in the mean time, you know," she added, with a smile, "you can dream."

"Farewell, dear Alceste! you cannot imagine how it grieves me to part."

"Adieu!—shall I say Contarini?"

X.

To say that I was in love, that I was in love at first sight—these are weak, worldly phrases to describe the profound and absorbing passion that filled my whole being. There was a mystical fulfilment in our meeting, the consciousness of which mingled with my adoration, and rendered it quite supernatural. This was the Adrian bride that I had come to greet. This was the great and worthy object of so many strange desires, and bewildering dreams, and dark coincidences. I returned to my palace—I threw myself into a chair, and sat for hours in mute abstraction. At last, the broad light of morning broke into the chamber—I looked up, glanced round at the ghastly chandeliers, thought of the coming eve, and retired.

In the evening I hurried to the opera. I did not see Alceste. I entered the box of the countess. A young man rose as I entered, and retired. "You see," I said, "your magic has in a moment converted me into a man of the world."

"I am not the enchantress," said the countess, "although I willingly believe you are enchanted."

"What an agreeable assembly you introduced me to last night!"

"I hope that I shall find you a constant guest."

"I fear that you will find me too faithful a votary. I little imagined, in the morning, that I could lay claim to relationship with so interesting a person as your charming young friend."

"Alceste is a great favourite of mine."

"She is not here, I believe, to-night?"

"I think not—Count Delfini's box is opposite, and empty."

"Count Delfini is, I believe, some connexion—"

"Her uncle. They will be soon, as you are perhaps aware, nearer connected."

"Indeed!" I said.

"You know that Alceste is betrothed to his son, Count Grimani. By-the-by, he quitted the box as you entered. You know him?"

I sank back in my chair—I turned pale.

"Do you admire this opera?" I inquired.

"It is a pretty imitation."

"Very pretty."

"We shall soon change it."

"Very soon."

"They have an excellent opera at St. Petersburg, I understand. You have been there?"

"Yes—no—I understand very excellent. This house is very hot." I rose up, bowed, and abruptly departed.

I instantly quitted the theatre, covered myself up in my cloak, threw myself down in my gondola, and groaned. In a few minutes I arrived home. I was quite unexpected. I ran up stairs. Lausanne was about to light the candles. I sent him away. I was alone in the large, dark chamber, which seemed only more vast and gloomy for the bright moon.

"Thank God!" I exclaimed, "I am alone. Why do I not die! Betrothed! It is false; she cannot be another's. She is mine; she is my Adrian bride. Destiny has delivered her to me. Why did I pass the Alps! Heaven frowned upon the passage. Yet I was expected. I was long expected. Poh! she *is* mine. I would cut her out from the heart of a legion. Is she happy? Her 'heaven is never serene.' Mark that. I will be the luminary to dispel these clouds. Betrothed! Infamous jargon! She belongs to me. Why did I not stab him! Is there ne'er a bravo in Venice that will do the job? Betrothed! What a word! what an infamous, what a ridiculous word! She is mine, and she is betrothed to another. Most assuredly, if she be only to be attained by the destruction of the city, she shall be mine. A host of Delfinis shall not balk me.

"Now this is no common affair. It shall be done, and it shall be done quickly. I cannot doubt she loves me. It is as necessary that she should love me, as that I should adore her. We are bound together by Fate. We belong to each other: 'I have been long expected.'

"Ah! were these words a warning or a prophecy? Have I arrived too late? Let it be settled at once, this very evening. Suspense is madness. She is mine, most assuredly she is mine. I will not admit for a moment that she is not mine. That idea cannot exist in my thoughts. It is the end of the world, it is doomsday for me. Most assuredly, she is my Adrian bride, my *bride*, not my *betrothed* merely, but my *bride*.

"Let me be calm. I am calm. I never was calmer in my life. Nothing shall ruffle, nothing shall discompose me. I will have my rights. This difficulty will make our future lives more sweet. We shall smile at it in each other's arms. Grimani Delfini! If there be blood in that name, it shall flow. Sooner than another should possess her, she should herself be sacrificed. A solemn sacrifice, a sweet and solemn sacrifice, consecrated by my own doom! I would lead her to the altar like Iphigenia. I—

"O! inscrutable, inexorable destiny, which must be fulfilled! Doom that mortals must endure, and cannot direct—lo! I kneel down before thee, and I pray!—Let it end, let it end, let it end at once! This suspense is insanity. Is she not mine! Didst thou not whisper it in the solitude of the north, didst thou not confirm it amid the thunder of the Alps, didst thou not reanimate my drooping courage, even amid this fair city I so much love, this land of long and frequent promise? And shall it not be! Do I exist, do I breathe, and think, and dare—am I a man, and a man of strong passions and deep thoughts—and shall I, like a vile beggar upon my knees, crave the rich heritage that is my own right? If she be not mine, there is no longer Venice, no longer human existence, no longer a beautiful and everlasting world. Let it all cease; let the whole globe crack and shiver; let all nations and all human hopes expire at once; let chaos come again, if this girl be not my bride!"

I determined to go to the Malbrizzi palace. My spirit rose as I ascended the stairs. I felt confident she was there. Her form was the first that occurred to me as I entered the saloon. Several persons were around her, among them Grimani Delfini. I did not care. I had none of the jealousy of petty loves. She was unhappy, that was sufficient; and if there were no other way of disentangling the mesh, I had a sword that should cut this Gordian knot in his best blood. I saluted her. She presented me to her cousin. I smiled upon one who, at all events, should be my victim.

"I hope that we shall make Venice agreeable to you, count," said Grimani.

"There is no doubt," I replied.

We conversed for some time on indifferent subjects. My manner was elated. I entered into the sparkling contest of conversation with success. The presence of Alceste was my inspiration. I would not quit her side, and in time, we were once more alone.

"You are ever gay," she remarked.

"My face is most joyful when my heart is most gloomy. Happiness is tranquil. Why were you not at the opera?"

"I go out very little."

"I went there only to meet you. I detest these assemblies. You are always surrounded by a crowd of moths. Will you dance?"

"I have just refused Grimani."

"I am glad of it. I abhor dancing. I only asked you to monopolize your company."

"And what have you been doing to-day? Have you seen all our spectacles!"

"I have just risen. I did not go to bed last night. I sat up musing over our strange meeting."

"Was it so strange?"

"It was stranger than you imagine."

"You are mysterious."

"Every thing is mysterious, although I have been always taught the reverse."

"I believe, too," she remarked, with a pensive air and in a serious tone, "that the courses of this world are not so obvious as we imagine."

"The more I look upon you, the more I am convinced that yesterday was not our first meeting. We have been long acquainted.

"In dreams?"

"What you please. Dreams, visions, prophecies, I believe in them all. You have often appeared to me, and I have often heard of you."

"Dreams are doubtless very singular."

"They come from heaven. I could tell you stories of dreams that would indeed surprise you."

"Tell me."

"When I was about to pass the Alps,—but really it is too serious a narrative for such a place. Do you know the villa of the temple on the Brenta?"

"Assuredly, for it is my own."

"Your own! Then you are indeed mine."

"What can you mean?"

"The temple, the temple—"

"And did you write upon the wall?"

"Who else? Who else? But why I wrote —that I would tell you."

"Let us walk to these rooms. There is a terrace, where we shall be less disturbed."

"And where we have been long expected."

"Ah!"

XI.

"It is wonderful, most wonderful." and she leaned down and plucked a flower.

"I wish I were that flower," I said.

"It resembles me more than you, Contarini," and she threw it away.

"I see no resemblance."

"It is lost."

I picked it up and placed it in my bosom.

"It is found," I replied, "and cherished."

"We are melancholy," said Alceste, "and yet we are not happy. Your philosophy—is it quite correct?"

"I am happy you should resemble me, because I wish it."

"Good wishes do not always bring good fortunes."

"Destiny bears to us our lot, and destiny is perhaps our own will."

"Alas! my will is brighter than my doom!"

"Both should be beautiful, and shall—"

"O talk not of the future. Come, Contarini, come, come, away."

XII.

Shall I endeavour to recall the soft transport which this night suffused itself over my being? I existed only for one object; one idea only was impressed upon my brain. The next day passed in a delicious listlessness and utter oblivion of all cares and duties. In the evening, I rose from the couch on which I had the whole day reclined musing on a single thought, and flew to ascertain whether that wizard Imagination had deceived me, whether she were, indeed, so wondrous fair and sweet, and that this earth could indeed be graced by such surpassing loveliness.

She was not there. I felt her absence as the greatest misfortune that had ever fallen upon me. I could not anticipate existing four-and-twenty hours without her presence. I lingered in expectation of her arrival. I could hear nothing of her. Each moment I fancied she must appear. It seemed impossible that so bitter a doom awaited me, as that I should not gaze this night upon her beauty. She did not come. I remained to the last, silent and anxious, and returned home to a sleepless bed.

The next morning I called at the Delfini palace, to which I had received an invitation. Morning was an unusual time to call, but for this I did not care. I saw the old count and countess, and her ladyship's cavalier, who was the most frivolous and ancient Adonis I had ever witnessed. I talked with them all, all of them with the greatest good humour, in the hope that Alceste would at length appear. She did not. I ventured to inquire after her. I feared she might be unwell. She was quite well, but engaged with her confessor. I fell into one of my silent rages, kicked the old lady's poodle, snubbed the cavalier, and stalked away.

In the evening, I was careful to be at the Malbrizzi palace. The Delfinis were there, but not Alceste. I was already full of suspicions, and had been brooding the whole morning over a conspiracy.

"Alceste is not here," I observed to the countess, "is she unwell?"

"Not at all. I saw her this morning. She was quite well.—I suppose Count Grimani is jealous"

"Hah!" thought I, "has it already come to that?

Let us begin, then. I feel very desperate. This affair must be settled. Fed by her constant presence and her smiles, the flame of my passion could for a time burn with a calm and steady blaze —but I am getting mad again. I shall die if this state of things last another day. I have half a mind to invite him to the terrace, and settle it at once. Let me see, cannot I do more ?"

I mused a moment, quitted the saloon, called the gondola, and told them to row me to the Delfini palace.

We glided beneath that ancient pile. All was dark, save one opened window, whence proceeded the voice of one singing. I knew that voice. I motioned to the gondoliers to rest upon their oars.

"'Tis the Signora Contarini," whispered Tita, who was acquainted with the family.

We floated silently beneath her window. Again she sang.

I marked a rose bedewed with tears, a white and virgin rose; and I said, "O! rose, why do you weep, you are too beautiful for sorrow?" And she answered, "Lady, mourn not for me, for my grief comes from Heaven."

She was silent. I motioned to Tita, who, like many of the gondoliers, was gifted with a fine voice, to answer. He immediately sang a verse from one of the favourite ballads of his city. While he sang, I perceived her shadow, and presently I observed her in the middle of the apartment. I plucked from my breast a flower, which I had borne for her to the Malbrizzi palace, and cutting off a lock of my hair, I tied it round the rose, and threw it into the chamber.

It fell upon the table. She picked it up, she stared at it for some moments, she smiled, she pressed it to her lips.

I could restrain myself no longer. I pushed the gondola alongside the palace, clambered up the balcony, and entered the room.

She started, she nearly shrieked, but restrained herself.

"You are surprised, Alceste, perhaps you are displeased. They are endeavouring to separate us; I cannot live without you."

She clasped her hands, and looked up to heaven with a glance of anguish.

"Yes! Alceste," I exclaimed, advancing, "let me express what my manner has never attempted to conceal; let me express to you my absolute adoration. I love you, my Alceste, I love you with a passion as powerful as it is pure, a passion which I cannot control, a passion which ought not to be controlled."

She spoke not, she turned away her head and deprecated my advances with her extended arms.

"Alceste, I know all. I know the empty, the impious ceremony that has doomed you to be the bride of a being whom you must abhor. My Alceste is not happy. She herself told me her heaven was not serene—the heaven in whose light I would forever lie."

I advanced, I stole her hand, I pressed it to my lips. Her face was hidden in her arm, and that reclined upon a pillar.

There was for a moment silence. Suddenly she withdrew her hand, and said, in a low, but distinct voice, "Contarini, this must end."

"End! Alceste, I adore you. You—you dare not say you do not love me. Our will is not our own Destiny has linked us together, and Heaven has interposed to consecrate our vows. And shall a form, a dull, infamous form, stand between our ardent and hallowed loves !"

"It is not that, Contarini, it is not that, though that were much. No, Contarini, I am not yours."

"Not mine, Alceste! not mine? Look upon me. Think who I am, and dare to say you are not mine. Am I not Contarini Fleming? Are not you my Adrian bride? Heaven has delivered you to me."

"Alas! alas! Heaven keeps me from you."

"Alceste, you see kneeling before you one who is indeed nothing, if fame be what some deem. I am young, Alceste, the shadow of my mind has not yet fallen over the earth. Yet there is that within me,—and at this moment I prophesy,—there is that within me which may yet mould the mind and fortunes of my race—and of this heart, capable of these things, the fountains are open, Alceste, and they flow for you. Disdain them not, Alceste; pass them not by with carelessness. In the desert of your life, they will refresh you—yes, yes, they can indeed become to you a source of all felicity.

"I love you with a love worthy of your being; I love you as none but men like me can love. Blend not the thought of my passion with the common-place affections of the world. Is it nothing to be the divinity of that breathing shrine of inspiration, my teeming mind? O! Alceste, you know not the world to which I can lead you, the fair and glorious garden in which we may wander for ever!"

"I am lost!" she exclaimed, "but I am yours."

I caught her in my arms; yea! I caught her in my arms, that dark-eyed daughter of the land I loved. I sealed her sweet lips with passionate kisses. Her head rested on my breast; and I dried with embraces her fast-flowing tears.

XIII.

I HAD quitted Alceste so abruptly that I had made no arrangements for our future meeting. Nor indeed for some time could I think of any thing but my present and overflowing joy. So passionately was I entranced with all that had happened, so deeply did I muse over all that had been said and done, so sweetly did her voice linger in my ear, and so clearly did her fond form move before my vision, that hours elapsed before I felt again the craving of again beholding her. I doubted not that I should find her at the Malbrizzi palace. I was disappointed, but my disappointment was not bitter like the preceding eve. I felt secure in our secret loves, and I soon quitted the assembly again to glide under her window All was dark. I waited, Tita again sang. No light appeared, no sound stirred.

I resolved to call at the palace, to which I had received the usual general invitation. The family were out, and at the Pisani palace. I returned to Madame Malbrizzi's. I looked about for my young Austrian acquaintance. I observed him, I fell into conversation. I inquired if he knew Count Pisani, and on his answering in the affirmative, I requested him to accompany me there. We soon arrived at the Pisani palace. I met the Delfinis, but no Alceste. I spoke to the countess. I listened to several stories about her lap-dog; I even anticipated her ancient cavalier in picking up her glove. I ventured to inquire after Alceste. They believed she was not quite well. I quitted the palace, and repaired again to the magical window. Darkness and silence alone greeted me. I returned home, more gloomy than anxious.

In the morning, Lausanne brought me a letter. I broke the seal with a trembling hand and with a faint blush. I guessed the writer. The words seemed traced by love. I read.

"I renounce our vows, I retract my sacred pledge, I deliver to the winds our fatal love.

"Pity me, Contarini, hate me, despise me, but forget me.

"Why do I write? Why do I weep? I am nothing, O! I am nothing. I am blotted out of this fair creation, and the world that should bring me so many joys, brings me only despair.

"Do not hate me, Contarini, do not hate me. Do not hate one who adores you. Yes! adore —for even at this dread moment, when I renounce your love, let me, let me pour forth my adoration.

"Am I insensible? am I unworthy of the felicity, that for an instant we thought might be mine? O! Contarini, no one is worthy of you, and yet I fondly believe my devotion might compensate for my imperfectness.

"To be the faithful companion of his life, to be the partner of his joy and sorrow, to sympathize with his glory, and to solace his grief—I ask no more, I ask no more thou Heaven! Wilt thou not smile upon me? Wilt thou, for whom I sacrifice so much, wilt thou not pity me?

"All is silent. There is no sign. No heavenly messenger tells me I may be happy. Alas! alas! I ask too much, I ask too much. It is too great a prize. I feel it, I believe it. My unworthiness is great, but I am its victim.

"Contarini, let this console you. I am unworthy of you. Heaven has declared I am unworthy of you. Were I worthy of you, Heaven would not be cruel. O! Contarini, let this console you. You are destined for higher joys. Think not of me, Contarini, think not of me, and I—I will be silent.

"Silent! and where? O! world, that I now feel that I could love, beautiful, beautiful world—thou art not for me, thou art not for me, and Heaven, Heaven, to whom I offer so much, surely, surely, in this agony it will support me.

"I must write, although my pen refuse to inscribe my wo; I must write, although my fast-flowing tears bathe out the record of my misery. O! my God! for one moment uphold me. Let the future at least purchase me one moment of present calm! Let me spare, at least, him! Let me at least, in this last act of my love, testify my devotion by concealing my despair.

"You must know all, Contarini, you must know all. You must know all, that you may not hate me. Think me not light, think me not capricious. It is my constancy that is fatal, it is my duty that is my death.

"You love our country, Contarini, you love our Italy. Fatal, fatal Italy! O! Contarini, fly, fly away from us. Cross again those Alps that Heaven frowned upon you as you passed. Unhappy country! I am the victim of thy usages, who was born to breathe amid thy beauty. You know the customs of this land. The convent is our school—it leads to the cloister, that is too often our doom. I was educated at a Tuscan convent. I purchased my release from it, like many of my friends, and the price was my happiness, which I knew not then how to prize. The day that I quitted the convent, I was the betrothed bride of Grimani Delfini. I was not then terrified by that, the memory of which now makes me shudder. It is a common, though an unhallowed incident.

"I entered that world of which I had thought so much. My mind developed with my increased sphere of knowledge. Let me be brief. I soon could not contemplate without horror the idea of being the bride of a man I could not love. There was no refuge. I postponed, by a thousand excuses, our union. I had recourse to a thousand expedients to dissolve it. Vain struggling of a slave! In my frenzy, the very day that you entered Italy, I returned to Florence on the excuse of visiting a friend, and secretly devoted myself to the cloister. The abbess, allured by the prospect of attaining my property for her institution, became my confidant, and I returned to Venice only to make in secret the necessary preparations for quitting it for ever.

"The Delfinis were on the Brenta. I repaired one day to the villa which you visited, and which, though uninhabited, became, from having been the favourite residence of my father, a frequent object of my visits. As I walked along the terrace, I perceived for a moment and at a distance, a stranger crossing the lawn. I retired into the chapel, where I remained more than an hour. I quitted the chapel and walked to the temple. I was attracted by some writing on the wall. I read it, and although I could ascribe to it no definite meaning, I could not help musing over it. I sat down in a chair at the head of the table. Whether I were tired by the walk, or overpowered by the heat, I know not, but an unaccustomed drowsiness crept over my limbs, and I fell asleep. I not only fell asleep, but, O! Contarini, I dreamed, and my dream was wonderful and strange.

"I found myself alone in the cloisters of a convent, and I heard afar the solemn chant of an advancing procession. It became louder and louder, and soon I perceived the nuns advancing, with the abbess at their head. And the abbess came forward to claim me, and to my horror, her countenance was that of Grimani Delfini. And I struggled to extricate myself from her grasp, and suddenly the stranger of the morning rushed in and caught me in his arms, and the cloister melted away, and I found myself in a beautiful country, and I woke.

"The sun had set. I returned home, pensive and wayward. Never had I thought of my unhappy situation with more unhappiness. And each night the figure of the stranger appeared to me in my dreams, and each day I procrastinated my return to Florence. And in the agitation which these strange dreams produced, I determined to go and pray at the tombs of my fathers. I quitted the villa Delfini with a single female attendant, and returned to it the same day. I entered the church through a private door from the adjoining building, which was a house of charity founded by our family.

"You know the rest, Contarini, you know the rest. We met. The stranger of my dreams stood before me. My heart before that meeting was already yours, and when you whispered to me that you too—

"Wo! wo! why are we not happy! You said that Heaven had brought us together. Alas! Contarini, Heaven, Heaven has parted us. I avoided you, Contarini, I flew from the spell which each instant grew stronger. You sought me. I yielded. Yes! I yielded, but long vigils shall atone for that fatal word.

"Go, Contarini, go forth in glory and in pride. I will pray for you, I will ever think of you, I will ever think of my best, my only beloved. All the prosperity human imagination can devise, and heavenly love can grant, hover over you! You will be happy, you must be happy. For my sake you will be happy—and I—I am alone, but I am alone with my Redeemer, "ALCESTE.

"Ere you have received this, I shall have crossed the Apennines—pursuit is hopeless; and my Contarini will, I am sure, respect my vow."

It was read. My spirit was never more hushed in my life—I was quite calm. She might be in a convent, and it might be necessary to burn the convent down, and both of us might probably perish in the flames. But what was death to the threatened desolation? I sent for Lausanne. "Lausanne," I said, "I have a very high opinion of your talents and energy. I have hitherto refrained from putting them to the test, for particular reasons. A circumstance has occurred in which I require not only their greatest exertion, but devotion and fidelity. If you accomplish my wish, you are no longer my servant, you are my friend for life. If you fail, it matters little, for I shall not survive. But if you betray me, Lausanne—" and I looked through his very soul.

"The consequences may be fatal to me. I understand you. When I entered your service, you are under a mistake if you consider my fidelity restricted."

"It is well; I place implicit trust in you. Signora Contarini has quitted Venice suddenly. Her present abode is a secret. She informs me that she has departed for Tuscany, and is by this time in a convent. This may be to mislead me, or to gain time—I wish to ascertain it."

"There will be no difficulty, my lord," said Lausanne, with a smile. "There are no secrets in Venice to the rich."

"It is well. I shall remain in this room until I hear from you. I care not how much is expended. Away; and for God's sake, Lausanne, bring me good news."

XIV.

I WALKED up and down the room without stopping. Not an idea crossed my mind. In two hours Lausanne returned.

"Well, well?" I exclaimed.

"There is, I think, little doubt that the signora departed for the villa Delfini. She may now have quitted it. I sent Tita to the palace, as he is acquainted with the household. This is all he could elicit."

"The gondola, the gondola. Rest you here, Lausanne, and let me know when I return what ships are about to leave the port. Tell the banker I shall want money—a considerable sum; two thousand sequins; and let the bills be ready for my signature. And, Lausanne," I added in a low tone, "I may require a priest. Have your eye upon some fellow who will run over the ceremony without asking questions. If I be any time absent, say I have gone to Trieste."

My gondoliers skimmed along. We were soon at Fusina. I shook my purse to the postillion. The horses were ready in an instant. I took Tita with me, as he knew the servants. We dashed off at a rate which is seldom achieved on those dull, sandy roads. We hurried on for three or four hours. I told Tita to have his eye for any of the Delfini household. As we were passing the gate of the villa of the temple, he turned round on the box and said, "By the blood of the holy Baptist, your excellency, there is the little Maria, Signora Alceste's attendant. She just now entered that side door. I knew her by the rose-coloured ribands which I gave her last carnival."

"Did she see us?"

"I think not, for the baggage would have smiled."

"Drive back a hundred yards."

It was sunset. I got out of the carriage, and stole into the gardens of the villa unperceived. I could see no lights in the building. From this I inferred that Alceste was perhaps only paying a farewell visit to her father's house. I ran along the terrace, I observed no one. I gained the chapel. I instinctively trod very lightly. I glanced in at the window. I perceived a form kneeling before the altar. There was a single candle. The kneeling figure leaned back with clasped hands. The light fell upon the countenance. I beheld the face of Alceste Contarini.

I opened the door gently, but it roused her. I entered.

"I come," I said, "to claim my bride."

She screamed, she jumped upon the altar, and clung to the great ebony cross. It was the same figure, and the same attitude, that I beheld in my vision in the church.

"Alceste," I said, "you are mine. There is no power in heaven or earth, there is no infernal influence that can prevent you from being mine. You are as much part of me as this arm with which I now embrace you." I tore her from the cross, I carried her fainting form out of the chapel.

The moon had risen. I rested on a bank, and watched with blended passion and anxiety her closed eyes. She was motionless, and her white arms drooped down apparently without life. She breathed, yes! she breathed. That large eye opened, and darkened into light. She gazed around with an air of vacancy. A smile, a faint, sweet smile played upon her face. She slightly stretched her beautiful frame, as if again to feel her existence, and moved her beautiful arms, as if to try whether she yet retained power over her limbs. Again she smiled, and exclaiming "Contarini!" threw them round my neck.

"O! my Alceste, my long-promised Alceste, you are indeed mine."

"I am yours, Contarini. Do with me what you like."

XV.

WE walked to the temple, in order that she might compose herself before her journey. I sat down in the same chair, but not alone. Alceste was in my arms. Happiness is indeed tranquil, for our joy was full, and we were silent. At length I whispered to her that we must go. She rose, and we were about to leave the temple, when she would go back and kiss my inscription.

She remembered the maid, whom I had forgotten. I sent Tita to tell his friend that a carriage had arrived from Madame Malbrizzi's for his mistress, who was obliged suddenly to return, and that she was to remain behind. I wrapped Alceste in my cloak and placed her in my arms in the carriage, and then returned to Venice.

The gondola glided swiftly to my palace. I carried Alceste out, and bore her in my arms to her apartment. She entreated that I would not, for a moment, quit her. I was obliged therefore to receive Lausanne's report at the door. There was no vessel immediately about to depart, but a ship had quitted the port that morning for Candia, and was still beating about in the offing. He had himself seen the captain, who was content to take passengers, provided they would come out to him. This suited my plans. Lausanne had induced the captain to lie-to till the morning. A priest, he told me, was waiting.

I broke to Alceste, lying exhausted upon the sofa, the necessity of our instant departure, and our instant union. She said it was well; that she should never be at ease till she had quitted Venice, and that she was ready. I postponed our marriage until the night, and insisted upon her taking some refreshment, but she could not eat. I gave directions to Lausanne to prepare for our instant departure. I resolved to take Tita with me, with whom I was well pleased.

I was anxious about the marriage, because, although I believed it invalid in a Catholic country withou a dispensation, it would, as I conceived, hold good in Protestant law. I was careful of the honour of the Contarinis, and at this moment, was not unmindful of the long line of northern ancestry, which I did not wish my child to disgrace.

The ingenuity of Lausanne was always remarkable at conjunctures like the present. The magic of his character was his patience. This made him quicker and readier, and more successful than all other men. He prepared every thing, and anticipated wants of which we could not think.

Two hours before midnight, I was united, by the forms of the Catholic church, to Alceste Contarini, the head of the most illustrious house in Europe, and the heiress of a fortune, which, in spite of its decay, was not unworthy of her birth. Two servants were the only witnesses of an act, to fulfil which she imagined herself to peril her eternal welfare, and which exercised a more certain and injurious influence over her worldly fortunes and reputation.

At daybreak, Lausanne roused me, saying that the wind was favourable, and we must be off. He had already despatched Tita to the ship with all our baggage. I rose, wrote to my banker, informing him that I should be absent some time, and requesting him to manage every thing for my credit, and then I kissed my still sleeping wife. The morning light fell upon her soft face. A slight flush melted away as I gazed upon her, and she opened her eyes and smiled. Never had she looked more beautiful. I would have given half my fortune to have been permitted to remain at Venice in tranquillity and peace.

But doubly sweet is the love that is gained by danger, and guarded by secrecy. All was prepared. We stepped, perhaps for the last time, into a gondola. The gray sea was before us, we soon reached the ship, Tita and the captain were standing at the ladder-head. The moment that we embarked the sails were set, and a dashing breeze bore us along out of the gulf. Long ere noon, that Venice, with its towers and cupolas, which I had forfeited so much to visit, and all those pleasant palaces wherein I could have lived forever, had faded into the blue horizon.

XVI.

The ship was an imperial merchant brig. The wife of the captain was on board, a great convenience for Alceste, who was without female attendance, and with the exception of some clothes the provident Lausanne had obtained from Tita's sister, without a wardrobe. But these are light hardships for love, and the wind was favourable, and the vessel fleet. We were excellent sailors, and bore the voyage without inconvenience, and the novelty of the scene, and the beauty of the sea amused and interested us.

I imbibed from this voyage a taste for a sea life, which future wanderings on the waters have only confirmed. I never find the sea monotonous. The variations of weather, the ingenious tactics, the rich sunsets, the huge, strange fish, the casual meetings, and the original and racy character of mariners, and perhaps also the frequent sight of land, which offers itself in the Mediterranean, afford me constant amusement. I do not think that there is in the world a kinder-hearted and more courteous person than a common sailor. As for their attentions to Alceste they were even delicate, and I am sure, that although a passionate lover, I might have taken many a hint from their vigilant solicitude. Whenever she was present their boisterous mirth was instantly repressed. She never walked the deck that a ready hand was not quick in clearing her path of any impediments, and ere I could even discover she was weary, their watchful eyes anticipated her wants, and they proffered her a rude but welcome seat. Ah! what a charming voyage was this, when my only occupation was to look upon an ever-smiling face, and to be assured a thousand times each hour, that I was the cause of all this happiness.

Lausanne called me one morning on deck. Our port was in sight. I ran up; I beheld the highlands of Candia—a rich, wild group of lofty blue mountains, and in the centre, the snowy peak of Mount Ida. As we approached, the plain, extending from the base of the mountains to the coast, became perceptible, and soon a town and harbour.

We were surrounded by boats full of beings in bright and strange costumes. A new world, a new language, a new religion, were before us. Our deck was covered with bearded and turbaned men. We stared at each other in all this picturesque confusion, but Lausanne, and especially Tita, who spoke Greek, and knew Candia well, saved us from all anxiety. We landed, and, thanks to being in a Turkish province, there was no difficulty about passports, with which we were unprovided, and a few sequins saved the captain from explaining why his passengers were not included in his ship's papers. We landed, and were lodged in the house of a Greek, who officiated as a European vice consul.

The late extraordinary incidents of our lives had followed each other with such rapidity, that when we woke in the morning, we could scarcely believe that it was not at all a dream. We looked round our chamber with its strange furniture, and stared at the divans, and small, high windows, shadowed with painted glass, and smiled. Our room was darkened, but, at the end, opened an arch bright in the sun. Beautiful strange plants quivered in the light. The perfume of orange-trees filled our chamber, and the bees were clustering in the scarlet flowers of the pomegranate. Amid the pleasing distraction of these sweet sounds and scents we distinguished the fall of a fountain.

We stole forward to the arch like a prince and princess just disenchanted in a fairy tale. We stepped into a court paved with marble, and full of rare shrubs. The fountain was in the centre. Around it were delicate mats of Barbary, and small bright Persian carpets; and crouching on a scarlet cushion was a white gazelle.

I stepped out, and found our kind host, who spoke Italian. I sent his lovely daughter, Alexina, whose cheeks were like a cleft of pomegranate, to my wife. As for myself, by Lausanne's advice, I took a Turkish bath, which is the most delightful thing in the world, and when I was reduced to a jelly, I repaired to our host's divan, where his wife, and three other daughters, all equally beautiful, and dressed in long flowing robes of different coloured velvets richly embroidered, and caps of the same material, with tassels of gold, and covered with pearls, came forward. One gave me a pipe seven feet long, another fed me with sweetmeats, a third pressed her hand to her heart, as she presented me coffee in a small cup of porcelain, resting in a filagree frame, and a child, who sparkled like a fairy, bent her knee, as she proffered me a vase of sherbet. I felt like a pasha, and the good father translated my compliments.

I thought that Alceste would never appear, and I sent Lausanne to her door fifty times. At length she came, and in a Greek dress, which they had insisted upon her wearing. I thought we should have both expired with laughing. We agreed that we were perfectly happy.

This was all very delightful, but it was necessary to arrange our plans. I consulted Lausanne. I wished to engage a residence in a retired part of the island. We spoke to our host. He had a country house, which would exactly suit us, and desired a tenant. I sent Lausanne immediately to examine it. It was only fifteen miles away. His report was most satisfactory, and I, at once, closed with the consul's offer.

The house was a long, low building, in the eastern style, with plenty of rooms. It was situate on a very gentle, green hill, the last undulation of a chain of Mount Ida, and was perfectly embowered with gardens, and plantations of olive and orange. It was about two miles from the sea, which appeared before us in a wild and rocky bay. A peasant, who cultivated the gardens, with his wife and children, two daughters just breaking into womanhood, and a young son, were offered to us as servants. Nothing could be more convenient. Behold us at length at rest!

XVII.

I HAVE arrived at a period of my life which, although it afforded me the highest happiness that was ever the lot of man, of which the recollection is now my never-ceasing solace, and to enjoy the memory of which is alone worth existence, cannot prove very interesting to those who have been sufficiently engaged by my history to follow me to my retirement in ancient Crete.

My life was now monotonous, for my life was only love.

I know not the palling of passion, of which some write. I have loved only once, and the recollection of the being to whom I was devoted, fills me at this moment with as much rapture, as when her virgin charms were first yielded to my embrace. I cannot comprehend the sneers of witty rakes, at what they call constancy. If beings are united by any other consideration but love, constancy is of course impossible, and I think, unnecessary. To a man who is in love, the thought of another woman is uninteresting, if not repulsive. Constancy is human nature. Instead of love being the occasion of all the misery of this world, as is sung by fantastic bards, I believe that the misery of this world is occasioned by there not being love enough. This opinion, at any rate, appears more logical. Happiness is only to be found in a recurrence to the principles of human nature, and these will prompt very simple manners. For myself, I believe that permanent union of the sexes should be early encouraged; nor do I conceive that general happiness can ever flourish but in societies where it is the custom for all the males to marry at eighteen. This custom, I am informed, is not unusual in the United States of America, and its consequence is a simplicity of manners, and a purity of conduct, which Europeans cannot comprehend, but to which they must ultimately have recourse. Primeval barbarism, and extreme civilization, must arrive at the same results. Men, under those circumstances, are actuated by their organization; in the first instance, instinctively; in the second, philosophically. At present, we are all in the various gradations of the intermediate state of corruption.

I could have lived with Alceste Contarini in a solitude for ever. I desired nothing more than to enjoy existence with such a companion. I would have communicated to her all my thoughts and feelings. I would have devoted to her solitary ear the poetry of my being. Such a life might not suit others. Others influenced by a passion not less ardent, may find its flame fed by the cares of life, cherished by its duties and its pleasures, and flourishing amid the travail of society. All is an affair of organization. Ours would differ. Among all men, there are some points of similarity and sympathy. There are few alike, there are some perfectly unlike the mass. The various tribes that people this globe in all probability, spring from different animals. Until we know more of ourselves, what use are our systems? For myself, I can conceive nothing more idle or more useless than what is styled moral philosophy. We speculate upon the character of man; we divide and we subdivide; we have our generals, our sages, our statesmen. There is not a modification of mind that is not mapped in our great atlas of intelligence. We cannot be wrong, because we have studied the past, and we are famous for discovering the future when it has taken place. Napoleon is first consul, and would found a dynasty. There is no doubt of it. Read my character of Cromwell. But what use is the discovery, when the consul is already tearing off his republican robe, and snatching the imperial diadem? And suppose, which has happened, and may and will happen again, suppose a being of a different organization to Napoleon or Cromwell placed in the same situation,—a being gifted with a combination of intelligence hitherto unknown, where then is our moral philosophy, our nice study of human nature? How are we to speculate upon results, which are to be produced by unknown causes? What we want is to discover the character of a man at his birth, and found his education upon his nature. The whole system of moral philosophy is a delusion, fit only for the play of sophists in an age of physiological ignorance.

I leave these great speculations for the dreariness of future hours. Alceste calls me to the golden sands, whither it is our wont to take our sunset walk.

A Grecian sunset! The sky is like the neck of a dove, the rocks and waters are bathed with a violet light. Each moment it changes; each moment it shifts into more graceful and more gleaming shadows. And the thin white moon is above all, the thin white moon, followed by a single star—like a lady by a page.

XVIII.

We had no books, no single source of amusement but our own society, and yet the day always appeared a moment. I did indeed contrive to obtain for Alceste what was called a mandolin, and which, from its appearance, might have been an ancient lyre. But it was quite unnecessary. My tongue never stopped the whole day. I told Alceste every thing. All about my youthful scrapes and fancies, and Musæus and my battle, and Winter, and Christiana, and the confounded tragedy, and, of course, Manstein. If I for a moment ceased, she always said "go on." On I went, and told the same stories over again, which she reheard with the same interest. The present was so delightful to me, that I cared little to talk about the past, and always avoided the future. But Alceste would sometimes turn the conversation to what might happen, and as she now promised to heighten our happiness by bringing us a beautiful stranger to share our delightful existence, the future began to interest even me.

I had never written to my father since I arrived at Paris. Every time I drew a bill I expected to find my credit revoked, but it was not so. And I therefore willingly concluded that Lausanne apprized him of every thing, and that he thought fit not to interfere. I had never written to my father, because I cannot dissemble, and as my conduct ever since I quitted France had been one continued violation of his commands and wishes, why, correspondence was difficult, and could not prove pleasing. But Alceste would talk about my father, and it was therefore necessary to think of him. She shuddered at the very name of Italy, and willingly looked forward to a settlement in the north. For myself, I was exceedingly happy, and my reminiscences of my fatherland were so far from agreeable, that I was careless as to the future, and although I already began to entertain the possibility of a return, I still wished to pass some considerable time of our youth inviolate by the vulgar cares of life, and under the influence of a glowing sky.

In the mean time we rambled about the mountains on our little, stout Candiote horses, or amused ourselves in adorning our residence. We made a new garden. We collected every choice flower, and rare bird, and beautiful animal that we could assemble together. Alceste was wild for a white gazelle ever since we had seen one in the consul's court. They came from a particular part of Arabia, and are rare. Yet one was obtained, and two of its fawn-coloured brethren. I must confess that we found these elegant and poetical companions extremely troublesome and stupid. They are the least sentimental and domestic of all creatures. The most sedulous attention will not attach them to you, and I do not believe they are ever fairly tame. I dislike them, in spite of their liquid eyes and romantic reputation, and infinitely prefer what are now my constant and ever delightful company, some fine, faithful, honest, intelligent, thorough-bred English dogs.

We had now passed nearly eight months in this island. The end of the year was again advancing. O! the happy, the charming evenings, when fearing for my Alceste, that it grew too cool to walk, we sat within the house, and the large lamp was lit, and the faithful Lausanne brought me my pipe, and the confounded gazelle kicked it over, and the grinning Tita handed us our coffee, and my dear, dear Alceste sang me some delicious Venetian melody, and then I left off smoking, and she left off singing, and we were happier and happier every day.

Talk of fame and romance—all the glory and adventure in the world are not worth one single hour of domestic bliss! It sounds like a claptrap, but the solitary splendour with which I am now surrounded, tells me, too earnestly, it is truth.

XIX.

The hour approached that was to increase my happiness, my incredible happiness. Blessed, infinitely blessed as I was, bountiful Heaven was about to shower upon me a new and fruitful joy. In a few days I was to become a father. We had obtained from the town all necessary attendance: an Italian physician, whose manner gave us confidence, a sage woman of great reputation, were at our house. I had myself been cautious that my treasure should commit no imprudence. We were full of love and hope. My Alceste was not quite well. The physician recommended great quiet. She was taking her siesta, and I stole from her side, because my presence ever excited her, and she could not slumber.

I strolled down to the bay, and mused over the character of a father. My imagination dwelt only upon this idea. I discovered, as my revery proceeded, the fine relations that must subsist between a parent and a child. Such thoughts had made no impression upon me before. I thought of my own father, and the tears stole down my cheek. I vowed to return to him immediately, and give ourselves up to his happiness. I prayed to Heaven to grant me a man-child. I felt a lively confidence that he would be choicely gifted. I resolved to devote myself entirely to his education. My imagination wandered in dreams of his perfect character, of his high accomplishments, his noble virtues, his exalted fame. I conceived a philosopher who might influence his race, a being to whom the regeneration of his kind was perhaps allotted.

My thoughts had rendered me unconscious of the hour; the sun had set without my observation; the growing twilight called me to myself. I looked up, I beheld in the distance Alceste. I was surprised, displeased, alarmed. I could not conceive any thing more imprudent than her coming forth in the evening, and in her situation. I ran forward to reprimand her with a kiss, to fold her shawl more closely round her, and bear her in my arms to the house. I ran forward, speaking at the same time. She faintly smiled. I reached her. Lo! she was not there! A moment before, she was on the wide sands. There was no cavern near in which she could have entered. I stood amazed, thunderstruck. I shouted "Alceste."

The shout was answered. I ran back. Another shout; Tita came to me running. His agitated face struck me with awe. He could not speak; he seized my arm and dragged me along. I ran to the house. I did not dare to inquire the cause. Lausanne met me at the threshold. His countenance was despair. I stared like a bewildered man, I rushed to her room. Yet I remember the group leaning round our bed. They moved aside. I saw Alceste. She did not see me. Her eyes were closed, her face pale and changed, her mouth had fallen.

"What," I said, "what is all this? Doctor, doctor, how is she?"

The physician shook his head.

I could not speak. I wrung my hands, more from the inability of thought and speech, than grief, by which I was not influenced.

Speak, speak!" I at length said, "is she dead?"

"My lord——"

"Speak, speak, speak!"

"It appears to me to be desperate.

"It is impossible! Dead! She cannot be dead. Bleed her, bleed her, sir, before me. Dead! Did you say dead? Nonsense, nonsense! Alceste, Alceste, speak to me. Say you are not dead, only say you are not dead. Bleed her, sir, bleed her."

To humour me, he took up his lancet and opened another vein. A few dull drops oozed out.

"Ah!" I exclaimed, "See! she bleeds! She is not dead. Alceste, Alceste! you are not dead! Lausanne, do something, Lausanne. For God's sake, Lausanne, save her. Do something, Lausanne. My good Lausanne, do something!"

He affected to feel her pulse. I staggered about the room, wringing my hands.

"Is she better?" I inquired.

No one answered.

"Doctor, save her! Tell me she is better, and I give you half—my whole fortune."

The poor physician shook his head. He attempted nothing. I rushed to Lausanne, and seized his arm.

"Lausanne, I can trust you. Tell me the truth. Is it all over?"

"It has too long been over."

"Ah!" I waved my hands, and shrieked, and fell.

XX.

When my self-consciousness was restored, I found myself in another room. I was lying in a divan in the arms of Lausanne. I had forgotten every thing. I called Alceste. Then the remembrance rushed into my brain.

"Is it true," I said, "Lausanne, is it true?"

His silence was an answer. I rose, and walked up and down the room once or twice, and then I said, in a low voice, "Take me to the body, Lausanne."

I leaned upon his arm and entered the chamber of our joys. Even as I entered, I indulged the wild hope that I should find it unoccupied. I could not believe it. Yes, yes, she was dead!

Tall candles were burning in the room; the walls were hung with solemn drapery. I advanced to the bedside. I took her hand. I motioned to Lausanne to retire. We were alone, alone once more. But how alone? I doubted of every thing. I doubted of my existence. I thought my heart would burst. I wondered why any thing still went on. Why was not all over? I looked round with idiot eyes, and opened mouth. A horrid contortion was chiselled on my face.

Suddenly I seized the corpse in my arms, and fiercely embraced it. I thought I could reanimate it. I felt so much I thought I could reanimate it. I struggled with death. Was she dead? Was she really dead? It had a heavy leaden feel. I let her drop from my arms. She dropped like a lifeless trunk. I looked round with a silly grin.

It was morning time. The flames of the candles looked haggard. There was a Turkish dagger in the closet. I remembered it. I ran to the closet. I cut off her long tresses. I rolled them round my neck. I locked the door. I stole out of the window. I cunningly watched to observe whether I were followed. No one was stirring, or no one suspected me. I scudded away fleetly. I rushed up the hills. I never stopped. For hours I could never have stopped. I have a faint recollection of chasms, and precipices, and falling waters. I leaped every thing. I found myself at length on a peak of Mount Ida.

A wide view of the ocean opened before me. As I gazed upon it, my mind became inflamed,—the power of speech was restored to me,—the poetry of my grief prevailed.

"Fatal ocean! fatal ocean!" I exclaimed,—"A curse upon thy waves, for thou wafted us to death. Green hills! green valleys! a blight upon thy trees and pastures, for she cannot gaze upon them! And thou, red sun! her blood is upon thy beams. Halt in thy course, red sun! halt! and receive my curse!

"Our house has fallen, the glorious house has fallen; and the little ones may now rise. Eagle! fly away and tell my father he is avenged. For lo! Venice has been my doom, and here on this toppling crag, I seal all things, and thus devote Contarini Fleming to the infernal gods."

I sprang forward, I felt myself in the air. My brain spun round, my sight deserted me, I fell.

XXI.

When I can again recall existence, I found myself in my own house. I was reclining on the divan propped up by cushions. My left arm was in a sling: my head bandaged. I looked around me without thought, and then I relapsed into apathy. Lausanne was in the room, and passed before me. I observed him, but did not speak. He brought me refreshment, which I took without notice. The room was darkened. I knew nothing of the course of time, nor did I care or inquire. Sometimes Lausanne quitted the apartment, and then Tita took his place. Sometimes he returned, and changed my bandages and my dress, and I fell asleep. Awake I had no thought, and slumbering I had no dreams.

I remained in this state, as I afterward learned, six weeks. One day I looked up, and seeing Tita, spoke in a faint voice, and asked for Lausanne. He ran immediately for him, and while he was a moment absent, I rose from my couch and tore the curtain from the window. Lausanne entered and came up to me, and would have again led me to my seat, but I bid him "lighten the room."

I desired to walk forth into the air, and leaning on his arm, I came out of the house. It was early morn, and I believe the sense of the fresh air had attracted and revived me. I stood for a moment vacantly gazing upon the distant bay, but I was so faint that I could not stand, and Spiro, the little Greek boy, ran and brought me a carpet and a cushion, and I sat down. I asked for a mirror, which was unwillingly afforded me; but I insisted upon it. I viewed without emotion my emaciated form, and my pallid, sunken visage. My eyes were dead and hollow, my cheek-bones prominent and sharp, my head shaven, and covered with a light turban. Nevertheless, the feeling of the free, sweet air was grateful, and from this moment I commenced gradually to recover.

I never spoke, except to express my wants, but my appetite returned, my strength increased, and each day, with Lausanne's assistance, I walked for a short time in the garden. My arm, which had been broken, resumed its power; my head, which had been severely cut, healed. I ventured to walk only with the aid of a stick. Gradually I extended my course, and, in time, I reached the seaside. There, in a slight recess formed by a small headland, I would sit with my back against a high rock, feel comforted that earth was hidden from my sight, and gaze for hours in vacancy upon the ocean and the sky. At sunset I stole home. I found Lausanne always about, evidently expecting me When he perceived me returning, he was soon by my side, but by a way that I could not observe him, and, without obtrusion or any appearance of officiousness, led, or rather carried me to my dwelling.

One morning I bent my way to a small green valley, which opened on the other side of our gardens. It had been one of our most favourite haunts. I know not why I resorted to it this morning, for, as yet, her idea had never crossed my mind, any more than her name my lips. I had an indefinite conviction that I was a lost and fallen man. I knew that I had once been happy, that I had once mingled in a glorious existence; but I felt with regard to the past as if it were another system of being, as if I had suddenly fallen from a star, and lighted on a degenerate planet.

I was in our valley, our happy valley. I stood still, and my memory seemed to return. The tears stole down my face. I remembered the cluster of orange trees under which we often sat. I plucked some leaves, and I pressed them to my lips. Yet I was doubtful, uncertain, incredulous. I scarcely knew who I was. Not indeed that I was unable to feel my identity, not indeed that my intelligence was absolutely incapable of fulfilling its office, but there seemed a compact between my body and my mind that existence should proceed without thought.

I descended into the vale. A new object attracted my attention. I approached it without suspicion. A green mount supported a stone, on which was boldly, but not rudely sculptured,

"Alceste, Countess Contarini Fleming."

A date recorded her decease.

"It must have been many years ago," was my first impression; "I am Contarini Fleming, and I remember Alceste well, but not in this country, surely not in this country. And yet those orange trees—

"My wife, my lost, my darling wife, O! why am I alive! I thought that I was dead! I thought that I had flung myself from the mountain-top to join you—and it was all a dream!"

I threw myself upon the tomb, and my tears poured forth in torrents, and I tore up the flowers that flourished upon the turf, and kissed them, and tossed them in the air.

There was a rose, a beautiful white rose, delicate and fragrant; and I gathered it, and it seemed to me like Alceste. And I sat gazing upon this fair flower, and as my vision was fixed upon it, the past grew up before me, and each moment I more clearly comprehended it. The bitterness of my grief overcame me. I threw away the rose, and a moment after, I was sorry to have lost it. I looked for it. It was not at my feet. My desire for the flower increased. I rose from the tomb, I looked around for the lost treasure. My search led me to the other side of the tablet, and I read the record of the death of my still-born son.

XXII.

"We must leave this place, Lausanne, and at once."

His eye brightened when I spoke.

"I have seen all that you have done, Lausanne, it is well, very well. I owe you much. I would have given much for her hair, more than I can express. But you are not to blame. You had much to do."

He left the room for a moment, and returned,—returned with the long, the beautiful tresses of my beloved.

"O! you have made me so happy. I never thought that I should again know what joy was. How considerate! How very good!"

He broke to me gently that he had found the tresses around my neck. I rubbed my forehead, I summoned my scattered thoughts,—"I remember something," I replied, "but I thought it was a dream. I fancied that in a dream I had quitted the house."

He told me all. He told me that, after three days' search, he had found me among the mountains, hanging to the rough side of the precipice, shattered, stark, and senseless. The bushes had caught my clothes, and prevented a fatal fall.

XXIII.

A ship was about to leave the port for Leghorn. And why not go to Leghorn? Anywhere but Venice. Our arrangements were soon made. I determined to assent to the request of his father in taking little Spiro, who was a favourite of Alceste, and had charge of her gazelles. A Greek father is very willing to see his son anywhere but among the Turks. I promised his family not only to charge myself with his future fortunes, but also to remit them an annual allowance through the consul, provided they cherished the tomb of their late mistress, and in a fortnight I was again on board.

The mountains of Candia were long in sight, but I avoided them. Our voyage was very long, although not unpleasant. We were often becalmed. The air and change of scene benefited me much. I wonderfully resumed my old habits of revery, and as I paced the deck, which I did all day without ceasing, I mused over the past with feelings of greater solace than I ever anticipated could associate with it. I was consoled by the remembrance of our perfect love. I could not recall on either of our parts a single fretful word, a single occasion on which our conduct had afforded either of us an anxious, or even annoying moment. We never had enjoyed those lovers' quarrels which are said to be so sweet. Her sufferings had been intense, but they had been brief. It would have been consolatory to have received her last breath, yet my presence might have occasioned her greater agony. The appearance of her spirit assured me that, at the moment of her departure, her last thought was for me. The conviction of her having enjoyed positive happiness supported me. I was confident that had it been possible to make the decision, she would not have yielded her brief and beautiful career for length of days unillumined by the presence of him who remained to consecrate her memory by his enduring love—perhaps by his enduring page.

Ah! old feelings returned to me. I perceived that it was impossible to exist without some object, and fame and poetic creation offered themselves to my void heart. I remembered that the high calling to which I was devoted had been silently neglected. I recollected the lofty education and loftier results that travel was to afford, and for which travel was to prepare me. I reminded myself that I had already proved many new passions, become acquainted with many new modifications of feeling, and viewed many new objects. My knowledge of man and nature was very much increased. My mind was full of new thoughts, and crowded with new images.

As I thus mused, that separation of the mere individual from the universal poet, which ever occurred in these high communings, again took place. My own misfortunes seemed but petty incidents to one who could exercise an illimitable power over the passions of his kind. If, amid the common losses of common life, the sympathy of a single friend can bear its balm, could I find no solace, even for my great bereavement, in the love of nations, and the admiration of ages?

Thus reflecting, I suddenly dashed into invention, and in my almost constant walks on deck, I poured forth a crowd of characters, and incidents, and feelings, and images, and moulded them into a coherent, and, as I hoped, a beautiful form. I longed for the moment when I could record them on a scroll more lasting then my memory, and upheld by this great purpose, I entered with a calm, if not cheerful countenance, the famous port of Leghorn.

PART THE FOURTH.

I.

I WAS at length at Florence. The fair city so much vaunted by poets at first greatly disappointed me. I could not reconcile myself to those unfinished churches like barns, and those gloomy palaces like prisons. The muddy Arno was not poetical, and the sight of the whole place and the appearance of the surrounding hills, in spite of their white villas, seemed to me confined, monotonous, and dull. Yet there is a charm in Florence, which, although difficult precisely to define, is in its influence very great and growing, and I scarcely know a place that I would prefer for a residence. I think it is the character of art, which both from ancient associations, and its present possessions, is forcibly impressed upon this city. It is full of invention. You cannot stroll fifty yards, you cannot enter a church or a palace, without being favourably reminded of the power of human thought. It is a famous memorial of the genius of the Italian middle ages, when the mind of man was in one of its spring-tides, and in which we mark so frequently what at the present day we too much underrate—the influence of individual character.

In Florence, the monuments are not only of great men, but of the greatest. You do not gaze upon the tomb of an author, who is merely a great master of composition, but of one who formed the language. The illustrious astronomer is not the discoverer of a planet, but the revealer of the whole celestial machinery. The artist and the politician are not merely the first sculptors and statesmen of their time, but the inventors of the very art and the very craft in which they excelled.

The study of the fine arts mutually assists each other. In the formation of my style, I have been perhaps more indebted to music and to painting, even than to the great masters of literary composition. The contemplation of the Venetian school had developed in me a latent love of gorgeous eloquence, dazzling incident, brilliant expression, and voluptuous sentiment. These brought their attendant imperfections, exaggeration, effeminacy, the obtrusion of art, the painful want of nature. The severe simplicity of the Tuscan masters chastened my mind. I mused over a great effect produced almost by a single mean. The picture that fixed my attention by a single group illustrating a single passion, was a fine and profitable study. I felt the power of nature delineated by a great master, and how far from necessary to enforce her influence, were the splendid accessaries with which my meditated compositions would rather have encumbered than adorned her. I began to think more of the individual than the species, rather of the motives of man, than of his conduct. I endeavoured to make myself as perfect in the dissection of his mind, as the Florentine in the anatomy of his body. Attempting to acquire the excellence of my models, I should probably have imbibed their defects; their stiff, and sombre, and arid manner, their want of variety and grace. The Roman school saved me from this, and taught me that a very chaste or severe conception might be treated in a very glowing or genial style. But after all, I prefer the Spanish to the Italian painters. I know no one to rival Murillo. I know no one who has blended with such felicity the high ideal with the extreme simplicity of nature. Later in life, I found myself in his native city, in that lovely Seville, more lovely from his fine creations than even from the orange bowers that perfume its gates, and the silver stream that winds about its plain.

I well remember the tumult of invention in which I wandered day after day amid the halls and galleries of Florence. Each beautiful face that flitted before me was a heroine, each passion that breathed upon the canvass was to be transferred to the page. I conceived at one time the plan of writing a series of works in the style of each school. The splendour of Titian, the grace of Raffaelle, the twilight tints of that magician, Guercino, alternately threw my mind into moods analogous to their creations. A portrait of Ippolyto de' Medici in the Pitti palace, of whom I knew nothing, haunted me like a ghost, and I could only lay the spectre by resolving in time to delineate the spirit of Italian feudality. The seraphic Baptist in the wilderness recalled the solitude I loved. I would have poured forth a monologue amid the mountains of Judea, had not Endymion caught my enraptured vision, and I could dream only of the bright goddess of his shadowy love.

I thought only of art. I sought the society of artists and collectors. I unconsciously adopted their jargon. I began to discourse of copies, and middle tints, and changes of style. I was in great danger of degenerating into a dilettante. Little objects as well as great, now interested me. I handled a bronze and speculated upon its antiquity. Yet even these slight pursuits exercised a beneficial tendency upon a mind wild, irregular, and undisciplined; nor do I believe that any one can long observe even fine carvings and choice medals, without his taste becoming more susceptible, and delicate, and refined.

My mind was overflowing with the accumulated meditation and experience of two years; an important interval in all lives, passed in mine in constant thought and action, and in a continual struggle with new ideas and novel passions. The desire of composition became irresistible. I recurred to the feelings with which I entered Leghorn, and from which I had been diverted amid the distraction produced by the novelty, the beauty, and the variety of surrounding objects. With these feelings, I quitted the city, and engaged the Villa Caponi, situated on a green and gentle swell of the Apennines, near the tower of Galileo.

I'

If there were any thing in the world for which I now entertained a sovereign contempt, it was my unfortunate Manstein. My most malignant critic must have yielded to me in the scorn which I lavished on that immature production, and the shame with which I even recollected its existence. No one could be more sensible of its glaring defects, for no one thought more of them, and I was so familiar with its less defective parts, that they had lost all their relish, and appeared to me as weak, and vapid, and silly as the rest. I never labour to delude myself. I never gloss over my faults. I exaggerate them. I can afford to face truth, for I feel capable of improvement. And indeed I have never yet experienced that complacency with which, it is said, some authors regard their offspring, nor do I think that this paternal fondness will ever be my agreeable lot. I am never satisfied. No sooner have I executed some conception, than my mind soars above its creation, and meditates a higher flight in a purer atmosphere. The very exercise of power only teaches me, that it may be wielded for a greater purpose.

I prepared myself for composition in a very different mood to that in which I had poured forth my fervid crudities in the garden-house. Calm and collected, I constructed characters on philosophical principles, and mused over a chain of action which should develope the system of our existence. All was art. I studied contrasts and grouping, and metaphysical analysis was substituted for anatomical delineation. I was not satisfied that the conduct of my creations should be influenced merely by the general principles of their being. I resolved that they should be the very impersonations of the moods and passions of our mind. One was ill-regulated will; another offered the formation of a moral being; materialism sparkled in the wild gayety and reckless caprice of one voluptuous girl, while spirit was vindicated in the deep devotion of a constant and enthusiastic heroine. Even the lighter temperaments were not forgotten. Frivolity smiled and shrugged his shoulders before us, and there was even a deep personification of cynic humour.

Had I executed my work in strict unison with my plan, it would doubtless have been a very dull affair. For I did not yet possess sufficient knowledge of human nature to support me in such a creation, nor was I then habituated to those metaphysical speculations, which might have in some degree compensated, by their profundity, for their want of entertainment. But nature avenged herself, and extricated me from my dilemma.

I began to write; my fancy fired, my brain inflamed; breathing forms rose up under my pen, and jostled aside the cold abstractions, whose creation had cost such long musing. In vain I endeavoured to compose without enthusiasm, in vain I endeavoured to delineate only what I had preconceived, in vain I struggled to restrain the flow of unbidden invention. All that I had seen and pondered passed before me, from the proud moment that I stood upon Mount Jura to the present ravishing hour that I returned to my long estranged art.

Every tree, every cloud, every star and mountain, every fair lake and flowing river, that had fed my fancy with their sweet suggestions in my rambling hours, now returned and illumined my pages with their brightness and their beauty. My mind teemed with similes. Thought and passion came vailed in metaphoric garb. I was delighted, I was bewildered. The clustering of their beauty seemed an evidence of poetic power: the management of these bright guests was an art of which I was ignorant. I received them all. I found myself often writing only that they might be accommodated.

I gave up to this work many long and unbroken hours. I was determined that it should not suffer from a hurried pen. I often stopped to meditate It was in writing this book, that I first learned my art. It was a series of experiments. They were at length finished, and my volumes consigned to their fate and northern publisher.

The critics treated me with more courtesy. What seemed to me odd enough then, although no puzzle now, was, that they admired what had been written in haste, and without premeditation and generally disapproved of what had cost me much forethought, and been executed with great care. It was universally declared a most unequal work, and they were right, although they could not detect the causes of the inequality. My perpetual efforts at being imaginative were highly reprobated. Now my efforts had been entirely the other way. In short, I puzzled them, and no one offered a prediction as to my future career. My book, as a whole was rather unintelligible, but parts were favourites. It was pronounced a remarkable compound of originality and dulness. These critiques, whatever might be their tenor, mattered little to me. A long interval elapsed before they reached Florence, and during that period, I had effectually emancipated myself from the thraldom of criticism.

I have observed, that after writing a book, my mind always makes a great spring. I believe that the act of composition produces the same invigorating effect upon the mind, which some exertion does upon the body. Even the writing of Manstein produced a revolution in my nature, which cannot be traced by any metaphysical analysis. In the course of a few days, I was converted from a hollow-hearted worldling into a noble philosopher. I was indeed ignorant, but I had lost the double ignorance of the Platonists, I was no longer ignorant that I was ignorant. No one could be influenced by a greater desire of knowledge, a greater passion for the beautiful, or a deeper regard for his fellow-creatures. And I well remember when, on the evening that I wrote the last sentence of this more intellectual effort, I walked out upon the terrace with that feeling of satisfaction, which accompanies the idea of a task completed; so far was I from being excited by the hope of having written a great work, that I even meditated its destruction. For, the moment it was terminated, it seemed to me that I had become suddenly acquainted with the long-concealed principles of my art, which, without doubt, had been slenderly practised in this production. My taste, as it were in an instant, became formed, and I felt the conviction, that I could now produce some lasting creation.

I thought no more of criticism. The breath of man has never influenced me much, for I depend more upon myself than upon others. I want no false fame. It would be no delight to me to be considered a prophet, were I conscious of being an impostor. I ever wish to be undeceived; but if I possess the organization of a poet, no one can prevent me from exercising my faculty, any more than he can rob the courser of his fleetness, or the nightingale of her song.

III.

After finishing my work, I read more at Florence than I have at any period of my life. Having formed the principles on which in future I intended to proceed in composition, and considering myself now qualified to decide upon other artists, I determined critically to examine the literary fiction of all countries, to ascertain how far my intentions had been anticipated, and in what degree my predecessors might assist me.

It appears to me that the age of versification has passed. The mode of composition must ever be greatly determined by the manner in which the composition can be made public. In ancient days, the voice was the medium by which we became acquainted with the inventions of a poet. In such a method, where those who listened had no time to pause, and no opportunity to think, it was necessary that every thing should be obvious. The audience who were perplexed would soon become wearied. The spirit of ancient poetry, therefore, is rather material than metaphysical. Superficial, not internal; there is much simplicity and much nature, but little passion and less philosophy. To obviate the baldness, which is the consequence of a style where the subject and the sentiments are rather intimated than developed, the poem was enriched by music, and enforced by action. Occasionally were added the enchantment of scenery, and the fascination of the dance. But the poet did not depend merely upon these brilliant accessaries. He resolved that his thoughts should be expressed in a manner different from other modes of communicating ideas. He caught a suggestion from his sister art, and invented metre. And in this modulation, he introduced a new system of phraseology, which marked him out from the crowd, and which has obtained the title of "poetic diction."

His object in this system of words was to heighten his meaning by strange phrases, and unusual constructions. Inversion was invented to clothe a commonplace with an air of novelty; vague epithets were introduced to prop up a monotonous modulation; were his meaning to be enforced, he shrank from wearisome ratiocination and the agony of precise conceptions, and sought refuge in a bold personification, or a beautiful similitude. The art of poetry was to express natural feelings in unnatural language.

Institutions ever survive their purpose, and customs govern us when their cause is extinct. And this mode of communicating poetic invention still remained, when the advanced civilization of man, in multiplying manuscripts, might have made many suspect that the time had arrived when the poet was to cease to sing, and to learn to write. Had the splendid refinement of imperial Rome not been doomed to such rapid decay, and such mortifying and degrading vicissitudes, I believe that versification would have worn out. Unquestionably that empire, in its multifarious population, scenery, creeds, and customs, offered the richest materials for emancipated fiction; materials, however, far too vast and various for the limited capacity of metrical celebration.

That beneficent Omnipotence, before which we must bow down, has so ordered it, that imitation should be the mental feature of modern Europe; and has ordained that we should adopt a Syrian religion, a Grecian literature, and a Roman law. At the revival of letters, we behold the portentous spectacle of national poets communicating their inventions in an exotic form. Conscious of the confined nature of their method, yet unable to extricate themselves from its fatal ties, they sought variety in increased artifice of diction, and substituted for the melody of the lyre the barbaric clash of rhyme.

A revolution took place in the mode of communicating thought. Now, at least, it was full time that we should have emancipated ourselves forever from sterile metre. One would have supposed that the poet who could not only write, but even print his inventions, would have felt that it was both useless and unfit that they should be communicated by a process invented when his only medium was simple recitation. One would have supposed that the poet would have rushed with desire to the new world before him, that he would have seized the new means that permitted him to revel in a universe of boundless invention; to combine the highest ideal creation with the infinite delineation of teeming nature; to unravel all the dark mysteries of our bosoms, and all the bright purposes of our being; to become the great instructer and champion of his species; and not only delight their fancy, and charm their senses, and command their will, but demonstrate their rights, illustrate their necessities, and expound the object of their existence; and all this too in a style charming and changing with its universal theme, now tender, now sportive, now earnest, now profound, now sublime, now pathetic, and substituting for the dull monotony of metre, the most various, and exquisite, and inexhaustible melody.

When I remember the trammels to which the poet has been doomed, and the splendour with which consummate genius has invested them, and when, for a moment, I conceive him bursting asunder his bonds, I fancy I behold the sacred bird snapping the golden chain that binds him to Olympus, and soaring even above Jove!

IV.

I HAD arrived at Florence in a very feeble and shattered state of health, of which, however, as I had never been an habitual invalid, I thought little. My confidence in my energy had never deserted me. Composition, however, although I now wrote with facility, proved a greater effort than I had anticipated. The desire I felt of completing my purpose had successfully sustained me throughout, but, during its progress, I was too often conscious of an occasional, but increasing languor, which perplexed and alarmed me. Perfect as might be my conception of my task, and easy as I ever found its execution when I was excited, I invariably experienced, at the commencement, a feeling of inertness, which was painful and mortifying. As I did not dream of physical inability, I began to apprehend that, however delightful might be the process of meditation, that of execution was less delicious. Sometimes I even for a moment feared that there might be a lurking weakness in my nature, which might prevent me from ever effecting a great performance.

I remember one evening as I was meditating in my chamber, my watch lying upon the table, and the hour nine, I felt, as I fancied, disturbed by the increased sound of that instrument. I moved it to the other side of the table, but the sound increased, and assured that it was not occasioned by the supposed cause, and greatly disturbed, I rang for Lausanne, and mentioned the inconvenience. Lausanne persisted in hearing nothing, but as the sound became even more audible, and as I now believed that some reptile might be in the room, he examined it in all parts. Nothing was perceived; the hum grew louder, and it was not until I jumped up from my seat to assist him in his examination, that I discovered by the increased sound, occasioned by my sudden rise, that the noise was merely in my own ears. The circumstance occasioned me no alarm. It inconvenienced me for the evening. I retired at an earlier hour, passed, as usual, a restless and dreamy night, but fell asleep towards the morning, and rose tolerably fresh.

I can write only in the morning. It is then I execute with facility all that I have planned the ensuing eve. And this day, as usual, I resumed my pen, but it was not obedient. I felt not only languid and indolent, but a sensation of faintness which I had before experienced and disregarded, came over me, and the pen fell from my hand. I rose and walked about the room. My extremities were cold, as of late in the morning I had usually found them. The sun was shining brightly over the sparkling hills. I felt a great desire to warm myself in his beams. I ordered my horse.

The ride entirely revived me. I fancied that I led perhaps too sedentary a life. I determined, immediately that my book was finished, that I would indulge in more relaxation. I returned home with more appetite than usual, for since my return from Candia, I had almost entirely lost my relish for food, and my power of digestion. In the evening I was again busied in musing over the scene which was to be painted on the coming morn. Suddenly I heard again the strange noise. I looked at my watch. It was exactly nine o'clock. It increased rapidly. From the tick of a watch, it assumed the loud confused moaning of a bell tolling in a storm, like the bell I had heard at the foot of the Alps. It was impossible to think. I walked about the room. It became louder and louder. It seemed to be absolutely deafening. I could compare it to nothing but the continuous roar of a cataract. I sat down, and looked around me in blank despair.

Night brought me no relief. My sleep, ever since the death of Alceste, had been very troubled and broken, and of late, had daily grown less certain, and less refreshing. Often have I lain awake the whole night, and usually have risen exhausted and spiritless. So it was on this morning. Cold, faint, and feeble, the principle of life seemed to wax fainter and fainter. I sent for my faithful companion: "Lausanne," I said, "I begin to think that I am very ill."

Lausanne felt my pulse, and shook his head. "There is no wonder," he replied. "You have scarcely any circulation. You want stimulants. You should drink more wine, and you should give up writing for a time. Shall I send for a physician?"

I had no confidence in medicine. I resolved to exert myself. Lausanne's advice I fancied sounded well. I drank some wine: I felt better; but as I never can write under any inspiration but my own, I resolved to throw aside my pen, and visit Pisa for a fortnight, where I could follow his prescription with the additional advantage of change of scene.

My visit to Pisa benefited me. I returned, and gave the last finish to my work.

V.

ALL the Italian cities are delightful; but an elegant melancholy pervades Pisa that is enchanting. What a marble group is formed by the cathedral, the wonderful Baptistery, the Leaning Tower, and the Campo Santo; and what an indication of the ancient splendour of the republic! I wish that the world consisted of a cluster of small states. There would be much more genius, and, what is of more importance, much more felicity. Federal unions would preserve us from the evil consequences of local jealousy, and might combine in some general legislation of universal benefit. Italy might then revive, and even England may regret that she has lost her heptarchy.

In the Campo Santo you trace the history of art. There too, which has not been observed, you may discover the origin of the Arabesques of Raffaelle. The Leaning Tower is a stumbling-block to architectural antiquaries. An ancient fresco in the Campo proves the intention of the artist. All are acquainted with the towers of Bologna; few are aware that in Saragossa the Spaniards possess a rival of the architectural caprice of the Pisans.

To this agreeable and silent city I again returned, and wandered in meditation and the stillness of its palaces. I consider this the period of my life in which whatever intellectual power I possess became fully developed. All that I can execute hereafter is but the performance of what I then planned, nor would a patriarchal term of life permit me to achieve all that I then meditated. I looked forward to the immediate fulfilment of my long hopes, to the achievement of a work which might last with its language, and the attainment of a great and permanent fame.

I was now meditating over this performance. It is my habit to contrive in my head the complete work, before I have recourse to the pen which is to execute it. I do not think that meditation can be too long, or execution too rapid. It is not merely characters and the general conduct of the story that I thus prepare, but the connexion of every incident, often whole conversations, sometimes even slight phrases. A very tenacious memory, which I have never weakened by having recourse to other modes of reminiscence, supports me in this process, which, however, I should confess is a very painful and exhausting effort.

I revolved this work in my mind for several months without ever having recourse to paper. It was never out of my consciousness. I fell asleep musing over it: in the morning my thoughts clustered immediately upon it, like bees on a bed of unexhausted flowers. In my rides, during my meals, in my conversations on common topics, I was indeed the whole time musing over this creation.

The profound thinker always suspects that he is superficial. Patience is a necessary ingredient of genius. Nothing is more fatal than to be seduced by the first flutter of the imagination into composition. This is the cause of so many weak and unequal works, of so many worthy ideas thrown away, and so many good purposes marred. Yet there is a bound to meditation; there is a moment when further judgment is useless. There is a moment when a heavenly light rises over the dim world you have been so long creating, and bathes it with life and beauty. Accept this omen that your work is good, and revel in the sunshine of composition.

I have sometimes half believed, although the suspicion is mortifying, that there is only a step between his state who deeply indulges in imaginative meditation and insanity. For I well remember that at this period of my life, when I indulged in meditation to a degree which would now be impossible, and I hope unnecessary, that my senses sometimes appeared to be wandering. I cannot describe the peculiar feeling I then experienced, for I have failed in so doing to several eminent surgeons and men of science with whom I have conversed respecting it, and who were curious to become acquainted with its nature. But I think it was, that I was not always assured of my identity, or even existence, for I sometimes found it necessary to shout aloud to be sure that I lived, and I was in the habit very often at night of taking down a volume, and looking into it for my name, to be convinced that I had not been dreaming of myself. At these times there was an incredible acuteness, or intenseness, in my sensations. Every object seemed animated, and, as it were, acting upon me. The only way that I can devise to express my general feeling is, that I seemed to be sensible of the rapid whirl of the globe.

All this time my health was again giving way, and all my old symptoms gradually returning. I set them at defiance. The nocturnal demon having now come back in all its fulness, I was forced to confine my meditations to the morning, and in the evening I fled for refuge and forgetfulness to the bottle. This gave me temporary relief, but entirely destroyed my remaining power of digestion. In the morning I regularly fainted as I dressed. Still I would not give in, and only postponed the commencement of my work until my return to Florence, which was to occur in a few days.

I rode the journey through the luxuriant Val d'Arno, attended by Tita. Lausanne and Spiro had returned the previous day. It was late in the evening when I arrived at the villa. I thought, as I got off my horse, that the falls of Niagara could not overpower the infernal roaring that I alone heard. I entered, and threw myself on a sofa. It came at last. What it was I knew not. It felt like a rushing of blood into my brain. I moaned, threw out my arm, and wildly caught at the bell. Lausanne entered, and I was lying apparently lifeless.

VI.

During the whole course of my life, my brain had been my constant source of consolation. As long as I could work that machine, I was never entirely without an object and a pleasure. I had laughed at physical weaknesses while that remained untouched; and unquestionably I should have sunk under the great calamity of my life, had it not been for the sources of hope and solace which this faithful companion opened to me. Now it was all over: I was little better than an idiot.

Physician followed physician, and surgeon surgeon, without benefit. They all held different opinions, yet none were right. They satirized each other in private interviews, and exchanged compliments in consultations. One told me to be quiet, another to exert myself; one declared that I must be stimulated, another that I must be soothed. I was, in turn, to be ever on horseback, and ever on a sofa. I was bled, blistered, boiled, starved, poisoned, electrified, galvanised, and at the end of a year found myself with exactly the same oppression on my brain, and the additional gratification of remembering that twelve months of existence had worn away without producing a single idea. Such are the inevitable consequences of consulting men who decide by precedents which have no resemblance, and never busy themselves about the idiosyncrasy of their patients.

I had been so overwhelmed by my malady, and so conscious that upon my cure my only chance of happiness depended, that I had submitted myself to all this treatment without a murmur, and religiously observed all their contradictory directions. Being of a sanguine temperament, I believed every assertion, and every week expected to find myself cured. When, however, a considerable period of time had elapsed without any amelioration, I began to rebel against these systems which induced so much exertion and privation, and were productive of no good. I was quite desperate of cure, and each day I felt more keenly, that if I were not cured, I could not live. I wished therefore to die unmolested. I discharged all my medical attendants, and laid myself down like a sick lion in his lair.

I never went out of the house, and barely out of a single room. I scarcely ever spoke, and only for my wants. I had no acquaintance, and I took care that I should see no one. I observed a strict diet, but fed every day. Although air, and medicine, and exercise were to have been productive of so much benefit to me, I found myself, without their assistance, certainly not worse, and the repose of my present system, if possible, rendered my wretched existence less burthensome.

Lausanne afterwards told me that he supposed I had relapsed into the state in which I fell immediately after my great calamity, but this was not the case. I never lost my mind or memory: I was conscious of every thing, I forgot nothing. But I had lost the desire of exercising them. I sat in moody silence, revolving in revery, without the labour of thought, my past life and feelings.

I had no hopes of recovery. It was not death that terrified me, but the idea that I might live, and for years, in this hopeless and unprofitable condition. When I contrasted my recent lust of fame, and plans of glory, and indomitable will, with my present woful situation of mysterious imbecility, I was appalled with the marvellous contrast, and I believed that I had been stricken by some celestial influence for my pride and wanton self-sufficiency.

VII.

I WAS in this gloomy state, when one morning Lausanne entered my room; I did not notice him, but continued sitting with my eyes fixed on the ground, and my chin upon my breast. At last he said, "My lord, I wish to speak to you."

"Well!"

"There is a stranger at the gate, a gentleman who desires to see you."

"You know I see no one," I replied rather harshly.

"I know it, and have so said. But this gentleman—"

"Good God! Lausanne, is it my father?"

"No. But it is one who may perhaps come from him."

"I will see him."

The door opened, and there entered Winter.

Long years, long and active years had passed since we parted. All had happened since. I thought of my boyhood, and it seemed innocent and happy, compared with the misery of the past and present. Nine years had not much altered my friend, but me—

"I fear, count," said Winter, "that I am abusing the privilege of an old friend in thus insisting upon an entrance, but I heard of your residence in this country and your illness at the same time, and being at Florence I thought you would perhaps pardon me."

"You are one of the few persons whom I am glad to see under all circumstances, even under those in which I now exist."

"I have heard of your distressing state."

"Say my hopeless state. But let us not converse about it. Let us speak of yourself. Let me hope you are as happy as you are celebrated."

"As for that, well enough. But if we are to talk about celebrity, let me claim the honours of a prophet, and congratulate a poet whom I predicted."

"Alas! dear Winter," I said, with a faint smile, "talk not of that, for I shall die without doing you honour."

"There is no one of my acquaintance who has less chance of dying."

"How so?" I remarked, rather quickly, for when a man really believes he is dying, he does not like to lose the interest which such a situation produces. "If you knew all—"

"I know all—much more, too, than your physician who told me."

"And you believe, then, that I cannot look forward even to death, to terminate this miserable existence?"

"I do not consider it miserable, and therefore I should be sorry if there were any thing to warrant such an anticipation."

"And I can assure you, chevalier," and I spoke very sincerely and solemnly, "that I consider existence, on the terms I now possess it, an intolerable burthen. And nothing but the chance, for I cannot call it hope, of amelioration, prevents me from terminating it."

"If you remember right, you considered existence equally an intolerable burthen when, as a boy, you first experienced feelings which you were unable to express."

"Well! what inference do you draw?"

"That it is not the first time you have quarrelled with nature."

"How so?" I eagerly replied, and I exerted myself to answer him, "is disease nature?"

"Is your state disease?"

"I have no mind."

"You reason."

"My brain is affected."

"You see."

"You believe, then, that I am a hypochondriac?"

"By no means! I believe your feelings are real and peculiar, but it does not therefore follow that they are evil."

"Perhaps," I said, with a dry smile, "you believe them beneficent?"

"I do certainly," he replied.

"In what respect?"

"I believe, that as you would not give nature a holyday, she is giving herself one."

I was silent, and mused. "But this infernal brain?" I replied.

"Is the part of the machinery that you have worked most; and therefore the weakest."

"But how is it to be strengthened?"

"Not by medicine. By following exactly a contrary course to that which enfeebled it."

"For fifteen months an idea has not crossed my brain."

"Well! you are the better for it; and fifteen months more—"

"Alas! what is life! At this age I hoped to be famous."

"Depend upon it, you are in the right road, but rest assured you must go through every trial that is peculiar to men of your organization. There is no avoiding it. It is just as necessary as that life should be the consequence of your structure. To tell you the truth, which is always best, I only came here to please your father. When he wrote to me of your illness, I mentioned to him that it must have its course, that there was nothing to be alarmed about, and that it was just as much a part of your necessary education as travel or study. But he wished me to see you, and so I came."

"My poor father! Alas! my conduct to him—"

"Has been just what it ought to be, just what it necessarily must have been, just exactly what my own was to my father. As long as human beings are unphilosophically educated, these incidents will take place."

"Ah! my dear Winter, I am a villain. I have never even written to him."

"Of course you have not. Your father tried to turn you into a politician. Had he not forced you to write so many letters then, you would not have omitted to write to him now. The whole affair is simple as day. Until men are educated with a reference to their organization, there will be no end to domestic fracas."

"You ever jest, my friend. I have not ventured on a joke for many a long month."

"Which is a pity; for, to tell you the truth, although your last work is of the tender and sublime, and maketh fair eyes weep, I think your forte is comic."

"Do you, indeed?"

"Ah! my dear Contarini, those two little volumes of Manstein—"

"O! mention not the name. Infamous, unadulterated trash!"

"Ah! exactly as I thought of my first picture, which after all has a freshness and a freedom I have never excelled,—but Manstein, my dear Contarini, it certainly was very impertinent. I read it at Rome. I thought I should have died. All our friends. So very true!"

"Will you stay with me? I feel a good deal better since you have been here, and what you tell me of my father delights me. Pray, pray stay. Well! you are indeed kind. And if I feel very ill, I will keep away."

"O! I should like to see you in one of your fits."

VIII.

"TAKE a glass of wine," said Winter at dinner.

"My dear friend, I have taken one."

"Take another. Here is your father's health."

"Well, then, here is yours. How is the finest of old men?"

"Flourishing and happy."

"And your mother?"

"Capital!"

"And you have never returned?"

"No! and never will, while there are such places as Rome and Naples."

"Ah! I shall never see them."

"Pooh! the sooner you move about the better."

"My good friend, it is impossible."

"Why so? Do not confound your present condition with the state you were in a year ago. Let me feel your pulse. Capital! You seem to have an excellent appetite. Don't be ashamed to eat. In cases like yours, the art is to ascertain the moment to make exertion. I look upon yours as a case of complete exhaustion. If there be any thing more exhausting than love, it is sorrow, and if there be any thing more exhausting than sorrow, it is poetry. You have tried all three. Your body and your mind both required perfect repose. I perceive that your body has sufficiently rested. Employ it; and in another year you will find your mind equally come round."

"You console me. But where shall I go? Home?"

"By no means. You require beauty and novelty. At present I would not go even to the south of this country. It will remind you too much of the past. Put yourself entirely in a new world. Go to Egypt. It will suit you. I look upon you as an Oriental. If you like, go to South America. Tropical scenery will astonish and cure you. Go to Leghorn, and get into the first ship that is bound for a country with which you are unacquainted."

IX.

WINTER remained with me several days, and before he had quitted Florence I had written to my father. I described to him my forlorn situation, my strong desire to see him, and I stated the advice which did not correspond with my wishes. I asked for his counsel, but said nothing of the great calamity. I was indeed myself extremely unwilling to return home in my present state, but this unwillingness I concealed.

I received an answer from my father by a special courier, an answer the most affectionate. He strongly recommended me to travel for some time, expressed his hope and confidence that I should entirely recover, and that I should return and repay him for all his anxiety. All that he required was, that I should frequently correspond with him. And ever afterward, I religiously respected his request.

A ship was about to sail from Leghorn to Cadiz. Spain appeared an interesting country, and one of which I knew nothing. It is the link between Europe and Africa. To Spain therefore I resolved to repair; and in a few days I again quitted Italy, and once more cast my fortunes on the waters!

PART THE FIFTH.

I.

EUROPE and AFRIC! I have wandered amid the tombs of Troy, and stood by the altar of Medea, yet the poetry of the Hellespont, and the splendour of the Symplegades must yield to the majesty of the Straits of Calpe.

Like some lone Titian, lurid and sublime, his throne the mountains and the clouds his crown, the melancholy Mauritania sits apart, and gazes on the mistress he has lost.

And lo! from out the waves that kiss her feet, and bow before her beauty, she softly rises with a wanton smile. Would she call back her dark-eyed lover, and does the memory of that bright embrace yet dwell within the hallowed sanctuary of her heart?

It was a glorious union. When were maidens fairer and more faithful—when were men more gentle and more brave? When did all that can adorn humanity more brightly flourish, and more sweetly bloom? Alas! for their fair cities, and fine gardens, and fresh fountains! Alas! for their delicate palaces, and glowing bowers of perfumed shade!

Will you fly with me from the dull toil of vulgar life? Will you wander for a moment amid the plains of Granada? Around us are those snowy and purple mountains, which a caliph wept to quit. They surrounded a land still prodigal of fruits, in spite of a Gothic government. You are gazing on the rows of blooming aloes, that are the only enclosures, with their flowery forms high in the warm air; you linger among those groves of Indian fig: you stare with strange delight at the first sight of the sugar-cane. Come away, come away, for on yon green and sunny hill, rises the ruby gate of that precious pile whose name is a spell, and whose vision is romance.

Let us enter Alhambra!

See! here is the Court of Myrtles, and I gather you a sprig. Mark how exquisitely every thing is proportioned, mark how slight, and small, and delicate! And now we are in the Court of Columns, the far-famed Court of Columns. Let us enter the chambers that open round this quadrangle. How beautiful are their deeply carved and purple roofs, studded with gold, and the wall entirely covered with the most fanciful fret-work, relieved with that violet tint, which must have been copied from their Andalusian skies. Here you may sit in the coolest shade, reclining on your divan with your beads or pipe, and view the most dazzling sunlight in the court, which assuredly must scorch the flowers, if the faithful lions ever ceased from pouring forth that element which you must travel in Spain or Africa to honour. How many chambers! The Hall of the Ambassadors ever the most sumptuous. How fanciful is its mosaic ceiling of ivory and tortoise-shell, mother-of-pearl and gold! And then the Hall of Justice with its cedar roof, and the Harem, and the baths—all perfect. Not a single roof has yielded, thanks to those elegant horse-shoe arches and those crowds of marble columns, with their oriental capitals. What a scene! Is it beautiful? O! conceive it in the time of the Boabdils —conceive it with all its costly decorations, all the gilding, all the imperial purple, all the violet relief, all the scarlet borders, all the glittering inscriptions and precious mosaics, burnished, bright, and fresh. Conceive it full of still greater ornaments, the living groups with their splendid, and vivid, and picturesque costume, and above all their rich and shining arms, some standing in conversing groups, some smoking in sedate silence, some telling their beads, some squatting round a storier. Then the bustle and the rush, and the coming horsemen, all in motion, and all glancing in the most brilliant sun.

Enough of this! I am alone. Yet there was one being with whom I could have loved to roam in these imaginative halls, and found no solitude in the sole presence of her most sweet society.

Alhambra is a strong illustration of what I have long thought, that however there may be a standard of taste, there is no standard of style. I must place Alhambra with the Parthenon, the Pantheon, the Cathedral of Seville, the Temple of Dendera. They are different combinations of the same principles of taste. Thus we may equally admire Æschylus, Virgil, Calderon and Ferdousi. There never could have been a controversy on such a point, if mankind had not confused the ideas of taste and style. The Saracenic architecture is the most inventive and fanciful, but at the same time the most fitting and delicate that can be conceived. There would be no doubt about its title to be considered among the finest inventions of man if it were better known. It is only to be found in any degree of European perfection in Spain. Some of the tombs of the Mamlouk sultans in the desert round Cairo, wrongly styled by the French "the tombs of the caliphs," are equal, I think, to Alhambra. When a person sneers at the Saracenic, ask him what he has seen? Perhaps a barbarous, although picturesque building, called the Ducal Palace, at Venice. What should we think of a man, who decided on the architecture of Agrippa by the buildings of Justinian, or judged the age of Pericles by the restoration of Hadrian? Yet he would not commit so great a blunder. There is a Moorish palace, the Alcazar at Seville, a huge mosque at Cordova turned into a cathedral, with partial alteration, Alhambra at Granada, these are the great specimens in Europe, and sufficient for all study. There is a shrine and chapel of a Moorish saint at Cordova, quite untouched, with the blue mosaic and the golden honeycomb roof, as vivid and as brilliant as when the santon was worshipped. In my life have I never seen any work of art more exquisite. The materials are the richest, the ornaments the most costly, and in detail, the most elegant and the most novel, the most fanciful and the most flowing, that I ever contemplated. And yet nothing at the same time can be conceived more just than the proportion of the whole, and more mellowed than the blending of the parts, which indeed Palladio could not excel.

II.

A Spanish city sparkling in the sun, with its white walls and verdant jalousies, is one of the most cheerful and most brilliant of the works of man. Figaro is in every street, and Rosina in every balcony.

The Moorish remains, the Christian churches, the gay, national dress, a gorgeous priesthood, ever producing, in their dazzling processions and sacred festivals, an effect upon the business of the day, the splendid pictures of a school of which we know nothing, theatres, alamedas, tertullas, bull fights, boleros,—here is matter enough for amusement within the walls, and now let us see how they pass their time out of them.

When I was in the south of Spain the whole of Andalusia was overrun with robbers. These bands, unless irritated by a rash resistance, have of late seldom committed personal violence, but only lay you on the ground and clear out your pockets. If however you have less than an ounce of gold, they shoot you. That is their tariff, which they have announced at all the principal towns, and it must be confessed is a light one. A weak government resolves society into its original elements, and robbery in Spain has become more honourable than war, inasmuch as the robber is paid, and the soldier is in arrear. The traveller must defend himself. Some combine, some compromise, merchants travel in corsarios or caravans well armed, persons of quality take a military escort, who, if cavalry scamper off the moment they are attacked, and if infantry, remain and participate in the plunder. The government is only anxious about the post, and to secure that pay the brigands black mail.

The country is thinly populated, with few villages or farmhouses, but many towns and cities. It chiefly consists of immense plains of pasture lands which, sunburnt in the summer, were a good preparation for the desert and intervening mountainous districts, such as the Sierra Morena, famous in Cervantes, the Sierra Nivada of Granada, and the Sierra da Ronda, a country like the Abruzzi, entirely inhabited by brigands and smugglers, and which I once explored. I must say that the wild beauty of the scenery entirely repaid me for some peril and very great hardship. Returning from this district towards Cadiz, you arrive at Oven, one of the finest mountain passes in the world. Its precipices and cork woods would have afforded inexhaustible studies to Salvator. All this part of the country is full of pictures, and of a peculiar character. I recommend Castellar to an adventurous artist.

I travelled over Andalusia on horseback, and in spite of many warnings, without any escort, or any companions but Lausanne and Tita, and little Spiro, and the muleteers who walk and occasionally increase the burden of a sumpter steed. In general, like all the Spanish peasants, they are tall, finely made fellows, looking extremely martial with their low, round, black velvet hats and coloured sashes, embroidered jackets and brilliant buttons. We took care not to have too much money, and no baggage that we could not stow in our saddle bags. I even followed the advice of an experienced guide, and was as little ostentatious as possible of my arms, for to a Spanish bandit, foreign pistols are sometimes a temptation, instead of a terror. Such prudent humility will not, however, answer in the East, where you cannot be too well, or too magnificently armed.

We were, in general, in our saddles at four o'clock, and stopped, on account of the heat, from ten till five in the evening, and then proceeded for three or four hours more. I have travelled through three successive nights, and seen the sun set and rise, without quitting my saddle, which all men cannot say. It is impossible to conceive any thing more brilliant than an Andalusian summer moon. You lose nothing of the landscape, which is only softened, not obscured, and absolutely the beams are warm. Generally speaking, we contrived to reach, for our night's bivouac, some village, which usually boasts a place called a posada. If this failed, there was sometimes a convent, and were we unfortunate in this expedient, we made pillows of our saddles, and beds of our cloaks. A posada is in fact a khan, and a very bad one. The same room holds the cattle, the kitchen, the family, and boards and mats for travellers to sleep on. Your host affords no provisions, and you must cater as you proceed, and, what is more, cook when you have catered. Yet the posada, in spite of so many causes, is seldom dirty; and for the Spaniards, notwithstanding their reputation, I claim the character of the most cleanly nation in Europe. Nothing is more remarkable than the delicacy of the lower orders. All that frequent whitewash and constant ablution can effect against a generating sun, they employ. You would think that a Spanish woman had no other occupation than to maintain the cleanliness of her chamber. Most assuredly they are a clean people. They have too much self-respect not to be clean. I once remember Lausanne rating a muleteer, who was somewhat tardy in his preparations. "What!" exclaimed the peasant, reproachfully, "would you have me go without a clean shirt?" Now when we remember that this man only put on his clean shirt to toil on foot for thirty or forty miles, we may admire his high feeling, and doubt whether we might match this incident even by that wonder, an English postilion.

Certainly the Spaniards are a noble race. They are kind and faithful, courageous and honest, with a profound mind, that will nevertheless break into rich humour, and a dignity which, like their passion, is perhaps the legacy of their oriental sires.

But, see! we have gained the summit of the hill. Behold! the noble range of the Morena mountains extends before us, and at their base is a plain worthy of such a boundary. Yon river, winding amid bowers of orange, is the beautiful Guadalquivir, and that city, with its many spires and mighty mosque, is the famous Cordova!

III.

The court-yard was full of mules, a body of infantry were bivouacking under the colonnades. There were several servants, all armed, and a crowd of muleteers with bludgeons.

"'Tis a great lady from Madrid, sir," observed Tita, who was lounging in the court.

I had now been several days at Cordova, and intended to depart at sunset for Granada. The country between these two cities is more infested by brigands than any tract in Spain. The town was rife with their daring exploits. Every traveller during the last month had been plundered, and only the night before my arrival, they had, in revenge for some attempt of the governor to interfere, burned down a farmhouse a few miles without the gates.

When I entered the hotel, the landlord came up to me, and advised me to postpone my departure for a few hours, as a great lady from Madrid was about to venture the journey, and depart at midnight towards Malaga with a strong escort. He doubted not that she would consent with pleasure to my joining their party. I did not feel, I fear, as grateful for his proposition as I ought to have been. I was tired of Cordova—I had made up my mind to depart at a particular hour. I had hitherto escaped the brigands—I began to suspect that their activity was exaggerated. At the worst, I apprehended no great evil. Some persons always escaped, and I was confident in my fortune.

"What is all this?" I inquired of Lausanne.

"'Tis a great lady from Madrid," replied Lausanne.

"And have you seen her?"

"I have not, sir, but I have seen her husband."

"O! she has a husband—then I certainly will not stop. At sunset we go."

In half an hour's time the landlord again entered my room, with an invitation from the great lady and her lord to join them at dinner. Of course I could not refuse, although I began to suspect that my worthy host, in his considerate suggestions, had perhaps been influenced by other views than merely my security.

I repaired to the saloon. It was truly a Gil Blas scene. The grandee, in an undress uniform, and highly imposing in appearance, greeted me with dignity. He was of middle age, with a fine form and a strongly marked, true Castilian countenance, but very handsome. The senora was exceedingly young, and really very pretty, with infinite vivacity and grace. A French valet leaned over the husband's chair, and a duenna, broad and supercilious, with beady jet eyes, mahogany complexion, and cocked-up nose, stood by her young mistress, refreshing her with a huge fan.

After some general and agreeable conversation, the senor introduced the intended journey, and understanding that I was about to proceed in the same direction, offered me the advantage of his escort. The dama most energetically impressed upon me the danger of travelling alone, and I was brutal enough to suspect that she had more confidence in foreign aid than in the courage of her countrymen.

I was in one of those ungallant fits that sometimes come over men of shattered nerves. I had looked forward with moody pleasure to a silent moonlit ride. I shrunk from the constant effort of continued conversation. It did not appear that my chivalry would be grievously affected in an almost solitary cavalier deserting a dame environed by a military force and a band of armed retainers. In short, I was not seduced by the prospect of security, and rash enough to depart alone.

The moon rose. I confess our anxiety. The muleteer prophesied an attack. "They will be out," said he, "for the great lady; we cannot escape." We passed two travelling friars on their mules, who gave us their blessing; and I observed to-night by the road-side more crosses than usual, and each of these is indicative of a violent death. We crossed an immense plain, and entered a broken mule-track through uneven ground. We were challenged by a picquet, and I, who was ahead, nearly got shot for not answering. It was a corsario of armed merchants returning from the fair of Ronda. We stopped and made inquiries, but could learn nothing, and we continued our journey for several hours in silence, by the most brilliant moon. We began to hope we had escaped, when suddenly a muleteer informed us that he could distinguish a trampling of horse in the distance. Ave Maria! a cold perspiration came over us. Decidedly they approached. We drew up out of pure fear. I had a pistol in one hand and my purse in the other, to act according to circumstances. The band were clearly in sight. I was encouraged by finding that they were a rather uproarious crew. They turned out to be a company of actors travelling to Cordova. There were dresses and decorations, scenery and machinery, all on mules and donkeys—the singers rehearsing an opera, the principal tragedian riding on an ass, and the buffo most serious, looking as grave as night, with a cigar, and in greater agitation than all the rest. The women were in side-saddles like sedans, and there were whole panniers of children. Some of the actresses were chanting an ave, while, in more than one instance, their waists were encircled by the brawny arm of a more robust devotee. All this irresistibly reminded me of Cervantes.

Night waned, and, instead of meeting robbers, we discovered that we had only lost our way. At length we stumbled upon some peasants sleeping in the field amid the harvest, who told us that it was utterly impossible to regain our road; and so, our steeds and ourselves being equally wearied, we dismounted, and turned our saddles into pillows.

I was roused, after a couple of hours' sound slumber, by the Rosario, a singing procession, in which the peasantry congregate to their labours. It is most effective, full of noble chants and melodious responses, that break upon the still fresh air, and your fresher feelings, in a manner truly magical. This is the country for a national novelist. The out-door life of the natives induces a variety of most picturesque manners, while their semi-civilization makes each district retain, with barbarous jealousy, their peculiar customs.

I heard a shot at no great distance. It was repeated. To horse, to horse! I roused Lausanne and Tita. It occurred to me directly. Shots were interchanged. We galloped in the direction of the sound, followed by several peasants, and firing our pistols. Two or three runaway soldiers met us. "Carraho! Scoundrels, turn back!" we cried. In a few minutes we were in sight of the combat. It was a most unequal one, and nearly finished. A robber had hold of the arm of the great lady of Madrid, who was dismounted, and seated on a bank. Her husband was leaning on his sword, and evidently agreeing to a capitulation. The servants seemed still disposed to fight. Two or three wounded men were lying on the field—soldiers, and mules, and muleteers, running about in all directions.

Tita, who was an admirable shot, fired the moment he was within reach, and brought down his man. I ran up to the lady, but not in time to finish her assailant, who was off in a flash. The robbers, surprised, disorderly, and plundering, made no fight, and we permitted them to retreat with some severe loss.

Exclamations, gratitude, hysterics. Lausanne in the mean time produced order. The infantry rallied, the mules re-assembled, the baggage was again arranged. The travellers were the Marquis and Marchioness of Santiago, who were about to pay a visit to their relative, the Governor of Malaga. I remained with them until we reached Granada, when the most dangerous portion of this journey was completed, and I parted from these agreeable persons, with a promise to visit them on my arrival at their place of destination.

IV

There is not a more beautiful and solemn temple in the world than the great cathedral of Seville. When you enter from the glare of a Spanish sky, so deep is the staining of the glass, and so small and few the windows, that, for a moment, you feel in darkness. Gradually the vast design of the Gothic artist unfolds itself to your vision: gradually rises up before you the profuse sumptuousness of the high altar, with its tall images, and velvet and gold hangings, its gigantic railings of brass and massy candlesticks of silver—all revealed by the dim and perpetual light of the sacred and costly lamps.

You steal with a subdued spirit over the marble pavement. All is still, save the hushed muttering of the gliding priests. Around you are groups of kneeling worshippers, some prostrate on the ground, some gazing upwards with their arms crossed in mute devotion, some beating their breasts and counting their consoling beads. Lo! the tinkling of a bell. The mighty organ bursts forth. Involuntarily you fall upon your knees, and listen to the rising chanting of the solemn choir. A procession moves from an adjoining chapel. A band of crimson acolytes advance, waving their censers and the melody of their distant voices responds to the deep-toned invocations of the nearer canons.

There are a vast number of chapels in this cathedral on each side of the principal nave. Most of them are adorned with masterpieces of the Spanish school. Let us approach one. The light is good, and let us gaze through this iron railing upon the picture it encloses.

I see a saint falling upon his knees, and extending his enraptured arm to receive an infant god. What mingled love, enthusiasm, devotion, reverence, blend in the countenance of the holy man! But, O! that glowing group of seraphim, sailing and smiling in the sunny splendour of that radiant sky—who has before gazed upon such grace, such ineffable and charming beauty? And in the background is an altar, whereon is a vase holding some lilies, that seem as if they were just gathered. There is but one artist who could have designed this picture, there is but one man who could have thus combined ideal grace with natural simplicity, there is but one man who could have painted that diaphonous heaven and those fresh lilies. Inimitable Murillo!

V.

A Spanish bull-fight taught me fully to comprehend the rapturous exclamation of "Panem et Circenses!" The amusement apart, there is something magnificent in the assembled thousands of an amphitheatre. It is the trait in modern manners which most effectually recalls the nobility of antique pastime. The poetry of a bull-fight is very much destroyed by the appearance of the cavaliers. Instead of gay, gallant knights, bounding on caracoling steeds, three or four shapeless, unwieldy beings, cased in armour of stuffed leather, and looking more like Dutch burgomasters than Spanish chivalry, enter the lists on limping rips. The bull is, in fact, the executioner for the dogs, and an approaching bull-fight is a respite for any doomed steed throughout all Seville.

The tauridors, in their varying, fanciful, costly, and splendid dresses, compensate, in a great measure, for your disappointment. It is difficult to conceive a more brilliant band. These are ten or a dozen footmen, who engage the bull unarmed, distract him as he rushes at one of the cavaliers by unfolding, and dashing before his eyes a glittering scarf, and saving themselves from an occasional chace by practised agility, which elicits great applause. The performance of these tauridors is, without doubt, the most graceful, the most exciting, and the most surprising portion of the entertainment.

The ample theatre is nearly full. Be careful to sit on the shady side. There is the suspense experienced at all public entertainments, only here upon a great scale. Men are gliding about selling fans and refreshments. The governor and his suite enter their box. A trumpet sounds! all is silent.

The knights advance, poising their spears, and for a moment trying to look graceful. The tauridors walk behind them, two by two. They proceed around, and across the lists. They bow to the viceregal party, and commend themselves to the Virgin, whose portrait is suspended above.

Another trumpet! a second, and a third blast. The governor throws the signal. The den opens, and the bull bounds in. The first spring is very fine. The animal stands for a moment still, staring, stupified. Gradually his hoof moves; he paws the ground; he dashes about the sand. The knights face him with their extended lances at due distance. The tauridors are all still. One flies across him, and waves his scarf. The enraged bull makes at the nearest horseman. He is frustrated in his attack. Again he plants himself, lashes his tail, and rolls about his eye. He makes another charge, and this time, the glance of the spear does not drive him back. He gores the horse, rips up its body, the steed staggers and falls. The bull rushes at the rider, and his armour will not now preserve him, but, just as his awful horn is about to avenge his future fate, a skilful tauridor skims before him, and flaps his nostrils with his scarf. He flies after his new assailant, and immediately finds another. Now, you are delighted by all the evolutions of this consummate band: occasionally they can only save themselves by leaping the barrier. The knight, in the mean time, rises, escapes, and mounts another steed.

The bull now makes a rush at another horseman. The horse dexterously veers aside. The bull rushes on, but the knight wounds him severely in the flank with his lance. The tauridors now appear armed with darts. They rush with extraordinary swiftness and dexterity at the now infuriated animal, plant their galling weapons in different parts of his body, and scud away. To some of their darts are affixed fireworks, which ignite by the pressure of the stab. The animal is then as bewildered as infuriated. The amphitheatre echoes to his roaring, and witnesses the greatest efforts of his rage. He flies at all, staggering and streaming with blood; at length, breathless, and exhausted, he stands at bay, his black swollen tongue hanging out, and his mouth covered with foam.

'Tis horrible. Throughout, a stranger's feelings are for the bull: although this even the fairest Spaniard cannot comprehend. As it is now evident that the noble victim can only amuse them by his death, there is a universal cry for the matador; and the matador, gayly dressed, appears amid a loud cheer. The matador is a great artist. Strong nerves must combine with quickness, and great experience, to form an accomplished matador. It is a rare character, highly prized. Their fame exists after their death, and different cities pride themselves on producing, or possessing the eminent.

The matador plants himself before the bull, and shakes a red cloak suspended over a drawn sword. This last insult excites the lingering energy of the dying hero. He makes a violent charge, the mantle falls over his face, and the sword enters his spine, and he falls amid thundering shouts. The death is instantaneous, without a struggle and without a groan. A car, decorated with flowers and ribands, and drawn by oxen, now appears, and bears off the body in triumph.

I have seen eighteen horses killed in a bull-fight, and eight bulls. But the sport is not always in proportion to the slaughter. Sometimes the bull is a craven, and then, if after having recourse to every mode of excitement he will not charge, he is kicked out of the arena, amid the jeers and hisses of the audience. Every act of skill on the part of the tauridors elicits applause, nor do the spectators hesitate, if necessary, to mark their temper by a contrary method. On the whole, it is a magnificent but barbarous spectacle, and however disgusting the principal object, the accessaries of the entertainment are so brilliant and interesting, that, whatever may be their abstract disapprobation, those who have witnessed a Spanish bull-fight, will not be surprised at the passionate attachment of the Spanish people to their national pastime.

VI.

There is a calm voluptuousness about Spanish life that wonderfully accorded with the disposition in which I then found myself; so that, had my intellect been at command, I do not know any place where I would more willingly have indulged it. The imagination in such a country is ever at work, and beauty and grace are not scared away by those sounds and sights, those constant cares and changing feelings, which are the proud possession of lands which consider themselves more blessed.

You rise early, and should breakfast lightly, although a table covered with all fruits, renders that rather difficult to those who have a passion for the most delightful productions of nature, and would willingly linger over a medley of grape, and melon, and gourd, and prickly pear. In the morning, you never quit the house, and these are hours which might be delightfully employed under the inspiration of a climate which is itself poetry, for it sheds over every thing a golden hue, which does not exist in the objects themselves illuminated. I could then indulge only in a calm revery, for I found the least exertion of mind instantly aggravate all my symptoms. But to exist, and to feel existence more tolerable, to observe and to remember, to record a thought that suddenly starts up, or catch a new image which glances over the surface of the mind—this was still left to me. But the moment that I attempted to meditate or combine, to ascertain a question that was doubtful, or in any way to call the higher powers of intellect into play, that moment I felt a lost man. My brain seemed to palpitate with frenzy. An indescribable feeling of idiocy came over me, and for hours I was plunged into a state of the darkest despair. When the curse had subsided to its usual dull degree of horror, my sanguine temper called me again to life and hope. My general health had never been better, and this supported me under the hardships of Spanish travelling. I never for a moment gave way to my real feelings, except under a paroxysm, and then I fled to solitude. But I resolved to pursue this life only for a year, and if at the end of that period I found no relief, the convent and the cloister should at least afford me repose. This was a firm determination.

But 'tis three o'clock, and all this time we should be at dinner. The Spanish kitchen is not much to my taste, being rich and rather gross. And yet for a pleasant, as well as a picturesque dish, commend me to an olla podrida! After dinner, comes the famed siesta. I generally slept for two hours. I think this practice conducive to health in hot climates. The aged however are apt to carry it to excess. By the time you have risen, and made your toilet, it is the hour to steal forth, and call upon any agreeable family, whose tertulla you may choose to honour, which you do, after the first time, uninvited, and with them you take your chocolate. This is often in the air; under the colonnade of the patio, or interior quadrangle of the mansion. Here you while away the time with music and easy talk, until it is cool enough for the Alameda, or public promenade. At Cadiz and Malaga, and even at Seville, up the Guadalquivir, you are sure of a delightful breeze from the water. The sea-breeze comes like a spirit. The effect is quite magical. As you are lolling in listless languor in the hot and perfumed air, an invisible guest comes dancing into the party, and touches all with an enchanted wand. All start, all smile. It has come, it is the sea-breeze. There is much discussion, whether it be as strong as, or whether weaker than the night before. The ladies furl their fans, and seize their mantillas; the cavaliers stretch their legs, and give signs of life. All rise. You offer your arm to Dolores or Catalina, and in ten minutes you are on the Alameda. What a change! All is now life and liveliness. Such bowing, such kissing, such fluttering of fans, such gentle criticisms of gentle friends! But the fan is the most wonderful part of the whole scene. A Spanish lady, with her fan, might shame the tactics of a troop of horse. Now she unfurls it with the slow pomp and conscious elegance of the bird of Juno; now she flutters it with all the languor of the listless beauty, now with all the liveliness of a vivacious one. Now, in the midst of a very tornado, she closes it with a whirr which makes you start. Pop! In the midst of your confusion, Dolores taps you on the elbow; you turn round to listen, and Catalina pokes you in your side. Magical instrument! In this land it speaks a particular language, and gallantry requires no other mode to express its most subtle conceits, or its most unreasonable demands, than this delicate machine. Yet we should remember that here, as in the north, it is not confined to the delightful sex. The cavalier also has his fan, and that the habit may not be considered an indication of effeminacy, learn that, in this scorching clime, the soldier will not mount guard without this solace.

But night wears on. We seat ourselves, we take a fanal, and fanciful refreshment which also, like the confectionary of Venice, I have since discovered to be oriental. Again we stroll. Midnight clears the public walk, but few Spanish families retire until a much later hour. A solitary bachelor, like myself, still wanders, lingering where the dancers softly move in the warm moonlight, and indicate, by the grace of their eager gestures, and the fulness of their languid eyes, the fierceness of their passion. At length the castanet is silent, the tinkling of the last guitar dies away, and the cathedral clock breaks up your revery. You, too, seek your couch, and amid a sweet flow of loveliness, and light, and music, and fresh air, thus dies a day in Spain.

VII.

The Spanish women are very interesting. What we associate with the idea of female beauty, is not perhaps very common in this country. There are seldom those seraphic countenances, which strike you dumb, or blind, but faces in abundance which will never pass without commanding admiration. Their charms consist in their sensibility. Each incident, every person, every word, touches the fancy of a Spanish lady, and her expressive features are constantly confuting the creed of the Moslemin. But there is nothing quick, harsh, or forced about her. She is extremely unaffected, and not at all French. Her eyes gleam rather than sparkle, she speaks with vivacity, but in sweet tones, and there is in all her carriage, particularly when she walks, a certain dignified grace which never deserts her, and which is very remarkable.

The general female dress in Spain is of black silk, called a *basquina*, and a black silk shawl, with which they usually envelope their heads, called a *mantilla*. As they walk along in this costume in an evening, with their soft dark eyes dangerously conspicuous, you willingly believe in their universal charms. They are remarkable for the beauty of their hair. Of this they are very proud, and indeed its luxuriance is only equalled by the attention which they lavish on its culture. I have seen a young girl of fourteen, whose hair reached her feet, and was as glossy as the curl of a contessa. All day long, even the lowest order are brushing, curling, and arranging it. A fruit-woman has her hair dressed with as much care as the Dutchess of Ossuna. In the summer, they do not wear their mantilla over their heads, but show their combs, which are of very great size. The fashion of these combs varies constantly. Every two or three months you may observe a new form. It is the part of the costume of which a Spanish woman is most proud. The moment that a new comb appears, even a servant wench will run to the melter's with her old one, and thus, with the cost of a dollar or two, appear the next holiday in the newest style. These combs are worn at the back of the head. They are of tortoise-shell, and with the very fashionable, they are white. I sat next to a lady of high distinction at a bull-fight at Seville. She was the daughter-in-law of the captain general of the province, and the most beautiful Spaniard I ever met. Her comb was white, and she wore a mantilla of blonde, without doubt extremely valuable, for it was very dirty. The effect, however, was charming. Her hair was glossy black, her eyes like an antelope's, and all her other features deliciously soft. She was further adorned, which is rare in Spain, with a rosy cheek, for in Spain our heroines are rather sallow. But they counteract this slight defect by never appearing until twilight, which calls them from their bowers, fresh, though languid, from the late siesta.

The only fault of the Spanish beauty is, that she too soon indulges in the magnificence of embonpoint. There are, however, many exceptions. At seventeen, a Spanish beauty is poetical. Tall, lithe, and clear, and graceful as a jennet, who can withstand the summer lightning of her soft and languid glance! As she advances, if she do not lose her shape, she resembles Juno rather than Venus. Majestic she ever is, and if her feet be less twinkling than in her first bolero, look on her hand, and you'll forgive them all.

VIII.

At Malaga, I again met the Santiagos, and through their medium, became acquainted with a young French nobleman, who had served in the late expedition against Algiers, and retired from the army in consequence of the recent revolution in his native country. The rapturous tone in which he spoke of the delights of oriental life, and of his intention to settle permanently in Egypt, or some other part of the Ottoman empire, excited in me a great desire to visit those countries, for which my residence in a Grecian isle had somewhat prepared me. And on inquiry at the quay, finding that there was a vessel bound for the Ionian isles at present in harbour, and about to sail, I secured our passage, and in a few days quitted the Iberian peninsula.

IX.

In sight of the ancient Corcyra, I could not forget, that the island I beheld had given rise to one of the longest and most celebrated, and most fatal of ancient wars. The immortal struggle of the Peloponnesus was precipitated, if not occasioned, by a feeling of colonial jealousy. There is a great difference between ancient and modern colonies. A modern colony is a commercial enterprise, an ancient colony was a political settlement. In the emigration of our citizens, hitherto, we have merely sought the means of acquiring wealth; the ancients, when their brethren quitted their native shores, wept and sacrificed, and were reconciled to the loss of their fellow-citizens solely by the constraint of stern necessity, and the hope that they were about to find easier subsistence, and to lead a more cheerful and commodious life. I believe that a great revolution is at hand in our system of colonization, and that Europe will soon recur to the principles of the ancient polity.

Old Corcyra is now the modern Corfu—a lovely isle, with all that you hope to meet in a Grecian sea—gleamy waters, woody bays, the cyprus, the olive, and the vine, a clear sky and a warm sun. I learned here that a civil war raged in Albania and the neighbouring provinces of European Turkey, and, in spite of all advice, I determined, instead of advancing into Greece, to attempt to penetrate to the Turkish camp, and witness, if possible, a campaign. With these views, I engaged a small vessel to carry me to Prevesa.

X.

I was now in the Ambracian Gulf, those famous waters, where the soft triumvir gained greater glory by defeat than attends the victory of harsher warriors.—The site is not unworthy of the beauty of Cleopatra. From the sinuosity of the land, this gulf appears like a vast lake, walled in on all sides by mountains more or less distant. The dying glory of a Grecian eve bathed with warm lights, a thousand promontories, and gentle bays, and infinite undulations of purple outline. Before me was Olympus, whose austere peak glittered yet in the sun; a bend of the shore alone concealed from me the islands of Ulysses and of Sappho.

As I gazed upon this scene, I thought almost with disgust of the savage splendour and turbulent existence in which perhaps I was about to mingle; I recurred to the feelings in the indulgence of which I could alone find felicity, and from which an inexorable destiny seemed resolved to shut me out.

Hark! the clang of the barbaric horn, and the wild clash of the cymbal. A body of Turkish infantry marched along the shore. I landed, and learned, for the first time, of the massacre of the principal rebel beys at Monastir, at a banquet given by the grand-vizier on pretence of arranging all differences. My host, a Frank, experienced in the Turkish character, checked me, as I poured forth my indignation at this savage treachery. "Live a little longer in these countries before you hazard an opinion as to their conduct. Do you indeed think that the rebel beys of Albania were so simple as to place the slightest trust in the vizier's pledge. The practice of politics in the East may be defined by one word—dissimulation. The most wary dissembler is the most consummate statesman. The Albanian chiefs went up to the divan in full array, and accompanied by a select body of their best troops. They were resolved to overawe the vizier, perhaps they even meditated, with regard to him, the very stroke which he had put in execution against themselves. He was the most skilful dissembler, that is all. His manner threw them off their guard. With their troops bivouacking in the court-yard, they did not calculate that his highness could contrive to massacre the troops by an ambush, and would dare, at the same moment, to attack the leaders by their very attendants at the banquet. There is no feeling of indignation in the country at the treachery of the conqueror, though a very strong sentiment of rage, and mortification, and revenge."

I learned that the grand-vizier had rejoined the main army, and was supposed to have advanced to Yanina, the capital; that in the mean time, the country between this city and the coast was overrun with prowling bands, the remnants of the rebel army, who, infuriate and flying, massacred, burned, and destroyed all persons and all property. This was an agreeable prospect. My friend dissuaded me from my plans, but, as I was unwilling to relinquish them, he recommended me to sail up to Salora, and from thence journey to Arta, where I might seek assistance from Kalio Bey, a Moslemin chief, one of the most powerful and wealthy of the Albanian nobles, and ever faithful to the Porte.

To Salora I consequently repaired, and the next day succeeded in reaching Arta, a town once as beautiful as its site, and famous for its gardens, but now a mass of ruins. The whole place was razed to the ground, the minaret of the principal mosque alone untouched, and I shall never forget the effect of the muezzin with his rich, and solemn, and sonorous voice, calling us to adore God in the midst of all this human havoc.

I found the Bey of Arta keeping his state, which, notwithstanding the surrounding desolation, was not contemptible, in a tenement which was not much better than a large shed. He was a very handsome, stately man, grave but not dull, and remarkably mild and bland in his manner. His polished courtesy might perhaps be ascribed to his recent imprisonment in Russia, where he was treated with so much consideration that he mentioned it to me. I had lived in such complete solitude in Candia, and had there been so absorbed by passion, that I really was much less acquainted with Turkish manners than I ought to have been. I must confess that it was with some awe that for the first time in my life I entered the divan of a great Turk, and found myself sitting cross-legged on the right hand of a bey, smoking an amber-mouthed chiboque, sipping coffee, and paying him compliments through an interpreter.

There were several guests in the room, chiefly his officers. They were, as the Albanians in general, finely formed men, with expressive countenances, and spare forms. Their picturesque dress is celebrated, though to view it with full effect it should be seen upon an Albanian. The long hair and the small cap, the crimson velvet vest and jacket, embroidered and embossed with golden patterns of the most elegant and flowing forms, the white and ample kilt, the ornamented buskins, and the belt full of silver-sheathed arms,—it is difficult to find humanity in better plight.

There was a considerable appearance of affairs, and of patriarchal solitude in the divan of Kalio Bey. It is possible that it was not always as busy, and that he was not uninfluenced by the pardonable vanity of impressing a stranger with his importance and beneficence. Many persons entered, and casting off their slippers at the door, advanced and parleyed; to some was given money, to all directions, and the worthy bey doled out his piastres and his instructions with equal solemnity. At length, I succeeded in calling my host's attention to the purport of my visit, and he readily granted me an escort of twenty of his Albanians. He was even careful that they should be picked men, and, calculating that I might reach the capital in two days, he drew his writing materials from his belt, and gave me a letter to a Turkish bimbashee, or colonel, who was posted with his force in the mountains I was about to pass, and under the only roof which probably remained between Arta and Yanina. He pressed me to remain his guest, though there was little, he confessed, to interest me, but I was anxious to advance, and so, after many thanks, I parted from the kind Kalio Bey.

XI.

By daybreak we departed, and journeyed for many hours over a wild range of the ancient Pindus, stopping only once for a short rest at a beautiful fountain of marble. Here we all dismounted, and lighted a fire, boiled the coffee, and smoked our pipes. There were many fine groups, but little Spiro was not as delighted as I expected at finding himself once more among his countrymen.

An hour before sunset we found ourselves at a vast, but dilapidated khan, as big as a Gothic castle, situated on a high range, and built for the accommodation of travellers from the capital to the coast, by the great Ali Pasha, when his long, sagacious, and unmolested reign permitted him to develope, in a country which combines the excellences of Western Asia and Southern Europe, some of the intended purposes of a beneficent nature. This khan had now been converted into a military post, and here we found the Turkish commander, to whom Kalio Bey had given me a letter. He was a young man of very elegant and pleasing exterior, but unluckily could not understand a word of Greek, and we had no interpreter. What was to be done? Proceed we could not, for there was not an inhabited place before Yanina, and here was I sitting before sunset on the same divan with my host, who had entered the place to receive me, and would not leave the room while I was there, without the power of communicating an idea. I was in despair, and also very hungry, and could not therefore, in the course of an hour or two, plead fatigue as an excuse for sleep, for I was ravenous, and anxious to know what prospect of food existed in this wild and desolate mansion. So we smoked. It is a great resource. But this wore out, and it was so ludicrous smoking and looking at each other, and dying to talk, and then exchanging pipes by way of compliment, and then pressing our hands to our hearts by way of thanks. At last it occurred to me that I had some brandy, and that I would offer my host a glass which might serve as a hint for what should follow so vehement a schnaps. Mashallah! the effect was indeed miraculous. My mild friend smacked his lips, and instantly asked for another cup. We drank it in coffee-cups. A bottle of brandy was despatched in quicker time, and fairer proportions, than had ever solemnized the decease of the same portion of Burgundy. We were extremely gay. The bimbashee ordered some dried figs, talking all the time, and indulging in the most graceful pantomime, examining my pistols, inquiring about percussion locks, which greatly surprised him, handing his own more ornamented although less effective weapons, for my inspection, and finally making out Greek enough to misunderstand most ludicrously every observation communicated. But all was taken in good part, and I never met such a jolly fellow in the course of my life.

In the mean time I became painfully ravenous, for the dry, round, unsugary fig of Albania is a great whetter. At last I asked for bread. The bimbashee gravely bowed, and said, "Leave it to me, take no thought," and nothing more occurred. I prepared myself for hungry dreams, when to my great astonishment and delight, a capital supper was brought in, accompanied, to my equal horror, by wine. We ate with our fingers. It was the first time I had performed such an operation. You soon get used to it, and dash, but in turn, at the choice morsels with perfect coolness. One, with a basin and ewer, is in attendance, and the whole process is by no means so terrible as it would first appear to European habits. For drinking—we really drank with a rapidity which, with me, was unprecedented. The wine was not bad, but, had it been poison, the forbidden juice was such a compliment from a Moslemin, that I must quaff it all. We quaffed it in rivers. The bimbashee called for brandy. Unfortunately there was another bottle. We drank it all. The room turned round, the wild attendants, who sat at our feet, seemed dancing in strange whirls, the bimbashee shook hands with me, he shouted Italian, I Turkish. "Buono, buono," he had caught up,—"Pecche, pecche," was my rejoinder, which, let me inform the reader, although I do not even now know much more, is very good Turkish. He roared, he patted me on the back. I remember no more.

In the middle of the night I awoke. I found myself sleeping on the divan, rolled up in its sacred carpet. The bimbashee had wisely reeled to the fire. The thirst I felt was like that of Dives. All were sleeping except two, who kept up, during the night, the great wood-fire. I rose, lightly stepping over my sleeping companions, and the shining arms, that here and there informed me that the dark mass wrapped up in a capote was a human being. I found Abraham's bosom in a flagon of water. I think I must have drunk a gallon at the draught. I looked at the wood-fire, and thought of the blazing blocks in the hall of Jonsterna, asked myself whether I were indeed in the mountain fastness of a Turkish chief, and shrugging my shoulders went to sleep, and woke without a headach.

XII.

I PARTED from my jovial host the next morning very cordially, and gave him my pipe, as a memorial of having got tipsy together.

After having crossed one more range of steep mountains, we descended into a vast plain, over which we journeyed for some hours, the country presenting the same mournful aspect which I had too long observed: villages in ruins, and perfectly desolate—khans deserted, and fortresses razed to the ground—olive woods burnt up, and fruit trees cut down. So complete had been the work of destruction, that I often unexpectedly found my horse stumbling amid the foundation of a village, and what at first appeared the dry bed of a torrent, often turned out to be the backbone of the skeleton of a ravaged town. At the end of the plain, immediately backed by very lofty mountains, and jutting into the beautiful lake that bears its name, we suddenly came upon the city of Yanina: suddenly, for a long tract of gradually rising ground had hitherto concealed it from our sight. At the distance I first beheld it, this city, once, if not the largest, one of the most thriving and brilliant in the Turkish dominions, was still imposing, but when I entered, I soon found that all preceding desolation had been only preparatory to the vast scene of destruction now before me. We proceeded through a street winding in its course, but of very great length. Ruined houses, mosques with their tower only standing, streets utterly razed—these are nothing. We met great patches of ruin a mile square, as if an army of locusts had had the power of desolating the works of man, as well as those of God. The great heart of the city was a sea of ruin,—arches and pillars, isolated and shattered, still here and there jutting forth, breaking the uniformity of the annihilation, and turning the horrible into the picturesque. The great Bazaar, itself a little town, had been burned down only a few days before my arrival, by an infuriate band of Albanian warriors, who heard of the destruction of their chiefs by the grand vizier. They revenged themselves on tyranny by destroying civilization.

But while the city itself presented this mournful appearance, its other characteristics were any thing but sad. At this moment a swarming population, arrayed in every possible and fanciful costume, buzzed and bustled in all directions. As I passed on, and myself of course not unobserved, where a Frank had not penetrated for nine years, a thousand objects attracted my restless attention and roving eye. Every thing was so strange and splendid, that for a moment I forgot that this was an extraordinary scene even for the East, and gave up my fancy to full credulity in the now almost obsolete magnificence of oriental life. I longed to write an Eastern tale. Military chieftains, clothed in the most brilliant colours and sumptuous furs, and attended by a cortege of officers equally splendid, continually passed us. Now for the first time a dervish saluted me; and now a delhi, with his high cap, reined in his desperate steed, as the suite of some pasha blocked up some turning of the street. It seemed to me that my first day in a Turkish city brought before me all the popular characteristics of which I had read, and which I expected occasionally to observe during a prolonged residence. I remember, as I rode on this day, I observed a Turkish sheikh in his entirely green vestments, a scribe with his writing materials in his girdle, an ambulatory physician and his boy. I gazed about me with a mingled feeling of delight and wonder.

Suddenly a strange, wild, unearthly drum is heard, and at the end of the street, a huge camel, with a slave sitting cross-legged on its neck, and playing upon an immense kettledrum, appears, and is the first of an apparently interminable procession of his Arabian brethren. The camels were very large, they moved slowly, and were many in number. There were not less than a hundred moving on one by one. To me who had then never seen a caravan, it was a novel and impressive spectacle. All immediately hustled out of the way of the procession, and seemed to shrink under the sound of the wild drum. The camels bore corn for the vizier's troops encamped without the walls.

At length I reached the house of a Greek physician, to whom I carried letters. My escort repaired to the quarters of their chieftain's son, who was in the city in attendance on the grand vizier, and for myself I was glad enough once more to stretch my wearied limbs under a Christian roof.

XIII.

The next day, I signified my arrival to the kehaya bey of his highness, and delivered, according to custom, a letter, with which I had been kindly provided by an eminent foreign functionary. The ensuing morning was fixed for my audience. I repaired at the appointed hour to the celebrated fortress palace of Ali Pasha, which, although greatly battered by successive sieges, is still inhabitable, and still affords a very fair idea of its pristine magnificence. Having passed through the gates of the fortress, I found myself in a number of small dingy streets, like those in the liberties of a royal castle. These were all full of life, stirring and excited. At length I reached a grand square, in which, on an ascent, stands the palace. I was hurried through courts and corridors, full of guards, and pages, and attendant chiefs, and in short every variety of Turkish population; for among the orientals all depends upon one brain, and we, with our subdivisions of duty, and intelligent and responsible deputies, can form no idea of the labour of a Turkish premier. At length I came to a vast, irregular apartment, serving as the immediate antechamber of the hall of audience.

This was the first thing of the kind I had ever yet seen. In the whole course of my life I had never mingled in so picturesque an assembly. Conceive a chamber of very great dimensions, full of the choicest groups of an oriental population, each individual waiting by appointment for an audience, and probably about to wait for ever. It was a sea of turbans, and crimson shawls, and golden scarfs, and ornamented arms. I marked with curiosity the haughty Turk stroking his beard, and waving his beads; the proud Albanian strutting with his tarragan, or cloak, dependent on one shoulder, and touching with impatient fingers his silver-sheathed arms; the olive-visaged Asiatic, with his enormous turban and flowing robes, gazing, half with wonder and half with contempt, at some scarlet colonel of the newly-disciplined troops in his gorgeous, but awkward imitation of Frank uniforms; the Greek, still servile, though no more a slave; the Nubian eunuch, and the Georgian page.

In this chamber, attended by the drogueman, who presented me, I remained about ten minutes—too short a time. I never thought I could have lived to wish to kick my heels in a ministerial antechamber. Suddenly I was summoned to the awful presence of the pillar of the Turkish empire, the man who has the reputation of being the mainspring of the new system of regeneration, the renowned Redschid, an approved warrior, a consummate politician, unrivalled as a dissembler in a country where dissimulation is the principal portion of moral culture. The hall was vast, entirely covered with gilding and arabesques, inlaid with tortoise-shell and mother-of-pearl. Here, squatted up in a corner of the large divan, I bowed to a little ferocious-looking, shrivelled, care-worn man, plainly dressed, with a brow covered with wrinkles, and a countenance clouded with anxiety and thought. I entered the shed-like divan of the kind, and comparatively insignificant Kalio Bey with a feeling of awe; I seated myself on the divan of the grand vizier of the Ottoman empire, who, as my attendant informed me, had destroyed, in the course of the last three months, *not* in war, "upwards of four thousand of my acquaintance," with the self-possession of a morning visit. At a distance from us, in a group on his left-hand, were his secretary, and his immediate suite. The end of the saloon was lined with tchawooshes, or lackeys, in waiting, in crimson dresses with long silver canes.

Some compliments passed between us. I congratulated his highness on the pacification of Albania, and he rejoined, that the peace of the world was his only object, and the happiness of his fellow-creatures his only wish. Pipes and coffee were then brought, and then his highness waved his hand, and in an instant the chamber was cleared.

He then told me that he had read the letter, that the writer was one whom he much loved, and that I should join the army, although, of course, I was aware that, as a Frank, I could hold no command. I told him that such was not my desire, but that, as I intended to proceed to Stamboul, it would be gratifying to me to feel that I had co-operated, however humbly, in the cause of a sovereign whom I greatly admired. A Tartar now arrived with despatches, and I rose to retire, for I could perceive that the vizier was overwhelmed with business, and although courteous, moody and anxious. He did not press me to remain, but desired that I would go and visit his son, Amin Pasha, to whose care he had consigned me.

Amin, Pasha of Yanina, was a youth of eighteen, but apparently ten years older. He was the reverse of his father: incapable in affairs, refined in manners, plunged in debauchery, and magnificent in dress. I found him surrounded by his favourites and flatterers, lolling on his divan in a fanciful hussar uniform of blue cloth covered with gold and diamonds, and worn under a Damascus pelisse of thick maroon silk, lined with white fox furs. I have seldom met with a man of more easy address, and more polished breeding. He paid many compliments to the Franks, and expressed his wish to make a visit to the English at Corfu. As I was dressed in regimentals, he offered to show me his collection of military costumes, which had been made for him principally at Vienna. He also ordered one of his attendants to bring his manuscript book of cavalry tactics, which were unfortunately all explained to me. I mention these slight traits to show how eagerly the modern Turks pique themselves on European civilization. After smoking, and eating sweetmeats, a custom indicative of friendship, he proposed that I should accompany him to the camp, where he was about to review a division of the forces. I assented. We descended together, and I found a boy with a barb magnificently caparisoned, waiting at the portal: of both of these Amin begged my acceptance. Mounting, we proceeded to the camp, nor do I think that the cortege of the young pasha consisted of less than a hundred persons, who were all officers of his household, or of the cavalry regiment which he commanded.

XIV.

I GLADLY believe that the increased efficiency of the Turkish troops compensates for their shorn splendour and sorry appearance. A shaven head, covered with a tight red cloth cap, a small blue jacket of coarse cloth, huge trousers of the same material, puckered out to the very stretch of art, yet sitting tight to the knee and calf, mean accoutrements, and a pair of dingy slippers—behold the successor of the superb janissary! Yet they perform their manœuvres with precision, and have struggled even with the Russian infantry with success. The officer makes a better appearance. His dress, although of the same fashion, is of scarlet, and of the finest cloth. It is richly embroidered, and the colonel wears upon his breast a star and crescent of diamonds. At the camp of Yanina, however, I witnessed a charge of delhis with their cimeters, and a more effective cavalry I never wish to lead.

We returned to the city, and I found that apartments were allotted to me in the palace, whither Lausanne and the rest had already repaired. In the evening the vizier sent to me the first singer in Turkey, with several musicians. The singer chanted for an hour in a wild, piercing voice, devoid both of harmony and melody, a triumphant ballad on the recent massacre of Veli Bey and his rebel coadjutors. Nothing appears to me more frightful than Turkish music, yet it produces on those who are accustomed to it a very great effect, and my room was filled with strangers who hastened to listen to the enchanting and exciting strain. The Turkish music is peculiar and different from that of other Eastern nations. I have seldom listened to more simple and affecting melodies than those with which the boatmen are wont to soothe their labours.

The dancing girls followed, and were more amusing, but I had not then witnessed the Alwyn of Egypt.

A week flew away at Yanina in receiving and returning visits from pashas, agas, and selictars, in smoking pipes, sipping coffee, and tasting sweetmeats. Each day the vizier, or his son, sent me provisions ready prepared from their table, and indicated by some attention their considerate kindness. There is no character in the world higher bred than a Turk of rank. Some of these men, too, I found extremely intelligent, deeply interested in the political amelioration of their country, and warm admirers of Peter the Great. I remember with pleasure the agreeable hours I have spent in the society of Mehemet Aga, Selictar of the Pasha of Lepanto, a warrior to whom the obstinate resistance of Varna is mainly to be attributed, and a remarkably enlightened man. Yet even he could not emancipate himself from their fatalism. For I remember when once conversing with him on the equipments of the cavalry, a subject in which he was very much interested, I suggested to him the propriety of a corps of cuirassiers. "A cuirass cannot stop the ball that bears your fate," he replied, shrugging up his shoulder, and exclaiming Mashallah!

While I was leading this novel and agreeable life, news arrived that the Pasha of Scutari, who had placed himself at the head of the insurgent janissaries, and was the champion of the old party, had entered Albania at the head of sixty thousand men, to avenge the massacre of the beys.

XV.

THE grand vizier set off the same night with ten thousand men, reached Okhrida by forced marches, attacked and routed a division of the rebel troops before they supposed him to be apprized of their movements, and again encamped at Monastir, sending urgent commands to Yanina for his son to advance with the rest of the army. We met his Tartar on our march, and the divisions soon joined. After a day's rest, we advanced, and entered the pashalic of Scutari.

The enemy, to our surprise, avoided an engagement. The fierce, undisciplined warriors were frightened at our bayonets. They destroyed all before us, and hung with their vigilant cavalry on our exhausted rear. We had advanced on one side of Scutari; on the other we had penetrated into Romelia. We carried every thing before us, but we were in want of supplies, our soldiers were without food, and a skilful general and disciplined troops might have cut off all our communications.

Suddenly the order was given to retreat. We retreated slowly, and in excellent order. Two regiments of the newly-organized cavalry, with whom I had the honour to act, covered the rear, and were engaged in almost constant skirmishing with the enemy. This skirmishing is very exciting. We concentrated, and again encamped at Okhridi.

We were in hopes of now drawing the enemy into an engagement, but he was wary. In this situation the vizier directed that in the night a powerful division under the command of Mehemet, Pasha of Lepanto, he who stabbed Ali Pasha, should fall back to Monastir with the artillery, and take up a position in the mountains. The ensuing night his highness, after having previously spiked some useless guns, scattered about some tents and baggage-wagons, and given a general appearance of a hurried and disorderly retreat, withdrew in the same direction. The enemy instantly pursued, rushed on, and attacked us full of confidence. We contented ourselves by protecting our rear, but still retreated, and appeared anxious to avoid an engagement. In the evening, having entered the mountain passes, and reached the post of the Pasha of Lepanto, we drew up in battle array.

It was a cloudy morning among the mountains, and some time before the mist drew away. The enemy appeared to be in great force, filling the gorge through which we had retreated, and encamped on all the neighbouring eminences. When they perceived us, a large body instantly charged with the famous janissary shout, the terror of which I confess. I was cold, somewhat exhausted, for I had tasted no food for two days, and for a moment my heart sunk.

They were received, to their surprise, by a well-directed discharge of artillery from our concealed batteries. They seemed checked. Our ranks opened and a body of five thousand troops instantly charged them with the bayonet. This advance was sublime, and so exciting that, what with the shouts and cannonading, I grew mad, and longed to rush forward. The enemy gave way. Their great force was in cavalry, which could not act among the mountains. They were evidently astonished and perplexed. In a few minutes they were routed. The vizier gave orders for a general charge and pursuit, and in a few minutes I was dashing over the hills in rapid chase of all I could catch, cutting, firing, shouting, and quite persuaded that a battle was, after all, the most delightful pastime in the world.

The masses still charging, the groups demanding quarter, the single horsemen bounding over the hills, the wild scared steeds without a rider, snorting and plunging, the dense smoke clearing away, the bright arms and figures flashing, ever and anon, in the moving obscurity, the wild shouts, the strange and horrible spectacles, the solitary shots and shrieks now heard in the decreasing uproar, and the general feeling of energy, and peril, and triumph—it was all wonderful, and was a glorious moment in existence.

The enemy was scattered like chaff. To rally them was impossible; and the chiefs, in despair, were foremost in flight. They offered no resistance, and the very men who, in the morning, would have been the first to attack a battery, sabre in hand, now yielded in numbers without a struggle to an individual. There was a great slaughter, a vast number of prisoners, and plunder without end. My tent was filled with rich arms, and shawls, and stuffs, and embroidered saddles. Lausanne and Tita were the next day both clothed in splendid Albanian dresses, and little Spiro plundered the dead as became a modern Greek.

I reached my tent, I dismounted from my horse, I leaned upon it from exhaustion. An Albanian came forward, and offered a flask of Zitza wine. I drank it at a draught, and assuredly experienced the highest sensual pleasure. I took up two Cachemere shawls, and a gun mounted in silver, and gave them to the Albanian. Lucky is he who is courteous in the hour of plunder!

The vizier I understood to be at Okhrida, and I repaired to that post over the field of battle. The moon had risen, and tinged with its white light all the prominent objects of the scene of destruction; groups of bodies, and, now and then, a pallid face, distinct and fierce; steeds, and standards, and arms, and shattered wagons. Here and there a moving light showed that the plunderer was still at his work, and, occasionally seated on the carcass of a horse, and sometimes on the corpse of a human being, were some of the fortunate survivors, smoking with admirable coolness, as if there were not on earth such a fearful mystery as death.

I found the victorious Redschid seated on a carpet in the moonlignt in a cypress grove, and surrounded by attendants, to whom he was delivering instructions, and distributing rewards. He appeared as calm and grave as usual. Perceiving him thus engaged, I mingled with the crowd, and stood aside, leaning on my sword: but observing me, he beckoned me to advance, and pointing to his carpet, he gave me the pipe of honour from his own lips. As I seated myself by his side, I could not help viewing this extraordinary man with great interest and curiosity. A short time back, at this very place, he had perpetrated an act which would have rendered him infamous in a civilized land; the avengers meet him, as if by fate, on the very scene of his bloody treachery, and—he is victorious. What is life?

So much for the battle of Bitoglia or Monastir, a very pretty fray, although not as much talked of as Austerlitz or Waterloo, and which probably would have remained unknown to the great mass of European readers, had not a young Frank gentleman mingled, from a silly fancy, in its lively business.

XVI.

The effect of the battle of Bitoglia was the complete pacification of Albania, and the temporary suppression of the conspiracies in the adjoining provinces. Had it been in the power of the Porte to have supported, at this moment, its able and faithful servant, it is probable that the authority of the sultan would have been permanently consolidated in these countries. As it is, the finest regions in Europe are still the prey of civil war, in too many instances excited by foreign powers, for their miserable purposes, against a prince, who is only inferior to Peter the Great, because he has profited by his example.

For myself, perceiving that there was no immediate prospect of active service, I determined to visit Greece, and I parted from his highness with the hope that I might congratulate him at Stamboul.

XVII.

A country of promontories, and gulfs, and islands clustering in an azure sea, a country of wooded vales and purple mountains, wherein the cities are built on plains, covered with olive woods, and at the base of an Acropolis, crowned with a temple or a tower. And there are quarries of white marble, and vines, and much wild honey. And wherever you move is some fair and elegant memorial of the poetic past, a lone pillar on the green and silent plain once echoing with the triumphal shouts of sacred games, the tomb of a hero, or the fane of a god. Clear is the sky, and fragrant is the air, and, at all seasons, the magical scenery of this land is coloured with that mellow tint, and invested with that pensive character, which, in other countries, we conceive to be peculiar to autumn, and which beautifully associate with the recollections of the past. Enchanting Greece!

XVIII.

In the Argolic Gulf I found myself in the very heart of the Greek tragedy; Nauplia and Sparta, the pleasant Argos, and the rich Mycene, the tomb of Agamemnon, and the palace of Clytemnestra. The fortunes of the house of Atreus form the noblest of all legends. I believe in that destiny before which the ancients bowed. Modern philosophy, with its superficial discoveries, has infused into the breast of man a spirit of skepticism, but I think that, ere long, science will again become imaginative, and that, as we become more profound, we may become also more credulous. Destiny is our will, and our will is our nature. The son who inherits the organization with the father, will be doomed to the same fortunes as his sire, and again the mysterious matter in which his ancestors were moulded may, in other forms, by a necessary attraction, act upon his fate. All is mystery, but he is a slave who will not struggle to penetrate the dark veil.

I quitted the Morea without regret. It is covered with Venetian memorials, no more to me a source of joy, and bringing back to my memory a country on which I no longer loved to dwell. I cast anchor in a small but secure harbour. I landed. I climbed a hill. From it I looked over a vast plain, covered with olive woods, and skirted by mountains. Some isolated hills, of every picturesque form, rose in the plain at a distance from the terminating range. On one of these I beheld a magnificent temple bathed in the sunset. At the foot of the craggy steep on which it rested was a walled city of considerable dimensions, in front of which rose a Doric temple of exquisite proportion, and apparently uninjured. The violet sunset threw over this scene a colouring becoming its loveliness, and, if possible, increasing its refined character. Independent of all associations, it was the most beautiful spectacle that had ever passed before a vision always musing on sweet sights, yet I could not forget that it was the bright capital of my youthful dreams, the fragrant city of the violet crown, the fair, the sparkling, the delicate Athens!

XIX.

The illusion vanished when I entered Athens. I found it in scarcely a less shattered condition than the towns of Albania. Ruined streets, and roofless houses, and a scanty population. The women were at Egina in security; a few males remained behind to watch the fortune of war. The Acropolis had not been visited by travellers for nine years, and was open to inspection for the first time the very day I entered. It was still in possession of the Turks, but the Greek Commission had arrived to receive the keys of the fortress. The ancient remains have escaped better than we could hope. The Parthenon and the other temples on the Acropolis have necessarily suffered in the sieges, but the injury is only in detail; the general effect is not marred, although I observed many hundred shells and cannon-balls lying about.

The Theseum has not been touched, and looks, at a short distance, as if it were just finished by Cimon. The sumptuous columns of the Olympium still rise from their stately platform, but the Choragic monument is sadly maimed, although, as I was assured, by English sailors, and not Eastern barbarians. Probably the same marine monsters, who have commemorated their fatal visit to Egypt, and the name of the fell craft that wafted them there, by covering the granite pillar of Pompey with gigantic characters in black paint.

The durability of the Parthenon is wonderful. As far as I could observe, had it not been for the repeated ravages of man, it might at this day have been in as perfect condition as in the age of Pericles. Abstract time it has defied. Gilt and painted, with its pictures and votive statues, it must have been one of the most brilliant creations of human genius. Yet we err if we consider this famous building as an unparalleled effort of Grecian architecture. Compared with the temples of Ionia and the Sicilian fanes, compared even with the Olympium to its feet, the Parthenon could only rank as a church with a cathedral.

In art, the Greeks were the children of the Egyptians. The day may yet come when we shall do justice to the high powers of that mysterious and imaginative people. The origin of Doric and Ionic invention must be traced amid the palaces of Carnac and the temples of Luxoor. For myself I confess I ever gaze upon the marvels of art with a feeling of despair. With horror I remember that, through some mysterious necessity, civilization seems to have deserted the most favoured regions and the choicest intellects. The Persian, whose very being is poetry, the Arab, whose subtle mind could penetrate into the very secret shrine of nature, the Greek, whose acute perceptions seemed granted only for the creation of the beautiful—these are now unlettered slaves in barbarous lands. The arts are yielded to the flat-nosed Franks. And they toil, and study, and invent theories to account for their own incompetence. Now it is the climate, now the religion, now the government, every thing but the truth, every thing but the mortifying suspicion that their organization may be different, and that they may be as distinct a race from their models, as they undoubtedly are from the Kalmuck and the Negro.

XX.

Whatever may have been the faults of the ancient governments, they were in closer relation to the times, to the countries, and to the governed, than ours. The ancients invented their governments according to their wants; the moderns have adopted foreign policies, and then modelled their conduct upon this borrowed regulation. This circumstance has occasioned our manners and our customs to be so confused, and absurd, and unphilosophical. What business had we, for instance, to adopt the Roman law?—a law foreign to our manners, and consequently disadvantageous. He, who profoundly meditates upon the situation of modern Europe, will also discover how productive of misery has been the senseless adoption of oriental customs by northern people. Whence came that divine right of kings, which has deluged so many countries with blood?—that pastoral and Syrian law of tithes, which may yet shake the foundation of so many ancient institutions?

XXI.

Even as a child, I was struck by the absurdity of modern education. The duty of education is to give ideas. When our limited intelligence was confined to the literature of two dead languages, it was necessary to acquire those languages in order to obtain the knowledge which they embalmed. But now each nation has its literature, each nation possesses, written in its own tongue, a record of all knowledge, and specimens of every modification of invention. Let education, then, be confined to that national literature, and we should soon perceive the beneficial effects of this revolution upon the mind of the student. Study would then be a profitable delight. I pity the poor Gothic victim of the grammar and the lexicon. The Greeks, who were masters of composition, were ignorant of all languages but their own. They concentrated their study of the genius of expression upon one tongue. To this they owe that blended simplicity and strength of style, which the imitative Romans, with all their splendour, never attained

To the few, however, who have leisure or inclination to study foreign literatures, I will not recommend them the English, the Italian, the German, since they may rightly answer, that all these have been in great part founded upon the classic tongues, and therefore it is wise to ascend to the fountain head; but I will ask them for what reason they would limit their experience to the immortal languages of Greece and Rome? Why not study the Oriental? Surely, in the pages of the Persians and the Arabs, we might discover new sources of emotion, new modes of expression, new trains of ideas, new principles of invention, and new bursts of fancy.

These are a few of my meditations amid the ruins of Athens. They will disappoint those who might justly expect an ebullition of classic rapture from one who has gazed upon Marathon by moonlight, and sailed upon the free waters of Salamis. I regret their disappointment, but I have arrived at an age when I can think only of the future. A mighty era is at hand, prepared by the blunders of long centuries. Ardently I hope that the necessary change in human existence may be effected by the voice of philosophy alone: but I tremble and I am silent. There is no bigotry so terrible as the bigotry of a country that flatters itself that it is philosophical.

XXII.

Understanding that the Turkish squadron I left at Prevesa had arrived in the Negropont, I passed over, and paid a visit to its commander, with whom I was acquainted, Halil Pasha. Halil informed me that all remained quiet in Albania, but that Redschid did not venture to return. He added that he himself was about to sail from Stamboul immediately, and proposed that I should accompany him. His offer suited me, and as the wind was fair, in a few hours we were all on board.

I had a most splendid view of Sunium, its columns against a dark cloud looked like undriven snow, and we were soon among the Cyclades. Sixteen islands were in sight, and we were now making our course in the heart of them. An archipelago by sunset is lovely—small isles of purple and gold studding the glowing waters. The wind served well through the night, but we were becalmed the next day off Mitylene. In the afternoon, a fresh breeze sprung up and carried us to the Dardanelles.

We were yet, I believe, upwards of a hundred miles from Constantinople. What a road to a great city! narrower and much longer than the Straits of Gibraltar, but not with such sublime shores. Asia and Europe look more kindly on each other than Europe and her more sultry sister. I found myself, the next morning, becalmed off Troy: a vast hilly, uncultivated plain, a scanty rill, a huge tumulus, some shepherds and their flocks—behold the kingdom of Priam, and the successors of Paris!

A signal summoned us on board, the wind was fair and fresh. We scudded along with great swiftness, passing many towns and fortresses. Each dome, each minaret, I thought was Constantinople. At last it came; we were in full sight. Masses of habitations, grouped on gentle acclivities, rose on all sides out of the water, part in Asia, part in Europe; a gay and confused vision of rea buildings, and dark-green cypress groves, hooded domes, and millions of minarets. As we approached, the design became more obvious. The groups formed themselves into three considerable cities, intersected by arms of the sea. Down one of these, rounding the seraglio point, our vessel held her course. We seemed to glide into the heart of the capital. The water was covered with innumerable boats as swift as gondolas, and far more gay, curiously carved, and richly gilt. In all parts swarmed a showy population. The characteristic of the whole scene was brilliancy. The houses glittered, the waters sparkled, and flocks of white and sacred birds glanced in the golden air, and skimmed over the blue wave. On one side of the harbour was moored the Turkish fleet, dressed out in all their colours. Our course was ended, and we cast our anchor in the famous Golden Horn.

XXIII.

No picture can ever convey a just idea of Constantinople. I have seen several that are faithful, as far as they extend, but the most comprehensive can only exhibit a small portion of this extraordinary city. By land or by water, in every direction, passing up the Golden Horn to the valley of Sweet Waters, or proceeding on the other hand down the famous Bosphorus to Buyukdere, and Terapia, to the Euxine, what infinite novelty! New kiosks, new hills, new windings, new groves of cypress, and new forests of chestnut, open on all sides.

The two most wonderful things at Constantinople are the Bosphorus and the bazaar. Conceive the ocean a stream not broader than the Rhine, with shores with all the beauty and variety of that river, running between gentle slopes covered with rich woods, gardens, and summer palaces, cemeteries, and mosques, and villages, and bounded by sublime mountains. The view of the Euxine from the heights of Terapia, just seen through the end of the straits, is like gazing upon eternity.

The bazaar is of a very different order, but not less remarkable. I never could obtain from a Turk any estimate of the ground it covered. Several in the habit of daily attendance have mentioned to me that they often find themselves in divisions they have not before visited. Fancy a Parisian panorama passage, fancy perhaps a square mile covered with these arcades, intersecting each other in all directions, and full of every product of the empire, from diamonds to dates. This will give you some idea of the great bazaar at Constantinople. The dealers, in every possible costume, sit cross-legged on their stalls, and dealers in the same article usually congregate together. The armourers, the grocers, the pipemakers, the jewellers, the shawlsellers, the librarians, all have their distinct quarter. Now you walk along a range of stalls, filled with the most fanciful slippers, cloth and leather of all colours embroidered with gold, or powdered with pearls: now you are in the street of confectionary, and now you are cheapening a Damascus sabre in the bazaar of arms, or turning over a vividly illuminated copy of Hafiz in that last stronghold of Turkish bigotry, the quarter of the venders of the Koran. The magnificence, novelty, and variety of goods on sale, the whole nation of shopkeepers all in different dress, the crowds of buyers from all parts of the world—I only hint at these traits. Here every people has a characteristic costume; Turks, Greeks, Jews, and Armenians are the staple population, the latter are numerous. The Armenians wear round, and very unbecoming black caps, and flowing robes; the Jews a black hat wreathed with a white handkerchief; the Greeks black turbans. The Turks are fond of dress, and indulge in all combinations of costume. Of late, among the young men in the capital, it has been the fashion to discard the huge turban, and the ample robes, and they have formed an exceedingly ungraceful dress upon the Frank. But vast numbers cling to the national costume, especially the Asiatics, renowned for the prodigious height and multifarious folds of their head-gear.

XXIV.

Halil Pasha paid me a visit one day at my residence on the Bosphorus, and told me that he had mentioned my name to the sultan, who had expressed a desire to see me. As it is not etiquette for the padishah to receive Franks, I was of course as sensible of the high honour as I was anxious to become acquainted with the extraordinary man who was about to confer it.

The sultan was at this moment at a palace on the Bosphorus, not far from Tophana. Hither on the appointed day I repaired with Halil, and the drogueman of the Porte. We were ushered into a chamber, where a principal officer of the household received us, and where I smoked out of a pipe tipped with diamonds, and sipped coffee perfumed with roses in cups studded with precious stones.

When we had remained here for about half an hour, Mustapha, the private secretary and favourite of the sultan, entered, and after saluting us, desired us to follow him. We proceeded along a corridor, at the end of which stood two or three eunuchs, richly dressed, and then the door opened, and I found myself in an apartment of moderate size, painted with indifferent arabesques in fresco, and surrounded with a divan of crimson velvet and gold. Seated upon this, with his feet on the ground, his arms folded, and in a hussar dress, was the grand signor.

As we entered, he slightly touched his heart, according to the fashion of the Orientals, and Mustapha, setting us an example, desired us to seat ourselves. I fancied, and I was afterward assured of the correctness of my observation, that the sultan was very much constrained, and very little at his ease. The truth is, he is totally unused to interviews with strangers, and this was for him a more novel situation than for me. His constraint wore off as conversation proceeded. He asked a great many questions, and often laughed, turning round to Mustapha with a familiar nod when my replies pleased him. He inquired much about the Albanian war. Without flattering my late commander, it was in my power to do him service. He asked me what service I had before seen, and was evidently surprised when I informed him I was only an amateur. He then made many inquiries as to the European forces, and, as I answered them, I introduced some opinions on politics which interested him. He asked me who I was. I told him I was the son of the prime minister of ——, a power always friendly to the Ottoman. His eyes sparkled, and he repeated several times, "It is well, it is well:" meaning, I suppose, that he did not repent of the interview. He told me that in two years' time he should have two hundred thousand regular infantry. That if the Russian war could have been postponed another year, he should have beat the Muscovites; that the object of the war was to crush his schemes of regeneration; that he was betrayed at Adrianople as well as at Varna. He added that he had only done what Peter the Great had done before him, and that Peter was thwarted by unsuccessful wars, yet at last succeeded.

I, of course, expressed my conviction that his highness would be as fortunate.

The padishah then abruptly said that all his subjects should have equal rights, that there should be no difference between Moslemin and infidel, that all who contributed to the government had a right to the same protection,

Here Mustapha nodded to Halil, and we rose, and bowing, quitted the presence of a really great man.

I found, at the portal, a fine Arabian, two Cachemere shawls, a scarlet cloak of honour, with the collar embroidered with gold, and fastened with diamond clasps, a sabre, and two superb pipes. This was my reward for charging with the Turkish cavalry at Bitoglia.

XXV.

One of the most curious things at Constantinople is the power you have in the capital of the East of placing yourselves in ten minutes in a lively Frank town. Such is Pera. I passed there the winter months of December and January in very agreeable and intelligent society. My health improved, but my desire of wandering increased. I began to think that I should now never be able to settle in life. The desire of fame did not revive. I felt no intellectual energy, I required nothing more than to be amused. And having now passed four or five months at Stamboul, and seen all its wonders, from the interior of its mosques to the dancing dervishes, I resolved to proceed. So, one cold morning of February, I crossed over to Scutari, and pressed my wandering foot upon Asia.

PART THE SIXTH.

I.

I was now in the great peninsula of Asia Minor, a country admirably fortified by nature, abounding in vast, luxuriant, and enchanting plains, from which a scanty population derive a difficult subsistence, and watered by broad rivers rolling through solitude.

As I journeyed along I could not refrain from contrasting the desolation of the present with the refinement of the past, and calling up a vision of the ancient splendour of this famous country. I beheld those glorious Greek federations that covered the provinces of the coast with their rich cultivation and brilliant cities. Who has not heard of the green and bland Ionia, and its still more fruitful, although less picturesque sister, the rich Æolia? Who has not heard of the fane of Ephesus, and the Anacreontic Teios, Chios, with its rosy wine, and Cnidos, with its rosy goddess? Colophon, Priene, Phocæa, Samos, Miletos, the splendid Halicarnassus, and the sumptuous Cos—magnificent cities abounding in genius and luxury, and all that polished refinement that ennobles life? Everywhere around these free and famous citizens disseminated their liberty and their genius, in the savage Tauris, and on the wild shores of Pontus; on the banks of the Borysthenes, and by the waters of the rapid Tyras. The islands in their vicinity shared their splendour and their felicity; the lyric Lesbos, and Tenedos with its woods and vines, and those glorious gardens, the fortunate Cyprus and the prolific Rhodes.

Under the empire of Rome, the peninsula of Asia did not enjoy a less eminent prosperity. The interior provinces vied in wealth and civilization with the ancient colonies of the coast. Then the cavalry of Cappadocia and Paphlagonia were famous as the Lycian mariners, the soldiers of Pontus, and the bowmen of Armenia; then Galatia sent forth her willing and welcome tribute of corn, and the fruitful Bithynia rivalled the Pamphylian pastures, the vines of Phrygia, and the Pisidian olives. Tarsus, Ancyra, Sardos, Cæsarea, Sinope, Amisus, were the great and opulent capitals of these flourishing provinces. Alexandria rose upon the ruins of Tyre, and Nicæa and Nicomedia ranked with the most celebrated cities.

And now the tinkling bell of the armed and wandering caravan was the only indication of human existence!

It is in such scenes as these, amid the ruins of ancient splendour, and the recollection of vanished empire, that philosophers have pondered on the nature of government, and have discovered, as they fancied, in the consequences of its various forms, the causes of duration or of decay, of glory or of humiliation. Freedom, says the sage, will lead to prosperity, and despotism to destruction.

Yet has this land been regulated by every form of government that the ingenuity of man has devised. The federal republic, the military empire, the oriental despotism, have in turn controlled its fortunes. The deputies of free states have here assembled in some universal temple which was the bond of union between their cities; here has the proconsul presided at his high tribunal; and here the pasha reposes in his divan. The Pagan fane, and the Christian church, and the Turkish mosque, have here alike been erected to form the opinions of the people. The legends of Chaos and Olympus are forgotten, the sites of the Seven Churches cannot even be traced, and all that is left are the revelations of the son of Kahrida, a volume, the whole object of which is to convert man into a fanatic slave.

Is there then no hope? Is it an irrevocable doom, that society shall be created only to be destroyed? When I can accept such a dogma, let me also believe that the beneficent Creator is a malignant demon. Let us meditate more deeply, let us at length discover that no society can long subsist that is based upon metaphysical absurdities.

The law that regulates man must be founded on a knowledge of his nature, or that law leads him to ruin. What is the nature of man? In every clime and in every creed we shall find a new definition.

Before me is a famous treatise on Human Nature, by a professor of Konigsberg. No one has more profoundly meditated on the attributes of his subject. It is evident that in the deep study of his own intelligence, he has discovered a noble method of expounding that of others. Yet when I close his volumes can I conceal from myself that all this time I have been studying a treatise upon the nature—not of man, but—of a German?

What then! Is the German a different animal from the Italian? Let me inquire in turn whether you conceive the negro of the Gold Coast to be the same being as the Esquimaux, who tracks his way over the polar snows?

The most successful legislators are those who have consulted the genius of the people. But is it possible to render that which is the occasional consequence of fine observation, the certain result of scientific study?

One thing is quite certain, that the system we have hitherto pursued to attain a knowledge of man has entirely failed. Let us disembarrass ourselves of that "moral philosophy," which has filled so many volumes with words. History will always remain a pleasant pastime; it never could have been a profitable study. To study man from the past is to suppose, that man is ever the same animal, which I do not. Those who speculated on the career of Napoleon had ever a dog's-eared annalist to refer to. The past equally proved that he was both a Cromwell and a Washington. Prophetic past! He turned out to be the first. But suppose he had been neither; suppose he had proved a Sylla?

Man is an animal, and his nature must be studied as that of all other animals. The Almighty Creator has breathed his spirit into us, and we testify our gratitude for this choice boon by never deigning to consider what may be the nature of our intelligence. The philosopher, however, amid this darkness, will not despair. He will look forward to an age of rational laws and beneficent education. He will remember that all the truth he has attained has been by one process. He will also endeavour to become acquainted with himself by demonstration, and not by dogma.

II.

One fair spring morning, with a clear blue sky and an ardent but not intense sun, I came in sight of the whole coast of Syria; very high and mountainous, and the loftiest ranges covered with snow.

I had sailed from Smyrna through its lovely gulf, vaster and more beautiful than the Ambracian, found myself in a new archipelago, the Sporades, and having visited Rhodes and Cyprus, engaged, at the last island, a pilot, to take us to the most convenient Syrian port.

Syria is, in fact, an immense chain of mountains, extending from Asia Minor to Arabia. In the course of this great chain, an infinity of branches constantly detach themselves from the parent trunk, forming on each side, either towards the desert or the sea, beautiful and fertile plains. Washed by the Levantine wave, on one side we behold the once luxurious Antioch, now a small and dingy Turkish town. The traveller can no longer wander in the voluptuous woods of Daphne. The palace and the garden pass away with the refined genius and the delicate taste that create them, but nature is eternal, and even yet the valley of the Orontes offers, under the glowing light of an eastern day, scenes of picturesque beauty that Switzerland cannot surpass. The hills of Laodicea, once famous for their wine are now celebrated for producing the choicest tobacco of the East. Tripoli is a flourishing town, embosomed in wild groves of Indian figs, and famous for its fruits and silks. Advancing along the coast we reach the ancient Berytus, whose tobacco vies with Laodicea, and whose silk surpasses that of Tripoli. We arrive at all that remains of the superb Tyre; a small peninsula and a mud village. The famous Acre is still the most important place upon the coast, and Jaffa, in spite of so many wars, is yet fragrant amid its gardens and groves of lemon trees.

The towns on the coast have principally been built on the sites and ruins of the ancient cities whose names they bear. None of them have sufficient claims to the character of a capital; but on the other side of the mountains we find two of the most important of oriental cities—the populous Aleppo and the delicious Damascus; nor must we forget Jerusalem, that city sacred in so many creeds!

In ancient remains, Syria is only inferior to Egypt. All have heard of the courts of Baalbec, and the columns of Palmyra. Less known, because only recently visited, and visited with extreme danger, are the vast ruins of magnificent cities in the Arabian vicinity of the Lake Asphaltites.

The climate of this country is as various as its formation. In the plains is often experienced that intense heat so fatal to the European invader; yet the snow that seldom falls upon the level ground, or falls only to vanish, rests upon the heights of Lebanon, and, in the higher lands, it is not difficult at all times to discover exactly the temperature you desire. I travelled in Syria at the commencement of the year, when the short, but violent rainy season had just ceased. It is not easy to conceive a more beautiful and fruitful land. The plains were covered with that fresh green tint so rare under an Eastern sky, the orange and lemon trees were clothed both with fruit and blossom, and then too I first beheld the huge leaf of the banana, and tasted, for the first time, the delicate flavour of its unrivalled fruit. From the great extent of the country, and the consequent variation of clime, the Syrian can always command a succession, as well as a variety of luxuries. The season of the pomegranate will commence in Antioch when it ends in Jaffa, and when you have exhausted the figs of Beiroot, you can fly to the gardens of Damascus. Under the worst government that perhaps ever oppressed its subjects, Syria still brings forth the choice productions of almost every clime; corn and cotton, maize and rice, the sugar-cane of the Antilles, and the indigo and cochineal of Mexico. The plains of Antioch and of Palestine are covered with woods of the finest olives, the tobaccos of the coast are unrivalled in any country, and the mountains of Lebanon are clothed with white mulberry trees, that afford the richest silks, or with vineyards that yield a wine that justly bears the name of Golden.

The inhabitants of this country are various as its productions, and its mutable fortunes. The Ottoman conqueror is now the lord, and rules the posterity of the old Syrian Greeks and of the Arabs, who were themselves once predominant. In the mountains, the independent and mysterious Druses live in freedom under their own emir, and, in the ranges near Antioch, we find the Ansaree tribes, who, it is whispered, yet celebrate the most singular rites of paganism. In the deserts around Aleppo wander the pastoral Kourd and the warlike Turkman, and from Tadmor to Gaza, the whole Syrian desert is traversed by the famous Bedouin.

There is a charm in oriental life, and it is—repose. Upon me, who had been bred in the artificial circles of corrupt civilization, and who had so freely indulged the course of my impetuous passions, this character made a very forcible impression. Wandering over those plains and deserts, and sojourning in those silent and beautiful cities, I experienced all that serenity of mind which I can conceive to be the enviable portion of the old age of a virtuous life. The memory of the wearing cares, and corroding anxieties, and vaunted excitement of European life, filled me with pain. Keenly I felt the vanity and littleness of all human plans and aspirations. Truly may I say, that on the plains of Syria, I parted forever with my ambition. The calm enjoyment of existence appeared to me, as it now does, the highest attainable felicity; nor can I conceive that any thing could tempt me from my solitude, and induce me once more to mingle with mankind, with whom, I fear, I have too little in common, but the strong conviction that the fortunes of my race depended on my effort, or that I could materially advance the great amelioration of their condition, in the practicability of which I devoutly believe.

III.

I galloped over an illimitable plain, covered with a vivid, though scanty pasture, and fragrant with aromatic herbs. A soft, fresh breeze danced on my cheek, and brought vigour to my frame. Day after day I journeyed, and met no sign of human existence, no village, no culture, no resting-place, not even a tree. Day after day I journeyed, and the land indicated no termination. At an immense distance, the sky and the earth mingled in a uniform horizon. Sometimes, indeed, a rocky vein shot out of the soil; sometimes, indeed, the land would swell into long undulations; sometimes, indeed, from a dingle of wild bushes, a gazelle would rush forward, stare, and bound away.

Such was my first wandering in the Syrian desert! But remember it was the burst of spring. I could conceive nothing more delightful, nothing more unlike what I had anticipated. The heat was never intense, the breeze was ever fresh and sweet, the nocturnal heavens luminous and clear to a degree which it is impossible to describe. Instead of that uniform appearance, and monotonous splendour I had hitherto so often gazed on, the stars were of different tints and forms. Some were green, some white, some red; and, instead of appearing as if they only studded a vast and azure vault, I clearly distinguished them, at different distances, floating in ether.

I no longer wondered at the love of the Bedouins for their free and unsophisticated earth. It appeared to me, that I could have lived in the desert forever. At night we rested. Our camels bore us water in goat-skins, cakes of fuel, which they themselves produced, and scanty, although sufficient, provisions. We lit our fire, pounded our coffee, and smoked our pipes, while others prepared our simple meal, bread made at the instant, and on the cinders, a slice of dried meat, and a few dates.

I have described the least sterile of the deserts,

and I have described it at the most favourable period. In general, the soil of the Syrian wilderness is not absolutely barren. The rains cover it with verdure, but these occur only for a very few weeks, when the rigour of a winter day arrests the clouds, and they dissolve into showers. At all other seasons they glide over the scorched and heated plain, which has neither hills nor trees to attract them. It is then the want of water which is the occasion of this sterility. In the desert there is not even a brook, springs are rare, and generally brackish, and it is on the artificial wells, stored by the rains, that the wanderer chiefly depends.

From the banks of the Euphrates to the shores of the Red Sea; from the banks of the Nile to the Persian Gulf, over a spread of country three times the extent of Germany, nature, without an interval, ceases to produce. Beneficent nature! Let us not wrong her; for even in a land apparently so unfavoured, exists a numerous and happy race. As you wander along, the appearance of the desert changes. The wilderness, which is comparatively fertile in Syria, becomes rocky when you enter Arabia, and sandy as you proceed. Here, in some degree, we meet with the terrible idea of the desert prevalent in Europe; but it is in Africa, in the vast and unexplored regions of Lybia and Zahara, that we must seek for that illimitable and stormy ocean of overwhelming sand, which we associate with the popular idea of the desert.

The sun was nearly setting when an Arab horseman, armed with his long lance, was suddenly observed on an eminence in the distance. He galloped towards us, wheeled round and round, scudded away, again approached, and our guide, shouting, rode forward to meet him. They entered into earnest conversation, and then joined us. Abdallah, the guide, informed me that this was an Arab of the tribe I intended to visit, and that we were very near their encampment.

The desert was here broken into bushy knolls, which limited the view. Advancing and mounting the low ridge on which we had at first observed the Bedouin, Abdallah pointed out to me, at no great distance, a large circle of low black tents, which otherwise I might not have observed, or have mistaken them in the deceptive twilight for some natural formation. On the left of the encampment was a small grove of palm trees, and when he had nearly gained the settlement, a procession of women in long blue robes, covering with one hand their faces with their veils, and with the other supporting on their heads a tall and classically formed vase, advanced with a beautiful melody, to the fountain, which was screened by the palm trees.

The dogs barked, some dark faces and long matchlocks suddenly popped up behind the tents. The Bedouin, with a shout, galloped into the encampment, and soon reappeared with several of his tribe. We dismounted. I entered into the interior court of the camp, which was filled with camels and goats. There were few persons visible, although as I was conducted along to the tent of the chief, I detected many faces staring at me from behind the curtains of their tents. The pavilion of the sheikh was of considerable size. He himself was a man advanced in years, but hale and lively; his long white beard curiously contrasting with his dark visage. He received me sitting on a mat, his son standing on his right hand, without his slippers, and a young grandchild squatting by his side.

He welcomed me with the usual oriental salutation, touching his forehead, his mouth, and his heart, while he exclaimed, "Salam;" thus indicating that all his faculties and feelings were devoted to me. He motioned that we should seat ourselves on the unoccupied mats, and taking from his mouth a small pipe of date wood, gave it to his son to bear to me. A servant instantly began pounding coffee. I then informed him, through Abdallah, that having heard of his hospitality and nappy life, I had journeyed even from Damascus to visit him; that I greatly admired the Bedouin character, and I eulogized their valour, their independence, their justice, and their simplicity.

He answered that he liked to be visited by Franks, because they were wise men, and requested that I would feel his pulse.

I performed this ceremony with becoming gravity, and inquired whether he were indisposed. He said that he was well, but that he might be better. I told him that his pulse was healthy and strong for one of his age, and I begged to examine his tongue, which greatly pleased him, and he observed that he was eighty years of age, and could ride as well, and as long as his son.

Coffee was now brought. I ventured to praise it. He said it was well for those who had not wine. I observed that wine was not suited to these climes, and that although a Frank, I had myself renounced it. He answered that the Franks were fond of wine, but that for his part he had never tasted it, although he should like once.

I regretted that I could not avail myself of this delicate hint, but Lausanne produced a bottle of eau de Cologne, and I offered him a glass. He drank it with great gravity, and asked for some for his son, observing it was good raki, but not wine. I suspected from this that he was not totally unacquainted with the flavour of the forbidden liquor, and I dared to remark with a smile that raki had one advantage over wine, that it was not forbidden by the prophet. Unlike the Turks, who never understand a jest, he smiled, and then said that the book (meaning the Koran) was good for men who lived in cities, but that God was everywhere.

Several men now entered the tent, leaving their slippers on the outside, and some saluting the sheikh as they passed, seated themselves.

I now inquired after horses, and asked him whether he could assist me in purchasing some of the true breed. The old sheikh's eyes sparkled as he informed me that he possessed four mares of pure blood, and that he would not part with one, not even for fifty thousand piastres. After this hint I was inclined to drop the subject, but the sheikh seemed interested by it, and inquired if the Franks had any horses?

I answered that some Frank nations were famous for their horses, and mentioned the English, who had bred a superb race from the Arabs. He said he had heard of the English, and asked me which was the greatest nation of the Franks? I told him there were several equally powerful, but perhaps that the English nation might be fairly described as the most important. He answered. "Ay! on the sea, but not on the land."

I was surprised by the general knowledge indicated by this remark, and more so when he further observed that there was another nation stronger by land. I mentioned the Russians. He had not heard of them, notwithstanding the recent war with the Porte. The French? I inquired. He knew the French, and then told me he had been at the siege of Acre, which explained all this intelligence. He then inquired if I were an Englishman? I told him my country, but was not astonished that he had never heard of it. I observed that when the old man spoke, he was watched by his followers with the greatest attention, and they grinned with pride and exultation at his knowledge of the Franks, showing their white teeth, elevating their eyes, and exchanging looks of wonder.

Two women now entered the tent, at which I was surprised. They had returned from the fountian, and wore small black masks, which covered the upper part of their face. They knelt down at the fire, and made a cake of bread, which one of them handed to me. I now offered to the sheikh my own pipe, which Lausanne had prepared. Coffee was again handed, and a preparation of sour milk and rice, not unpalatable.

I offered the sheikh renewed compliments on his mode of life, in order to maintain conversation; for the chief, although like the Arabs in general, of a very lively temperament, had little of the curiosity of what are considered the more civilized orientals, and asked very few questions.

"We are content," said the sheikh.

"Then, believe me, you are in the condition of no other people," I replied.

"My children," said the sheikh, "hear the words of the wise man! If we lived with the Turks," continued the chieftain, "we should have more gold and silver, and more clothes, and carpets, and baths; but we should not have justice and liberty. Our luxuries are few, but our wants are less."

"Yet you have neither priests nor lawyers?"

"When men are pure, laws are useless: when men are corrupt, laws are broken."

"And for priests?"

"God is everywhere."

The women now entered with a more substantial meal, the hump of a young camel. I have seldom eaten any thing more delicate and tender. This dish was a great compliment, and could only have been offered by a wealthy sheikh. Pipes and coffee followed.

The moon was shining brightly when, making my excuses, I quitted the pavilion of the chieftain, and went forth to view the humours of the camp. The tall camels crouching on their knees in groups, with their outstretched necks, and still and melancholy visages, might have been mistaken for works of art, had it not been for the process of rumination. A crowd was assembled round a fire, before which a poet recited impassioned verses. I observed the slight forms of the men, short and meager, agile, dry, and dark, with teeth dazzling white, and quick, black glancing eyes. They were dressed in cloaks of coarse black cloth, apparently of the same stuff as their tents, and few of them, I should imagine, exceeded five feet two or three inches in height. The women mingled with the men, although a few affected to conceal their faces on my approach. They were evidently deeply interested in the poetic recital. One passage excited their loud applause. I inquired its purport of Abdallah, who thus translated it to me. A lover beholds his mistress, her face covered with a red vail. Thus he addresses her.

"O! withdraw that veil, withdraw that red veil! Let me behold the beauty that it shrouds! Yes! let that rosy twilight fade away, and let the full moon rise to my vision!"

Beautiful! Yet more beautiful in the languag of the Arabs, for in that rich tongue there are words to describe each species of twilight, and where we are obliged to have recourse to an epithet, the Arabs reject the feeble and unnecessary aid.

It was late ere I retired, and I stretched myself on my mat, musing over this singular people, who combined primitive simplicity of habits with the most refined feelings of civilization, and who in a great degree appeared to me to offer an evidence of that community of property, and that equality of condition, which have hitherto proved the despair of European sages, and fed only the visions of their fanciful Utopias.

IV.

A Syrian village is very beautiful in the centre of a fertile plain. The houses are isolated, and each surrounded by palm trees; the meadows divided by rich plantations of Indian fig, and bounded by groves of olive.

In the distance rose a chain of severe and savage mountains. I was soon wandering, and for hours, in the wild, stony ravines of these shaggy rocks. At length, after several paces, I gained the ascent of a high mountain. Upon an opposite height, descending as a steep ravine, and forming with the elevation on which I rested, a dark and narrow gorge, I behold a city entirely surrounded, by what I should have considered in Europe an old feudal wall, with towers and gates. The city was built upon an ascent, and, from the height on which I stood, I could discern the terrace and the cupola of almost every house, and the wall upon the other side rising from the plain; the ravine extending only on the side to which I was opposite. The city was in a bowl of mountains. In the front was a magnificent mosque, with beautiful gardens and many light and lofty gates of triumph; a variety of domes and towers rose in all directions from the buildings of bright stone.

Nothing could be conceived more wild, and terrible, and desolate than the surrounding scenery, more dark, and stony, and severe; but the ground was thrown about in such picturesque undulations, that the mind, full of the sublime, required not the beautiful; and rich, and waving woods, and sparkling cultivation would have been misplaced. Except Athens, I had never witnessed any scene more essentially impressive. I will not place this spectacle below the city of Minerva. Athens and the holy city in their glory must have been the finest representations of the beautiful and the sublime—the holy city, for the elevation on which I stood was the Mount of Olives, and the city on which I gazed was Jerusalem!

V.

The dark gorge beneath me was the vale of Jehoshaphat; farther on, was the fountain of Siloah. I entered by the gate of Bethlehem, and sought hospitality at the Latin convent of Terra Santa.

Easter was approaching, and the city was crowded with pilgrims. I had met many caravans in my progress. The convents of Jerusalem are remarkable. That of the Armenian Christians, at this time, afforded accommodation for four thousand pilgrims. It is a town of itself, and possesses within its walls streets and shops. The Greek convent held perhaps half as many. And the famous Latin convent of Terra Santa, endowed by all the monarchs of Catholic Christendom, could boast only of one pilgrim—myself! The Europeans have ceased to visit the holy sepulchre.

As for the interior of Jerusalem, it is hilly and clean. The houses are of stone, and well built, but, like all Asiatic mansions, they offer nothing to the eye but blank walls and dull portals. The mosque I had admired was the famous Mosque of Omar, built upon the supposed site of the temple. It is perhaps the most beautiful of Mohammedan temples; but the Frank, even in the Eastern dress, will enter it at the risk of his life. The Turks of Syria have not been contaminated by the heresies of their enlightened sultan. In Damascus, it is impossible to appear in the Frank dress without being pelted; and although they would condescend, perhaps, at Jerusalem, to permit an infidel dog to walk about in his national dress, he would not escape many a curse, and many a scornful expression of "Giaour!" There is only one way to travel in the East with ease, and that is with an appearance of pomp. The Turks are much influenced by the exterior, and although they are not mercenary, a well-dressed and well-attended infidel will command respect.

VI.

The church of the Holy Sepulchre is nearly in the middle of the city, and professedly built upon Mount Calvary, which it is alleged was levelled for the structure. Within its walls they have contrived to assemble the scenes of a vast number of incidents in the life of the Saviour, with a highly romantic violation of the unity of the place. Here the sacred feet were anointed, there the sacred garments parcelled, from the pillar of the scourging to the rent of the rock, all is exhibited in a succession of magical scenes. The truth is, the whole is an ingenious imposture of a comparatively recent date, and we are indebted to that favoured individual, the Empress Helen, for this exceedingly clever creation, as well as for the discovery of the true cross. The learned believe, and with reason, that Calvary is at present, as formerly, without the walls, and that we must seek for this celebrated elevation in the lofty hill now called Sion.

The church is a spacious building, surrounded by a dome. Attached to it are the particular churches of the various Christian sects, and many chapels and sanctuaries. Mass in some part or other is constantly celebrating, and companies of pilgrims may be observed in all directions visiting the holy places, and offering their devotions. Latin, and Armenian, and Greek friars are everywhere moving about. The court is crowded with the venders of relics and rosaries. The church of the Sepulchre itself is a point of common union, and in its bustle and lounging character, rather reminded me of an exchange than a temple.

One day as I was pacing up and down this celebrated building, in conversation with a very ingenious Neapolitan friar, experienced in the East, my attention was attracted by one who, from his sumptuous dress, his imposing demeanour, self-satisfied air, and the coolness with which, in a Christian temple, he waved in his hand a rosary of Mecca, I for a moment considered a Moslemin. "Is it customary for the Turks to visit this place?" I inquired, drawing the attention of my companion to the stranger.

"The stranger is not a Turk," answered the friar, "though I fear I cannot call him a Christian. It is Marigny, a French traveller. Do you not know him? I will introduce you. He is a man of distinguished science, and has resided some months in this city, studying Arabic."

We approached him, and the friar made us acquainted.

"Salem Aleikoum! Count. Here at least is no Inquisition. Let us enjoy ourselves. How mortifying, my good brother Antony, that you cannot burn me!"

The friar smiled, and was evidently used to this raillery.

"I hope yet to behold the Kaaba," said Marigny, "it is at least more genuine than any thing we here see."

"Truth is not truth to the false," said Brother Antony.

"What, you reason!" exclaimed Marigny "Stick to faith and infallibility, my good friend Antonio. I have just been viewing the rent in the rock. It is a pity, holy father, that I have discovered that it is against the grain."

"The greater the miracle," said the friar.

"Bravo! you deserve to be a bishop."

"The church has no fear of just reasoners," observed Brother Antony.

"And is confuted, I suppose, only by the unjust," rejoined Marigny.

"Man without religion is a wild beast," remarked the friar.

"Which religion?" inquired Marigny.

"There is only one true religion," said Brother Antony.

"Exactly; and in this country, Master Antony remember you are an infidel."

"And you, they say, are a Moslemin."

"They say wrong. I believe in no human revelation, because it obtrudes the mind of another man into my body, and must destroy morality which can only be discovered by my own intelligence."

"All is divine revelation," said a stranger who joined us.

"Ah! Werner," said Marigny, "you see we are at our old contests."

"All is divine revelation," repeated Werner, "for all comes from God."

"But what do you mean by God?"

"I mean the great luminous principle of existence, the first Almighty Cause from whom we are emanations, and in whose essence we shall again mingle."

"I asked for bread and you give me a stone. I asked for a fact, and you give me a word. I cannot annex an idea to what you say. Until my Creator gift me with an intelligence that can comprehend the idea of his existence, I must conclude that he does not desire that I should busy myself about it."

"That idea is implanted in our breasts," said Werner.

"Innate!" exclaimed Marigny, with a sneer.

"And why not innate?" replied Werner, solemnly. "Is it impossible for the Great Being who created us, to create us with a sense of his existence?"

"Listen to these philosophers," said Brother Antony; "I never heard two of them agree. I must go to mass."

"Mr. Werner and myself, count," said Marigny, "are about to smoke a pipe with Besso, a rich Hebrew merchant here. He is one of the finest-hearted fellows in the world, and generous as he is rich. Will you accompany us? You will greatly honour him, and find in his divan some intelligent society."

VII.

Marigny was a skeptic, and an absolute materialist, yet he was influenced by noble views, for he had devoted his life to science, and was now, at his own charge, about to penetrate into the interior of Africa, by Sennaar. Werner was a German divine, and a rationalist, tauntingly described by his companion as a devout Christian, who did not believe in Christianity. Yet he had resided in Palestine and Egypt nearly four years, studying their language and customs, and accumulating materials for a history of the miraculous creed whose miracles he explained. Both were men of remarkable intellectual powers, and the ablest champions of their respective systems.

I accompanied these new acquaintances to the house of Besso, and was most hospitably received and sumptuously entertained. I have seldom met a man with more easy manners and a more gracious carriage than Besso, who, although sincere in his creed, was the least bigoted of his tribe. He introduced us to his visiter, his friend, and correspondent, Sheriff Effendi, an Egyptian merchant, and who fortunately spoke the lingua Franca with facility. The other guest was an Englishman, by name Benson, a missionary, and a very learned, pious, and acute man.

Such was the party in whose society I generally spent a portion of my day during my residence at Jerusalem, and I have often thought, that were the conversations to which I have there listened recorded, a volume might be sent forth of more wit and wisdom than are now usually met with. The tone of discussion was, in general, metaphysical and scientific, varied with speculations principally on African travel, a subject with which Sheriff Effendi was well acquainted. In metaphysics, sharp were the contests between Benson, Marigny, and Werner, and on all sides ably maintained. I listened to them with great interest. Besso smiled, and Sheriff Effendi shrugged his shoulders.

Understanding this mild and intelligent Moslemin was in a few days about to join the caravan over the desert through Gaza to Egypt, I resolved to accompany him. I remember well that on the eve of our departure, one of those metaphysical discussions arose in which Marigny delighted. When it terminated, he proposed, that as our agreeable assembly was soon about to disperse, each of us should inscribe, on a panel of the wall, some sentence as a memorial of his sojourn.

Benson wrote first, "*For as in Adam all die, so in Christ all men shall be made alive.*"

Werner wrote, "*Glory to Christ! The supernatural has destroyed the natural.*"

Marigny wrote, "*Knowledge is human.*"

Besso wrote, "*I will not believe in those who must believe in me.*"

Sheriff Effendi wrote, "*God is great. Man should be charitable.*"

Contarini Fleming wrote, "*Time.*"

These are the words that were written in the house of Besso, the Hebrew, residing at Jerusalem, near the gate of Sion. Amen! Travel teaches toleration

VIII.

Perchance, while I am writing these pages, some sage may be reading, in the once mysterious inscriptions of the most ancient of people, some secret which may change the foundations of human knowledge. Already the chronology of the world assumes a new aspect, already in the now intelligible theology of Egypt, we have discovered the origin of Grecian polytheism, already we have penetrated beyond the delusive veil of Ptolemaic transmutation: Isis has yielded to Athor, and Osiris to Knepth. The scholar discards the Grecian nomenclature of Sesostris and Memnon. In the temples of Carnac, he discovers the conquests of Rameses, and in the palaces of Medinet Abou, the refined civilization of Amenoph.

Singular fate of modern ages, that beneficent Omnipotence has willed, that for all our knowledge, we should be indebted to the most insignificant of ancient states. Our divine instruction is handed down to us by an Arabian tribe, and our profane learning flows only from the clans of the Ægean!

Where are the records of the great Assyrian monarchy? Where are the books of the Medes and Persians? Where the learned annals of the Pharaohs?

Fortunate Jordan! Fortunate Ilissus! I have waded through the sacred waters; with difficulty, I traced the scanty windings of the classic stream. Alas! for the exuberant Tigris; alas! for the mighty Euphrates; alas! for the mysterious Nile!

A river is suddenly found flowing through the wilderness; its source is unknown. On one side are interminable wastes of sand; on the other a rocky desert and a narrow sea. Thus it rolls on for five hundred miles, throwing up on each side, to the extent of about three leagues, a soil fertile as a garden. Within a hundred and fifty miles of the sea it divides into two branches, which wind through an immense plain, once the granary of the world. Such is Egypt!

From the cataracts of Nubia to the gardens of the Delta, in a course of twelve hundred miles, the banks of the Nile are covered at slight intervals with temples and catacombs, pyramids and painted chambers. The rock temples of Ipsambol, guarded by colossal forms, are within the roar of the second cataract: avenues of sphinxes lead to Derr, the chief town of Nubia: from Derr to the first cataract, the Egyptian boundary, a series of rock temples conduct to the beautiful and sacred buildings of Philœ: Edfou and Esneh are a fine preparation for the colossal splendour and the massy grace of ancient Thebes.

Even after the inexhaustible curiosity and varied magnificence of this unrivalled record of ancient art, the beautiful Dendera, consummate blending of Egyptian imagination and Grecian taste, will command your enthusiastic gaze; and if the catacombs of Siout, and the chambers of Benihassan prove less fruitful of interest after the tombs of the kings, and the cemeteries of Gornou, before you are the obelisks of Memphis, and the pyramids of Gizeh, Saccarah, and Dashour!

IX.

The traveller who crosses the desert, and views the Nile with its lively villages, clustered in groves of palm, and its banks entirely lined with that graceful tree, will bless with sincerity "The Father of Waters." 'Tis a rich land, and indeed flowing with milk and honey. The Delta, in its general appearance, somewhat reminded me of Belgium. The soil everywhere is a rich black mud, without a single stone. The land is so uniformly flat, that those who arrive by sea do not detect it until within half a dozen miles, when a palm tree creeps upon the horizon, and then you observe the line of land that supports it. The Delta is intersected by canals which are filled with the rising Nile. It is by their medium, and not by the absolute overflowing of the river, that the country is periodically deluged.

The Arabs are gay, witty, vivacious, and very susceptible and acute. It is difficult to render them miserable, and a beneficent government might find in them the most valuable subjects. A delightful climate is some compensation for a grinding tyranny. Every night as they row along the moonlit river, the boatmen join in a melodious chorus, shouts of merriment burst from each illumined village, everywhere are heard the sounds of laughter and of music, and wherever you stop you are saluted by the dancing girls. These are always graceful in their craft; sometimes very agreeable in their persons. They are gayly, even richly dressed: in bright colours, with their hair braided with pearls, and their necks and foreheads adorned with strings of gold coin. In their voluptuous dance we at once detect the origin of the boleros, and fandangos, and castanets of Spain.

I admire very much the Arab women. They are very delicately moulded. Never have I seen such twinkling feet, and such small hands. Their complexion is clear, and not dark; their features beautifully formed, and sharply defined; their eyes liquid with passion, and bright with intelligence. The traveller is delighted to find himself in an oriental country where the women are not imprisoned, and scarcely veiled. For a long time I could not detect the reason why I was so charmed with Egyptian life. At last I recollected that I had recurred, after a long estrangement, to the cheerful influence of women.

X.

I followed the course of the Nile far into Nubia, and did not stop until I was under the tropic of Cancer. Shortly after quitting Egypt the landscape changes. It is perfectly African; mountains of burning sand, vegetation unnaturally vivid, groves of cocoa trees, groups of crocodiles, and an ebony population in a state of nudity, armed with spears of reeds, and shields of the hippopotamus and the giraffe.

The voyage back was tedious, and I was glad, after so much wandering, to settle down in Cairo.

XI.

Cairo is situated on the base of considerable hills, whose origin cannot be accounted for, but which are undoubtedly artificial. They are formed by the ruins and the rubbish of long centuries. When I witness these extraordinary formations, which are not uncommon in the neighbourhood of eastern cities, I am impressed with the idea of the immense antiquity of oriental society.

There is a charm about Cairo, and it is this,—that it is a capital in a desert. In one moment you are in the stream of existence, and in the other in boundless solitude, or, which is still more awful, the silence of tombs. I speak of the sepulchre of the Mamlouk sultans without the city. They form what may indeed be styled a city of the dead an immense necropolis, full of exquisite buildings, domes covered with fret-work, and minarets carved and moulded with rich and elegant fancy. To me, they proved much more interesting than the far-famed pyramids, although their cones in a distance are indeed sublime,—their gray cones soaring in the light blue sky.

The genius that has raised the tombs of the sultans, may also be traced in many of the mosques of the city—splendid specimens of Saracenic architecture. In gazing upon these brilliant creations, and also upon those of ancient Egypt, I have often been struck by the felicitous system which they display, of ever forming the external ornaments by inscriptions. How far excelling the Grecian and Gothic method! Instead of a cornice of flowers, or an entablature of unmeaning fancy, how superior to be reminded of the power of the Creator, or the necessity of government, the deeds of conquerors, or the discoveries of arts!

XII.

It was in these solitary rides in the Desert of Cairo, and in these lone wanderings amid the tombs of the sultans, that I first again felt the desire of composition. My mind appeared suddenly to have returned. I became restless, disquieted. I found myself perpetually indulging in audible soliloquy, and pouring forth impassioned monologues. I was pleased with the system of oriental life, and the liberty in which in Egypt Franks can indulge. I felt no inclination to return to Europe, and I determined to cast my lot in this pleasant and fruitful land. I had already spent in Cairo several months, and I now resolved to make it my permanent residence, when I received strange letters from my father. I style them strange, for there breathed throughout a tone of melancholy which with him was quite unusual, and which perplexed me. He complained of ill-health, and expressed a hope that my wanderings were drawing to a close, and that we might again meet. I had been nearly six years absent. Was it possible? Was it indeed six years since I stood upon Mount Jura? And yet in that time how much had happened! How much had I seen, and felt, and learned! What violent passions, what strange countries, what lively action, and what long meditation!

Strange as may have appeared my conduct to my father, I loved him devotedly. An indication of sentiment on his part ever called forth all my latent affection. It was the conviction from which I could never divest myself, that he was one who could spare no portion of his sense for the softer feelings, and that his conduct to me was rather in accordance with the system of society than instigated by what I should consider the feelings of a father—it was this conviction that had alone permitted me so long to estrange myself from his hearth. But now he called me back, and almost in sorrow. I read his letter over and over again, dwelt on all its affection, and on all its suppressed grief. I felt an irresistible desire to hasten to him without a moment's delay. I longed to receive his blessing and his embrace.

I quitted Cairo. The Mahmadie canal was not yet open. I was obliged, therefore, to sail to Rosetto. Thence I crossed the desert in a constant mirage, and arrived at the famous Alexandria. In this busy port I was not long in finding a ship. One was about to sail for Ancona. I engaged a passage, and soon the palms and sands of Egypt vanished from my sight.

XIII.

Our passage was tedious. The captain was afraid of pirates, and, alarmed in the night, suddenly changed his course, and made for the Barbary coast, by which we lost our wind. We were becalmed off Candia. I once more beheld Mount Ida.

I induced the captain to run into port. I landed once more on that fatal coast. The old consul and his family were still there, and received me with a kindness which reminded me of our first happy meeting. I slept in the same chamber. I woke in the morning—the sun was still shining, the bright plants still quivering in its beams. But the gazelle had gone—the white gazelle had died. And my gazelle—where was she?

I beheld our home—our once happy home. Spiro only was with me, and his family came forth with joy to greet him. I left them. I hastened with tremulous steps to the happy valley. I passed by the grove of orange trees. My strength deserted me. I leaned, nearly fainting, against a tree. At last, I dared to advance a step, and look forward.

I beheld it. Yes! I beheld it, green and verdant, and covered with white roses, but I dared not approach. I wafted it a kiss and a blessing, and rushed like a madman to the shore.

At Ancona, I entered the lazaretto to perform a long quarantine. I instantly wrote to my father, and I despatched a courier to my banker at Florence. I received from him, in a few days, a packet. I opened it with a sad foreboding. A letter in my father's handwriting reassured me. I tore it open—I read.

XIV.

"My beloved Contarini, the hand of death is upon me. Each day my energies decrease. I can conceal from others, but not from myself, my gradual, but certain decay. We shall not meet again, my child—I have a deep conviction we shall not meet again. Yet I would not die without expressing to you my love, without yielding to feelings which I have too long suppressed.

"Child of my affections! receive my blessing. Offspring of my young passion! let me press you, in imagination, to my lone bosom!

"Ah! why are you not with me? why is not my hand in yours? There is much to say—more, more than I can ever express—yet, I must write, for I would not die without my son doing justice to his father.

"As a child you doubted my love—as a man, in spite of all your struggles, I am conscious you never divested yourself of the agonizing idea. O my Contarini, what is this life, this life of error, and misconception, and wo!

"My feeble pen trembles in my hand. There is much, there is much to write, much, alas! that never can be written. Why are we parted?

"You think me cold—you think me callous—you think me a hollow-hearted worldling. O! my Contarini, recall the doubt and misery of your early years, and all your wild thoughts, and dark misgivings, and vain efforts—recall all these, and behold the boyhood of your father!

"I, too, believed myself a poet—I, too, aspired to emancipate my kind—I, too, looked forward to a glorious future, and the dazzling vista of eternal fame. The passions of my heart were not less violent than yours, and not less ardent was my impetuous love.

"Wo! wo! the father and the son have been alike stricken. I know all, my Contarini—I know all, my sweet, sweet child. I would have saved you from the bitter lot—I alone would have borne the deep despair.

"Was she fair, my Contarini? Was she beautiful? Alas! there was once one as bright and as glorious—you knew not your mother.

"I can remember the day but as yesterday when I first gazed upon the liquid darkness of her eye. It was at that fatal city I will not name—horrible Venice!

"I found her surrounded by a thousand slaves —I won her from amid this band—against the efforts and opposition of all her family, I won her. Yes! she was my bride—the beautiful daughter of this romantic land—a land to which I was devoted, and for which I would have perilled my life. Alas! I perilled my love! My imagination was fired by that wondrous and witching city. My love of freedom, my hatred of oppression, burned each day with a brighter and more vehement flame. I sighed over its past glory and present degradation, and when I mingled my blood with the veins of Contarini, I vowed I would revive the glory they had themselves created.

"Venice was at that time under the yoke of the French. The recollection of the republic was still fresh in men's minds; the son of the last doge was my relative and my friend. Unhappy Pasgualigo! thy memory demands a tear.

"We conspired. Even now my blood seems to flow with renewed force, when I recall the excitement of our secret meetings in the old Palazzo Contarini, on the Grand Lagune. How often has daylight on the waters reminded us of our long counsels!

"We were betrayed. Timely information permitted me to escape. I bore away my wife. We reached Mantua in safety. Perhaps it was the agitation of the event and the flight—since the tragedy of Candia, I have sometimes thought it might have been a constitutional doom. But that fatal night—why, why recall it? We have both alike suffered. No, no, not alike—for I had my child.

"My child, my darling child, even now your recollection maintains me, even now my cheek warms as I repose upon the anticipation of your glory.

"I will not dwell upon what I now endured. Alas! I cannot leave it to your imagination. Your reality has taught you all. I roved a madman amid the mountains of the Tyrol. But you were with me, my child, you were with me, and I looked upon your mild and pensive eyes, and the wildness of my thoughts died away.

"I recurred to those hopes of poetic fame which had soothed the dull wretchedness of my boyhood. Alas! no flame from heaven descended on my lyre. I experienced only mortification, and so complete was my wretchedness, so desolate my life, so void of hope and cheerfulness, and even the prospect of that common ease that the merest animals require, that had it not been for you, I would have freed myself from the indescribable burthen of my existence. My hereditary estates were confiscated; my friends, like myself, were in exile. We were, in fact, destitute, and I had lost all confidence in my energies.

Thus wo-begone, I entered Vienna, where, fortunately, I found a friend. Mingling in the artificial society of that refined city, those excited feelings, fed by my strange adventures and solitary life, subsided. I began to lose what was peculiar in me, and share much that was general. Worldly feelings sprang up. Some success brought back my confidence. I believed that I was not destitute of power, but had only mistaken its nature. It was a political age. A great theatre seemed before me. I had ever been ambitious. I directed my desires in a new channel, and I determined to be a statesman.

"I had attracted the attention of the Austrian minister. I became his secretary. You know the rest.

"I resolved that my child should be happy. I desired to save him from the misery that clouded my own youth. I would have preserved him from the tyranny of impetuous passions, and the harrowing wo that awaits an ill-regulated mind. I observed in him a dangerous susceptibility that alarmed me. I studied to prevent the indulgence of his feelings. I was kind, but I was calm. His imaginative temperament did not escape me. I perceived only hereditary weakness, and would have prevented hereditary wo. It was my aim to make him a practical man. O! Contarini, it was the anxiety of affection that prevented me from doing justice to your genius.

"My son, my child, my only beloved, could I but once press you in my arms, I should die happy. And even now the future supports me, and I feel the glory of your coming fame irradiating my tomb.

"Why, why cannot we meet? I could say so much, although I would say only I loved you. The pen falls from my hand, the feeble pen, that has signified nothing. Imagine what I would express, my Contarini—love me, love me. Cherish my memory while you receive my blessing."

"Let me fly, let me fly to him instantly!" was my exclamation. I felt the horrors of my imprisonment. I wrung my hands, and stamped from helplessness. There was a packet. I opened it—a lock of rich, dark hair, whose colour was not strange to me, and a beautiful miniature, that seemed a portrait of my beloved, yet I gazed upon the countenance of my mother.

XV.

There was yet a letter from my banker, which I long neglected to open. I opened it at last, and learned the death of my remaining parent.

The age of tears was past. That relief was denied me. I looked up to heaven in despair. I flew to a darkened chamber. I buried my face in my hands, and, lone and speechless, I delivered myself up for days to the silent agony of the past.

PART THE SEVENTH.

I.

I leaned against a column of the temple of Castor. On one side was the palace of the Cæsars; on the other, the colossal amphitheatre of Vespasian. Arches of triumph, the pillars of Pagan temples, and the domes of Christian churches, rose around me. In the distance was the wide Campagna, the Claudian Aqueduct, and the Alban Mount.

Solitude and silence reigned on that sacred road once echoing with the shouts and chariots of three hundred triumphs—solitude and silence, meet companions of imperial desolation! Where are the spoils of Egypt and of Carthage? Where the golden tribute of Iberia? Where the long Gallic trophies? Where are the rich armour and massy cups of Macedon? Where are the pictures and statues of Corinth? Where the libraries of Athens? Where is the broken bow of Parthia? Where the elephants of Pontus, and the gorgeous diadems of the Asian kings?

And where is Rome? All nations rose and flourished only to swell her splendour, and now I stand amid her ruins.

In such a scene, what are our private griefs and petty sorrows? And what is man? I felt my nothingness. Life seemed flat, and dull, and trifling. I could not conceive that I could again become interested in its base pursuits. I believed that I could no longer be influenced by joy or by sorrow. Indifference alone remained.

A man clambered down the steep of the Palatine. It was Winter, flushed and eager from a recent excavation.

"What, count," he exclaimed, "moralizing in the forum!"

"Alas! Winter, what is life?"

"An excellent thing, as long as one can discover as pretty a Torso as I have stumbled upon this morning."

"A Torso! a maimed memorial of the past. The very name is melancholy."

"What is the past to me? I am not dead. You may be. I exist in the present."

"The vanity of the present overpowers me."

"Pooh! I will tell you what, my friend, the period has arrived in your life when you must renounce meditation. Action is now your part. Meditation is culture. It is well to think until a man have discovered his genius, and developed his faculties, but then let him put his intelligence in motion. Act, act, act; act without ceasing, and you will no longer talk of the vanity of life."

"But how am I to act?"

"Create. Man is made to create, from the poet to the potter."

II.

My father bequeathed me his entire property which was more considerable than I had imagined, the countess and her children being amply provided for by her own estate. In addition to this, I found that he had claimed in my favour the Contarini estates, to which, independent of the validity of my marriage, I was entitled through my mother. After much litigation, the question had been decided in my behalf a few months before my return to Italy. I found myself, therefore, unexpectedly, a very rich man. I wrote to the countess, and received from her a very affectionate reply; nor should I omit that I was honoured by an autograph letter of condolence from the king, and an invitation to re-enter his service.

As I was now wearied with wandering, and desirous of settling down in life, and as I had been deprived of those affections which render home delightful, I determined to find, in the creations of art, some consolation and some substitute for that domestic bliss, which I value above all other blessings. I resolved to create a paradise.

I purchased a large estate in the vicinity of Naples, with a palace and beautiful gardens. I called in the assistance of the first artists in the country, and I availed myself, above all, of the fine taste of my friend Winter. The palace was a Palladian pile, built upon a stately terrace covered with orange and citron trees, and to which you ascended by broad flights of marble steps. The formation of the surrounding country was highly picturesque; hills beautifully peaked or undulating, richly wooded, covered with the cypress and the ilex, and crowned with the stone pine. Occasionally you caught a glimpse of the blue sea and the brilliant coast.

Upon the terrace, on each side of the portal, I have placed a collossal sphinx, which were excavated when I was at Thebes, and which I was fortunate enough to purchase. They are of cream-coloured granite, and as fresh and sharp as if they were finished yesterday. There is a soft majesty and a serene beauty in the countenances, which are very remarkable.

It is my intention to build in these beautiful domains a Saracenic palace, which my oriental collections will befit, but which I hope also to fill with the masterpieces of Christian art. At present, in a gallery, I have placed some fine specimens of the Venetian, Roman, and Eclectic schools, and have ranged between them copies in marble, by Bertolini, of the most celebrated ancient statues. In one cabinet by itself is the gem of my collection, a Magdalen, by Murillo, and in another, a sleeping Cupid, by Canova, over which I have contrived by a secret light to throw a rosy flush, that invests the ideal beauty of the sculptor with still more ideal life. At the end of the gallery I have placed the portraits of my father and of my mother, the latter copied by an excellent artist from the miniature. Between them is a frame of richly carved ivory, enclosing a black velvet veil, studded with white roses, worked in pearls.

Around me, I hope in time to create a scene which may rival in beauty and variety, although not in extent, the villa of Hadrian, whom I have always considered the most sumptuous and accomplished character of antiquity. I have already commenced the foundation of a tower which shall rise at least one hundred and fifty feet, and which I trust will equal in the beauty of design, and the solidity of the masonry, the most celebrated works of antiquity. This tower I shall dedicate to the future, and I intend that it shall be my tomb.

Lausanne has married, and will never quit me. He has promised also to form a band of wind instruments, a solace necessary to solitude. Winter is my only friend and my only visiter. He is a great deal with me, and has a studio in the palace. He is so independent, that he often arrives and quits it without my knowledge; yet I never converse with him without pleasure.

Here let me pass my life in the study and the creation of the beautiful. Such is my desire; but whether it will be my career is, I feel, doubtful. My interest in the happiness of my race is too keen to permit me for a moment to be blind to the storms that lower on the horizon of society. Perchance also the political regeneration of the country to which I am devoted may not be distant, and in that great work I am resolved to participate. Bitter jest, that the most civilized portion of the globe should be considered incapable of self-government!

When I examine the state of the European society with the unimpassioned spirit which the philosopher can alone command, I perceive that it is in a state of transition—a state of transition from feudal to federal principles. This I conceive to be the sole and secret cause of all the convulsions that have occurred, and are to occur.

Circumstances are beyond the control of man; but his conduct is in his own power. The great event is as sure as that I am now penning this prophecy of its occurrence. With us it rests whether it shall be welcomed by wisdom or by ignorance—whether its beneficent results shall be accelerated by enlightened minds, or retarded by our dark passions.

What is the arch of the conqueror, what the laurel of the poet! I think of the infinity of space, I feel my nothingness. Yet if I am to be remembered, let me be remembered as one who, in a sad night of gloomy ignorance and savage bigotry, was prescient of the flaming morning-break of bright philosophy,—as one who deeply sympathized with his fellow-men, and felt a proud and profound conviction of their perfectibility,—as one who devoted himself to the amelioration of his kind, by the destruction of error, and the propagation of truth.

Grace Aguilar.

HOME INFLUENCE. 12mo. Cloth. $1.00.

MOTHER'S RECOMPENSE. 12mo. Cloth. $1.00.

DAYS OF BRUCE. 2 vols., 12mo. Cloth. $2.00.

HOME SCENES AND HEART STUDIES. 12mo. Cloth. $1.00.

WOMAN'S FRIENDSHIP. 12mo. Cloth. $1.00.

WOMEN OF ISRAEL. 2 vols., 12mo. Cloth. $2.00.

VALE OF CEDARS. 12mo. Cloth. $1.00.

"Grace Aguilar's works possess attractions which will always place them among the standard writings which no library can be without. 'Mother's Recompense' and 'Woman's Friendship' should be read by both young and old."

W. Arthur.

THE SUCCESSFUL MERCHANT. 1 vol., 12mo. Cloth. $1.50.

J. B. Bouton.

ROUND THE BLOCK. A new American Novel. Illustrated. 1 vol., 12mo. Cloth. $2.00.

"Unlike most novels that now appear, it has no 'mission,' the author being neither a politician nor a réformer, but a story-teller, according to the old pattern; and a capital story he has produced, written in the happiest style."

F. Caballero.

ELIA; or, Spain Fifty Years Ago. A Novel. 1 vol., 12mo. Cloth. $1.75.

Mary Cowden Clarke.

THE IRON COUSIN. A Tale. 1 vol., 12mo. Cloth. $2.00.

"The story is too deeply interesting to allow the reader to lay it down till he has read it to the end."

Charles Dickens.

The Cheap Popular Edition of the Works of Charles Dickens.

Clear type, handsomely printed, and of convenient size. 18 vols., 8vo. Paper.

	Pages.	Cts.
OLIVER TWIST	172	25
AMERICAN NOTES	104	15
DOMBEY & SON	356	35
MARTIN CHUZZLEWIT	342	35
OUR MUTUAL FRIEND	330	35
CHRISTMAS STORIES	162	25
TALE OF TWO CITIES	144	20
HARD TIMES, and ADDITIONAL CHRISTMAS STORIES	200	25
NICHOLAS NICKLEBY	340	35
BLEAK HOUSE	340	35
LITTLE DORRIT	330	35
PICKWICK PAPERS	326	35
DAVID COPPERFIELD	351	35
BARNABY RUDGE	257	30
OLD CURIOSITY SHOP	221	30
SKETCHES	196	25
GREAT EXPECTATIONS	184	25
UNCOMMERCIAL TRAVELLER, PICTURES FROM ITALY, Etc.	300	35

THE COMPLETE POPULAR LIBRARY EDITION. Handsomely printed in good, clear type. Illustrated with 32 Engravings, and a Steel-plate Portrait of the Author. 6 vols., small 8vo. Cloth, extra. $10.50.

OUR MUTUAL FRIEND. With Illustrations by Marcus Stone. London edition. 2 vols., 12mo. Scarlet Cloth, $5.00; Half Calf, $9.00.

Mrs. Ellis.

HEARTS AND HOMES; or, Social Distinctions. A Story. 1 vol., 8vo. Cloth. $2.50.

"There is a charm about this lady's productions that is extremely fascinating. For grace and ease of narrative, she is unsurpassed; her fictions always breathe a healthy moral."

Margaret Field.

BERTHA PERCY; or, L'Esperance. 1 vol. 12mo. Cloth. $1.50.

"A book of great power and fascination. . . . . . In its pictures of home life, it reminds one of Fredrika Bremer's earlier and better novels, but it possesses much more than Fredrika Bremer's descriptive power."

Julia Kavanagh.

ADELE. A Tale. 1 thick vol. 12mo. Cloth. $2.00.
BEATRICE. 12mo. Cloth. $2.00.
DAISY BURNS. 12mo. Cloth. $2.00.
GRACE LEE. 12mo. Cloth. $2.00.
MADELINE. 12mo. Cloth. $1.50.
NATHALIE. A Tale. 12mo. Cloth. $2.00.
RACHEL GRAY. 12mo. Cloth. $1.50.
QUEEN MAB. 12mo. Cloth. $2.00.
SEVEN YEARS, and Other Tales. 12mo. Cloth. $1.50.
SYBIL'S SECOND LOVE. 12mo. Cloth. $2.00.
WOMEN OF CHRISTIANITY, Exemplary for Piety and Charity. 12mo. Cloth. $1.50.
DORA. Illustrated by Gaston Fay. 1 vol. 8vo. Paper, $1.00. Cloth, $1.50.

"There is a quiet power in the writings of this gifted author, which is as far removed from the sensational school as any of the modern novels can be."

Margaret Lee.

DR. WILMER'S LOVE; or, A Question of Conscience. A Novel. 1 vol., 12mo. Cloth. $2.00.

Olive Logan.

CHATEAU FRISSAC; or, Home Scenes in France. Authoress of "Photographs of Paris Life." 1 vol., 12mo. Cloth. $2.00.

Maria J. Macintosh.

AUNT KITTY'S TALES. 12mo. Cloth. $1.50.
CHARMS AND COUNTER CHARMS. 12mo. Cloth. $1.75.
EVENINGS AT DONALDSON MANOR. 1 vol., 12mo. Cloth. $1.50.
THE LOFTY AND LOWLY. 2 vols., 12mo. Cloth. $3.00.
TWO LIVES; or, To Seem and To Be. 12mo. Cloth. $1.50.
TWO PICTURES; or, How We See Ourselves, and How the World Sees Us. 1 vol., 12mo. Cloth. $2.00.

"Miss Macintosh is one of the best of the female writers of the day. Her stories are always full of lessons of truth, and purity, and goodness, of that serene and gentle wisdom which comes from no source so fitly as from a refined and Christian woman."

Alice B. Haven.

The COOPERS; or Getting Under Way. A Tale of Real Life. 1 vol., 12mo. Cloth. $1.50.

LOSS AND GAIN; or, Margaret's Home. 1 vol., 12mo. Cloth. $1.50.

The lamented Cousin Alice, better known as the author of numerous juvenile works of a popular character, only wrote two works of fiction, which evidence that she could have met with equal success in that walk of literature. They both bear the impress of a mind whose purity of heart was proverbial.

Helen Modet.

LIGHT. A Novel. 1 vol., 12mo. Cloth. $1.50.

Miss Warner.

THE HILLS OF THE SHATEMUC. 1 vol., 12mo. Cloth. $2.00.

MY BROTHER'S KEEPER. 1 vol., 12mo. Cloth. $1.75.

Sarah A. Wentz.

SMILES AND FROWNS. A Novel. 1 vol., 12mo. Cloth. $1.75.

Anonymous.

COMETH UP AS A FLOWER. An Autobiography. 1 vol., 8vo. Paper covers. 60 cents.

NOT WISELY, BUT TOO WELL. By the Author of "Cometh up as a Flower." 1 vol., 8vo. Paper covers. 60 cents.

The name of the author of the above is still buried in obscurity. The sensation which was created by the publication of "Cometh up as a Flower" remains unabated, as the daily increasing demand abundantly testifies. No work, since the appearance of "Jane Eyre," has met with greater success.

LADY ALICE; or, The New Una. A Novel. New edition. Paper. 50 cents.

MADGE; or, Night and Morning. A Novel. 1 vol., 12mo. Cloth. $1.75.

SHERBROOKE. By H. B. G., author of "Madge." 1 vol., 12mo. Cloth. $2.00.

MARY STAUNTON: or, The Pupils of Marvel Hall. By the Author of "Portraits of My Married Friends." 1 vol., 12mo. Cloth. $1.75.

MINISTRY OF LIFE. By the Author of "Ministering Children." Illustrated. 1 vol., 12mo. Cloth. $2.00.

THE VIRGINIA COMEDIANS; or, Old Days in the Old Dominion. 2 vols., 12mo. Cloth. $3.00.

WIFE'S STRATAGEM. A Story for Fireside and Wayside. By Aunt Fanny. Illustrated. 1 vol., 12mo. Cloth. $1.50.

Captain Marryat.

Marryat's Popular Novels and Tales. A new and beautiful edition. 12 vols., 12mo. Cloth. $21.

Or, separately:

PETER SIMPLE. 12mo. Cloth. $1.75.
JACOB FAITHFUL. 12mo. Cloth. $1.75.
NAVAL OFFICER. 12mo. Cloth. $1.75.
KING'S OWN. 12mo. Cloth. $1.75.
JAPHET IN SEARCH OF A FATHER. 12mo. Cloth. $1.75.
NEWTON FORSTER. 12mo. Cloth. $1.75.
MIDSHIPMAN EASY. 12mo. Cloth. $1.75.
PACHA OF MANY TALES. 12mo. Cloth. $1.75.
THE POACHER. 12mo. Cloth. $1.75.
THE PHANTOM SHIP. 12mo. Cloth. $1.75.
SNARLEYOW. 12mo. Cloth. $1.75.
PERCIVAL KEENE. 12mo. Cloth. $1.75.

Fine edition, printed on tinted paper. 12 vols., large 12mo. Cloth, $30.00; Half Calf, extra, $54.00.

THE CHEAP POPULAR EDITION OF MARRYAT'S NOVELS. To be completed in 12 volumes. Printed from new stereotype plates, in clear type, on good paper. **Price per volume, 50 cents.**

"Capt. Marryat is a classic among novel-writers. A better idea may be had of the sea, of ship-life, especially in the navy, from these enchanting books, than from any other source. They will continue to be read as long as the language exists."

Miss Jane Porter.

SCOTTISH CHIEFS. A Romance. New and handsome edition. With Engravings. 1 vol., large 8vo. Cloth. $3.00; Half Calf, extra, $5.50.

The great popularity of this novel has rendered it necessary to furnish this handsome edition in large, readable type, with appropriate embellishments for the domestic library.

E. M. Sewell.

AMY HERBERT. A Tale. 12mo. Cloth. $1.50.
CLEVE HALL. A Tale. 12mo. Cloth. $2.00.
THE EARL'S DAUGHTER. 12mo. Cloth. $1.50.
EXPERIENCE OF LIFE. 12mo. Cloth. $1.50.
A GLIMPSE OF THE WORLD. 12mo. Cloth. $1.75.
GERTRUDE. A Tale. 12mo. Cloth. $1.50.
IVORS. A Story of English Country Life. 2 vols. Cloth. $3.00.
KATHARINE ASHTON. 2 vols., 12mo. Cloth. $3.00.
MARGARET PERCIVAL. 2 vols., 12mo. Cloth. $3.00.
URSULA. A Tale of Country Life. 2 vols., 12mo. Cloth. $3.00.
LANETON PARSONAGE. A Tale. 3 vols., 12mo. Cloth. $4.50.
HOME LIFE. A Journal. 1 vol., 12mo. Cloth. $2.00.

"Scarcely any modern English authoress stands so high as Miss Sewell; and so long as the English language exists, such books as 'Amy Herbert,' 'Gertrude,' etc., will continually be sought for."

Sir Walter Scott.

WAVERLEY NOVELS. The Cheap Popular Edition of the Waverley Novels. To be completed in Twenty-five Volumes, from New Stereotype Plates, uniform with the New Edition of Dickens, containing all the Notes of the Author, and printed from the latest edition of the Authorized Text, on fine white paper, in clear type, and convenient in size. Each volume illustrated with a Frontispiece. Pronounced "A Miracle of Cheapness."

Order of Issue.

1. WAVERLEY .25
2. IVANHOE .25
3. KENILWORTH .25
4. GUY MANNERING .25
5. ANTIQUARY .25
6. ROB ROY .25
7. OLD MORTALITY .25
8. THE BLACK DWARF, and A LEGEND OF MONTROSE .25
9. BRIDE OF LAMMERMOOR .25
10. HEART OF MID-LOTHIAN .25
11. THE MONASTERY .25
12. THE ABBOT .25
13. THE PIRATE .25
14. FORTUNES OF NIGEL .25
15. PEVERIL OF THE PEAK .25
16. QUENTIN DURWARD .25
17. ST. RONAN'S WELL .25
18. REDGAUNTLET .25
19. THE BETROTHED, and HIGHLAND WIDOW .25
20. THE TALISMAN .25
21. WOODSTOCK .25
22. FAIR MAID OF PERTH .25
23. ANNE OF GEIERSTEIN .25
24. COUNT ROBERT OF PARIS .25
25. THE SURGEON'S DAUGHTER .25

The Complete Popular Library Edition of the Waverley Novels. Handsomely printed, in good clear type. Illustrated with numerous Engravings, and a Steel-plate Portrait of the Author. 6 vols., small 8vo. (Uniform with the "Popular Library Edition of Dickens.") Cloth, extra, $10.50.

WAVERLEY NOVELS. Black's Edition. Illustrated with 204 Steel Engravings. 25 vols., 8vo. Full Calf, extra, gilt edges, $175.00. Morocco, antique $250.00.

Thackeray.

The popular Novels of W. M. THACKERAY, comprising:

THE LUCK OF BARRY LYNDON.
CONFESSIONS OF FITZ-BOODLE.
MR. BROWN'S LETTERS.
JEAMES'S DIARY.
MEN'S WIVES.
PARIS SKETCH-BOOK.
PUNCH'S PRIZE NOVELISTS.
A SHABBY GENTEEL STORY.
THE YELLOWPLUSH PAPERS.
BOOK OF SNOBS.

12 vols. in 6, 12mo. Cloth, $10.50; Half Calf, extra, $20.00.